Smoke Jumping
on the Western Fire Line

Smoke Jumping on the Western Fire Line

Conscientious Objectors during World War II

Mark Matthews

Foreword by Senator George McGovern

UNIVERSITY OF OKLAHOMA PRESS : NORMAN

Library of Congress Cataloging-in-Publication Data

Matthews, Mark, 1951–

    Smoke jumping on the Western fire line : conscientious
objectors during World War II / by Mark Matthews ; foreword
by George McGovern.

      p. cm.
    Includes bibliographical references and index.
    ISBN 0-8061-3766-5 (hardcover)
    ISBN 0-8061-9104-1 (paper)
    1. Smokejumpers—West (U.S.)—Biography.
2. Smokejumping—West (U.S.)—History. 3. World War,
1939–1945—Conscientious objectors—United States.
4. Civilian Public Service—History. I. Title.
    SD421.24.M38   2006
    634.9'618—dc22   2005055530

*To the memory of Helen Viviane,
a tireless worker for peace
throughout her lifetime.*

Peace Jumpers

War came; the young men
all stood in line to go.
But we, when asked to take the oath,
simply answered, "No."

For what we said was simple,
though said by just a few:
"I will not shoot another man
because I'm ordered to."

No wonder some were puzzled,
or took it as a joke,
when COs wrote and volunteered
to jump into the smoke.

You said that what we were doing
could prove that we were men;
we had—and didn't need your words
to prove it once again.

You thought that we were renegades,
and the training much too hard;
we packed your words in our duffel bags
and left for Camp Menard.

But you shunned us in the cookhouse,
and cursed us to our souls;
your words were blurred by the heat and sweat,
as we practiced landing rolls.

You said we were too yellow
to jump with airborne troops;
we rolled your words in our shroud lines
when the rigger packed our chutes.

We turned aside your hatred,
and blunted your abuse;
we held your words in clenching teeth,
and climbed into the goose.

You told us we were cowards,
called each of us a liar;
we hooked your words to the static line,
and jumped into the fire.

And all you said hung over us
as we saw our chutes deploy;
we took your words to the fire line,
to save and not destroy.

You said we'd never understand
what war was all about;
we threw your words on the roaring flames
and put the fire out.

—Bruce "Utah" Phillips

Contents

Illustrations

Foreword

Senator George McGovern

This excellent, historically researched book tells the bittersweet story of deeply religious young men whose spirituality led them to reject military service in World War II in return for their service as smoke jumpers in fighting wildland fires in the forests of Montana and other western states.

They were paid only a bare subsistence wage, but their duties were dangerous, difficult, and sometimes terrifying. Many times their lives were threatened at a level equal to the dangers of combat warfare. What made the life of conscientious objectors in the firefighting service worse than combat military service is that almost invariably the smoke jumpers were decried as "draft dodgers," "yellowbellies," "cowards," and worse. Frequently, gangs of young toughs—themselves braving neither military service nor firefighting—would descend on the young Quakers, Mennonites, members of the Church of the Brethren, and other men of like persuasion to attack them with curses, stones, clubs, or all three. In some cases, the conscientious objectors (or COs) feared for their lives.

Interestingly, sometimes hostile members of the U.S. Forest Service, local civilians, or GIs home on leave would castigate and harass the smoke jumpers—only to eventually be won over by the deep conviction, the religious faith, and the hard work of the conscientious objectors.

For many of the young "conchies," the firefighting experience in the beautiful forests and mountains of the western states was a defining time in their lives. They demonstrated to themselves and to others that they were not cowards. Rather, they were willing to jump out of an airplane at the edge of a raging fire and fight with every resource they could muster to save America's matchless forests. Their religion told them not to kill people but to save them—and to nurture God's beautiful creation.

As this fine book makes clear, the smoke jumpers of the peace churches have demonstrated that in America a citizen can hold fast to his or her spiritual faith while serving the greater good of the nation—provided he or she is brave, determined, and strong.

Preface and Acknowledgments

In 1994, during my last year as a graduate student at the University of Montana's School of Journalism, my good friend Helen Viviane told me of an interesting slide show she had seen, on the Civilian Public Service (CPS) smoke jumpers at the Jeannette Rankin Peace Center in Missoula. Having professed nonresistant tendencies myself since the Vietnam War era and also having worked as a wildland firefighter for the U.S. Forest Service at the Ninemile Ranger District during the summers while attending school, I was immediately drawn to the saga of the CPS smoke jumpers. Following Helen's advice, I tracked down Roy Wenger, the former civilian director of CPS Camp No. 103, who was eighty-four at the time and living in Missoula.

Mr. Wenger graciously conducted a number of interviews with me and directed me to other former CPS smoke jumpers in Montana, including Phil Stanley and Wilmer Carlsen. He also lent me some vintage slides to accompany newspaper stories that eventually ran in the *Kaimin,* the University of Montana's daily newspaper, as well as the *Great Falls Tribune, High*

Country News, and the *Washington Post.* Mr. Wenger also gave me a treasure trove of testimonials written by more than one hundred CPS smoke jumpers that he had compiled into three self-published volumes. (Since the three volumes contain no page numbers, I have opted not to footnote the quotations taken from Wenger's collections. Therefore, the reader may assume that any quotation not referenced in the text originated from that collection.)

I also acquired a similar self-published book, titled *Static Lines and Canopies,* that had been compiled by another CPSer, Asa Mundell. (Quotations from that volume have been duly referenced.) Together the four works contain remembrances of more than 50 percent of the two hundred and fifty conscientious objectors who had trained as smoke jumpers during World War II.

Many of the biographical pieces were short and sketchy; some, poorly written and difficult to get through. But here and there I found insightful or descriptive sentences or paragraphs. And sometimes I discovered an entire piece that captivated me. (For example, I hope the reader takes the time to read the letters of George Robinson contained in the appendix, which are too colorful and detailed to break up for piecemeal quotations throughout the book.)

I gleaned the good writing and interesting anecdotes from the volumes and separated the fragments into categories. Each category eventually evolved into a chapter. I wanted to tell as much as possible of the story in the CPSers' own words, so I have quoted generously from the original reminiscences.

Also of invaluable help was former smoke jumper and trainer Earl Cooley. I interviewed Earl a number of times for this and other stories related to the history of smoke jumping. I also found Earl's entertaining book, *Trails and Trimotors,* chock-full of tales of pre-CPS days of smoke jumping—as well as the ensuing years.

I would also like to thank U.S. Forest Service employees Sue Alley, Steve Slaughter, Dave Ramirez, and Bill McCullough for the many opportunities of employment at the historic Ninemile Ranger Station during various summers from 1993 to the present. And I extend a warm thanks to all my fellow firefighters and other Forest Service workers, both seasonal and lifers, who have provided good fellowship and wise counsel throughout the years.

Much appreciation also goes to the anonymous reviewers who read the original manuscript and directed me toward rewarding revisions . . . and to Sally Bennett for her brilliant copyediting.

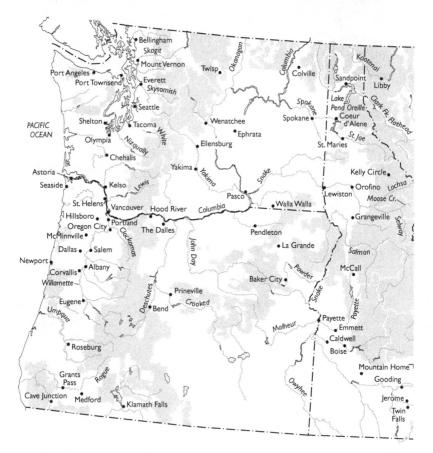

The northwestern United States, with national forests indicated by shading.

Blackfeet
Reservation
Cut Bank
Shelby
Kalispell
Flathead Lake
Conrad
Teton
Havre
Milk
Marias
Glasgow
Wolf Point
Sidney
Missouri
Polson
Sun
Great Falls
Glendive
Ninemile/
Camp
Menard
Seeley Lake/
Camp Paxon
Blackfoot
Missou
Judith
Lewistown
Missoula
Clark Fork
Helena
Dear Lodge
Hamilton
Bitterroot
Anaconda
Butte
Miles City
Musselshell
Yellowstone
Big Hole
Jefferson
Bozeman
Livingston
Billings
Hardin
Bighorn
Salmon
Salmon
Beaverhead
Dillon
Madison
Gallatin
Lemhi

St. Anthony
Rexburg
Rigby
Hailey
Idaho Falls
Blackfoot
Blackfoot
Pocatello
Rupert
American Falls
Soda Springs
Burley
Snake
Preston

N

National Forest

0   50   100 Miles

Smoke Jumping
on the Western Fire Line

Introduction

Civilian Public Service

Maynard Shetler would have been the first to admit how nervous he felt as he stooped within the doorless opening at the rear of the Ford Trimotor. As stiff winds buffeted the airplane, hot and cold chills played tag through his system, while his mouth felt as dry as cotton balls. Two thousand feet below, stretcher bearers ran toward an earlier parachutist who now lay in the middle of a hayfield. "I've got to do it," Shetler kept reminding himself. Nervously fingering the ripcord of the emergency parachute pack clipped to his chest, he envisioned the tail of the plane hooking onto his billowing chute and dragging him across the sky. As the spotter raised his hand to signal the plane's approach over the jump spot, Shetler finally abandoned his morbid fantasy, held his breath, and prepared to step into the sky.

"The slow sickness ran through my system, ending like lead in my stomach," he later recalled. "Down came the spotter's hand. Simultaneously I swallowed, summoned up all my energy, and put myself through the plane's door."[1]

That same year, 1944—during the height of World War II—thousands of other young American men, soldiers in the U.S. Army, had to overcome the same fears Maynard Shelter was confronting, before they floated down to battlefields across Europe and Asia. But Shetler fought a different kind of battle, one that did not involve enemy soldiers. In fact, standing before his draft board a couple of years earlier, Shetler had renounced any participation in the armed services. As a practicing Mennonite (a member of one of the three recognized "historic peace churches," a trio that also included the Church of the Brethren and the Religious Society of Friends), Shetler opted for the Civilian Public Service (CPS), in which he could perform jobs of "national importance." About 12,000 men throughout the war years lived at 218 CPS camps across the country, working on a variety of agricultural, forestry, medical, and conservation programs.[2] Here, at CPS Camp No. 103 near Huson, Montana, about 250 CPSers trained throughout the duration of the war to jump from airplanes to reach and confine wildfires for the U.S. Forest Service in five mountainous western states and Canada.

The conscientious objectors were not the first smoke jumpers, but they hit the silk (a phrase that came into use when parachutes were made of silk) during the critical formative years of that elite brigade. In some ways, the conscientious objectors functioned as guinea pigs. After observing the CPSers' experiences, Forest Service specialists developed current smoke jumper training, parachuting, and firefighting techniques that have since become standard practice. When the Second World War ended, the returning veterans who stepped into the conscientious objectors' shoes joined a well-oiled and smoothly orchestrated firefighting machine that remains the premier battalion of the wildland fire control program.

In home movies taken during their boot camp–like training sessions, the "conchies" look just like smoke jumpers of this new millennium. The only hints of the bygone era may be a shiny Studebaker or R.E.O. Speedwagon parked near a Ford Trimotor or Travelaire aircraft—plus the dearth of female and minority jumpers. They are handsome men with well-defined physiques. They smile broadly at the camera. One gains the impression of a lot of horseplay going on amid an atmosphere of genuine camaraderie. Their expressions exude a mixture of adventure and trepidation, especially on the part of those who have yet to hit the silk.

When the men were finally able to jump a real fire, other challenges waited on the ground. Although benign at most times, wildfire can turn into a dangerous adversary. Under the right (or wrong) conditions, walls of flame can explode two hundred feet into the air and rush up and down mountainsides faster than a man can run. As a crown fire leaps from treetop to treetop, its force is comparable to avalanches, tidal waves, or tornadoes—even atomic bombs. Unlimited numbers of firefighters or limitless pieces of equipment cannot stop a raging crown fire. Only wet weather can do that. In rare cases, the only recourse is to run for a safety zone. Under this premonition of danger, smoke jumping offered conscientious objectors an opportunity to prove that they were not cowards.

"Would you just stand there and let a Nazi rape and kill your mother or sister?" was a typical question skeptics often asked to corner a CPSer into taking a hypocritical stance. Many citizens believed that conscientious objectors had no logical argument to back their views. Intolerant Americans verbally insulted and sometimes physically attacked the conscientious objectors, who often heard the epithets "yellow-belly," "slacker," and "coward" shouted behind their backs and sometimes to their faces. They were frequently spit on or had to dodge stones thrown by teenagers or older irascible patriots.

Ironically, but not surprisingly, gentle practitioners of nonresistance—especially those belonging to the historic peace churches—have long faced similar persecution. Many CPSers

had heard legends passed down by family elders document-
ing atrocities endured by their ancestors in Europe that
included torture and execution for their religious beliefs.
Most families could trace the exodus of forced migration
across the map of Europe and Great Britain to the seaports
where early religious pilgrims disembarked for America.
They were part of a rich tradition of nonviolence that had its
roots in early Christian belief. The followers of these
churches took the gospels of the New Testament literally,
believing that the words of Jesus superseded the sometimes
violent accounts set forth in the Old Testament. In explaining
their stance of nonresistance, they quoted passages from the
Bible, such as Luke 6:27–36:

> But I say unto you, love your enemies, do good to them
> who hate you, bless them who curse you, and pray for
> them who despitefully use you. And to him who smites
> you on the one cheek, offer also the other; and to him
> who takes away your cloak, forbid not that he also take
> your coat. Give to every man who asks of you; and of
> him who takes away your goods, ask them not to be
> returned. And, as you would that men should do to you,
> do also to them likewise. . . . Love your enemies, and do
> good, and lend, hoping for nothing again; and your
> reward shall be great, and you shall be the children of
> the Highest; for he is kind unto the unthankful and to
> the evil. Be you therefore merciful, as your father also is
> merciful.

For members of the peace churches, there could be no clearer
directions on how to lead a good life. Factor in the sixth commandment—"Thou shalt not kill"—and what Christian could
ever defend the concept of war? Through the eyes of a conscientious objector, it was a wonder that "normal" people could

not understand them. CPS smoke jumper Gregg Phifer expressed those sentiments in 1944:

> Until you got to know us, you'd probably have a hard time putting your finger on what makes us what we are, what differences led us to CPS and our brothers—literally as well as figuratively—to the armed forces. . . . Have we not the same desire for home, friends, job? How different is our picture of the world we would like to live in? True enough, we believe the quicker and surer road to that goal lies apart from ways of violence and war. For that belief, "impractical" is the mildest of the charges hurled against us. But that is part of the price assessed by society against those who would redirect her energies into the way of peace.[3]

Besides pioneering the way for future generations of smoke jumpers, thousands of other CPSers performed other valuable services on the home front during a period marked by an extreme shortage of manpower. CPSers took over the chores formerly done by young men in the Civilian Conservation Corps in national forests and parks across the nation. They fought fires, graded roads, cut brush, built and maintained buildings. They grew seedlings in nurseries and later reset the young plants in the wild; they built bridges, dug latrines, and laid water lines. In short, they helped preserve and conserve the nation's natural resources and scenic treasures. Others worked in soil conservation projects to help reduce erosion at a time when scientists estimated that the United States was losing more than three billion tons of topsoil every year.[4] The diverse projects included contour cultivation, strip cropping, terracing, and construction of diversion ditches.

At the end of the war, the Bureau of Reclamation reported that it had fifty-seven projects in operation, many constructed by CPSers. The biggest projects enhanced food production and electrical energy output or furnished cities and towns with water. That meant building dams and digging ditches. Other projects provided flood control, regulated river channels, preserved fish and wildlife, or created recreational opportunities.[5]

Local farmers regularly recruited CPSers for emergency help during planting and harvesting time. A number of CPSers worked directly for state agricultural experiment stations, while others labored on dairy farms, doing the tasks typically performed by hired hands. A smaller number tested dairy herds and developed artificial insemination programs.

For those men who craved jobs with more social relevance, the government allowed CPSers to work as orderlies in hospitals and in training schools for the mentally ill and those with learning and physical disabilities. The need was great. In 1940, mental hospitals (as such facilities were then known) housed more than four hundred thousand patients. Few civilians wanted to work the long, unpleasant hours for short pay when they could earn generous salaries at munitions factories and shipyards. Yet CPSers welcomed the opportunity to help the less fortunate. By the fall of 1943, one out of every six men in CPS had worked with a mental hospital unit.[6] Other CPSers took part in public health projects such as the eradication of hookworm, and also volunteered for medical experiments.

Although the conscientious objector has never convinced the general public to a great degree to abandon fighting and killing—with the possible exception during the Vietnam War era—he has long played an important role in society. By taking a stance of nonresistance, he rubs against the collective conscience of society and presents a moral distraction to those who react emotionally to confrontation and to those who seek personal benefit and financial gain from the devastation of war. His gentle voice challenges those quick to unsheathe the sword and encourages them to stop and analyze their motives—if only for a brief moment.

Throughout its history, American society has grudgingly protected, to various degrees, the privilege to conscientiously object. That fact alone attests to the philosophy's deep subliminal social and political influences, according to former U.S. Supreme Court chief justice Harlan F. Stone. Stone pointed out the importance of protecting such rights when he wrote, "It may well be questioned whether the state which preserves its life by a settled policy of violation of the conscience of the individual will not in fact ultimately lose it by the process. Every ethical and practical consideration which should lead the state to endeavor to avoid the violation of the conscience of its citizens should therefore lead a wise and humane government to seek some practical solution of this difficult problem."[7]

CHAPTER ONE

Conscientious Objection in America

By the eighteenth century, thousands of members of the three historic peace churches had immigrated to America believing that the promise of religious freedom guaranteed by some colonies encompassed the right to follow the nonresistant teachings of Christ. A few colonies did excuse them from battlefield duty—but during an era before wholesale war reached America's shores.

The first real test for nonresistors occurred during the French and Indian War in western Pennsylvania, where many Mennonites and Brethren had settled at the urging of William Penn. The two sects politically supported the similarly nonresistant Quakers, who dominated the colony's assembly, and strove to keep peace with the Indians through negotiating fair treaties. However, by the mid-1750s, the burgeoning number of new settlers who did not belong to the peace churches had begun to clamor for protection from increasing frontier raids. At first, the Quaker-controlled legislature grudgingly approved war taxes, which it conveniently defined as general fund monies to be used at the king's discretion—or, as the

Bible said, "Rendering unto Caesar what is rightfully his." But not all members of the Society of Friends agreed with this ploy, and the internal pressure soon threatened to split the church as Quaker tax collectors and constables resorted to prosecuting fellow Friends. Consequently, the Quaker party began to dissolve, paving the way for the legislature to pass an act authorizing a militia in 1756, with a fine providing a way out for conscientious objectors.

There is no evidence that the Mennonites and Brethren living in the hinterlands at that time took up arms to defend themselves. To the contrary, the record, as in the case of the Mennonite Hochstetler family, details the sufferings caused by a strict adherence to nonresistance. As Indians attacked the Hochstetler farm in western Pennsylvania, the older sons pleaded with their father for permission to shoot back. The elder Hochstetler forbade them, reminding the boys of the scriptural teachings on nonresistance. In the end, the menfolk, after witnessing the killing of the mother and two younger children, were taken captive. The Indians also killed a number of nonresistant Brethren families at Morrison's Cove. Eventually the raids abated; but some twenty years later, the churches of nonresistance faced a more challenging crisis.

The American Revolution was a civil war that set American against American, as well as a rebellion that pitted patriot against king. Historians estimate that one-third of the colonists supported the revolution, while a little less than one-third remained loyal to the Crown. The remainder (including the majority of Mennonites, Quakers, and Brethren) attempted to stay neutral—although their sympathies often leaned toward the Crown.

The Mennonites and Brethren especially had good reasons for not supporting the revolt. Besides fearing that a new state might not tolerate their religious doctrines, they also believed that the Bible sanctified the authority of all monarchs. Many of them had affirmed obedience to King George III when they had first arrived in America, and they felt that they could not break their word. Also, because of their largely agrarian pursuits, the Mennonites and Brethren had few complaints about taxation without representation. Though some did run simple businesses, including the weaving of flax, the two sects had little interest in the mercantile policies of the British or the price of tea and other luxuries, which they avoided.

In November 1775, the Mennonites and Brethren jointly addressed the Assembly of Pennsylvania. Their statement was significant, since it was the first time the two churches worked together to present a unified stand. The two sects offered to pay war taxes and accepted the fact that the government sometimes had to transact business that stood outside of their own realms. They also assured the assembly that they meant no offense by their nonresistant stance.[1] The Society of Friends also objected to any change of government achieved by violence rather than by consent, but they spurned all overtures by the Crown to convince them to passively or actively undermine the rebels. Like the German sects, the Quakers just wanted to be left alone to tend to their spiritual struggles.[2]

As the rebellion progressed, most colonies continued to provide members of the peace churches an option to avoid military service by paying a fine. On July 18, 1775, Congress stepped in, passing an ambiguous resolution recommending that the nonresistant practitioners "contribute liberally in this time of universal calamity, to the relief of their distressed brethren in the several colonies." The intent was to make the nonassociators (those who remained neutral) pay for the supplies and wages of the military if they were not going to fight.

When push came to shove, the peace churches discouraged their members from hiring substitutes in lieu of military service. They also, with some few exceptions, consistently refused to take loyalty oaths to the revolutionary government—despite harsh legal and financial penalties levied against them. Some "fighting Quakers" did go to battle, but the majority of that sect remained pacifists, and the meetings disowned any members who took up arms. In Philadelphia, a group of disowned Quakers formed a new church called Free Quakers.

After the war, James Madison, in the first few drafts of the U.S. Constitution, wrote a provision in the Bill of Rights that "no person religiously scrupulous of bearing arms shall be compelled to render military service." However, the constitutional delegates, assuming those rights would be protected by the states, omitted that provision in the final draft.

Again, during the ensuing years of peace, national debate of conscientious objection seemed to fall silent. That neglect changed as the clouds of war amassed near the Mason-Dixon line over the issues of slavery and states' rights during the 1850s. By that time, Mennonites, Quakers, and Brethren were to be found in parts of the South, especially in Virginia and North Carolina. These people, who condemned slavery, suffered during the war because of their nonresistant stance much more than did their brethren to the north. Others had migrated into midwestern states, as well as into Missouri.

As the prospect for civil war became imminent, members of the peace churches in the South faced the likelihood of military conscription. A teenager at the time, Peter S. Hartman of Virginia later explained that his local Mennonite church "decided that if any of the members would voluntarily go to war, they would voluntarily go out of the church, without a church trial or anything of that kind." On the eve of war, the Congress of the Confederated States issued a call for soldiers in March 1861. Hartman noted, "On a Sunday at Weavers Church while there was preaching, a captain came and there notified every man between the ages of eighteen and forty-five to report for war. I never want to see another day like that—a whole congregation in tears."[3]

Most Mennonites voluntarily reported for duty, and authorities hauled away those who resisted. Hartman observed, "They forced our brethren into war. They could not help it."[4] But the military brass soon realized their mistake in coercing the pacifists to bear arms. When in battle, the Mennonite soldiers often sat on their hands. "After [the battle] was over, the captain came to him and asked him whether he shot," Hartman wrote of an acquaintance. "He said, 'No, I didn't see anything to shoot at.' 'Why, didn't you see all those Yankees over there?' 'No, they're people; we don't shoot people.'"[5] General Thomas "Stonewall" Jackson found that the nonresistors lacked a killer instinct: "It is impossible to get them to take correct aim. I, therefore, think it better to leave them at their homes that they may produce supplies for the army."[6]

During planting season, the Confederacy did allow many Mennonite soldiers to return to their farms, but more than one failed to report back for duty, according to Hartman. Many tried to escape west or to Northern states. Some made it; some did not. In the spring of 1862, seventy-two of these nonresistors came upon a handful of Confederate soldiers outside Petersburg, West Virginia. When the soldiers ordered the Mennonites to give up their arms, they offered up their Bibles. The vastly outnumbered soldiers escorted the meek prisoners south to Libby Prison in Richmond, Virginia, where they were held under insufferable conditions for six weeks.

That November, the Southern Provisional Congress passed a law permitting recognized members of the Society of Friends, Dunkers (i.e., Brethren), Christadelphians, and Mennonites to provide substitutes or pay a tax of five hundred dollars to secure exemption. Men who joined a church after the law was passed were ineligible. Brethren and Mennonites discouraged their members from hiring substitutes but grudgingly advised all to pay the war taxes. In some areas of the South, however, the Confederate law was not respected. Elder

P. R. Wrightsman reported that "local authorities arrested many of our Brethren and shut them up in prison and in the stockades in various places, even after they paid the five hundred dollar penalty."[7]

Southern Quakers also faced deprivation during the war, and Friends' meetings agonized over how to counsel their young men. In the end they left it up to the individual's conscience.[8] Some Quakers labored at salt mines, many paid exemption money, while others fled west—but as the Confederacy became more desperate for fighters, the majority were conscripted and sent to military camps even after paying the exemption tax. Those who refused to wear the gray uniform and carry a gun sometimes faced brutal treatment— depending on the nature of the local officers. Eventually many ended up at Andersonville and other horrific interment camps.

In one such camp, zealous officers starved Himelius Hockett for five days, branded him with a three-inch-wide letter "D", bound him to a ball and chain, and ordered him and a companion to unload ordnance cars. A guard waited nearby under orders to pierce him four inches deep with a bayonet if he refused. Instead, at his refusal, Hockett was hung by the thumbs almost clear off the ground. He later noted, "After I remained in this suffering position for some time, the corporal was told that he had no orders to tie up either of us, but to pierce us with bayonets, and that he had better obey orders. So I was untied and pierced with a bayonet."[9]

As the Civil War dragged on, a kind of Underground Railroad developed to help southern conscientious objectors reach security in Northern states. They referred to hiding places in isolated mountains as depots, while guides, known as pilots, conducted the men through the lines. Other conscientious objectors chose to hide out in the woods nearer to home, stealthily picking up food and clothing when needed.

Meanwhile, nonresistors living in the North, with its more stable government, more dominant manpower, and a president with Quaker heritage in his family, fared far better than their Southern compatriots. Congress passed a Federal Militia Act in July 1862, and the ensuing general order provided that exemption would follow the established state militia practice, without specifically citing religious scruples as sufficient cause. Indiana and Ohio provided exemption for conscientious objectors by a commutation payment of two hundred dollars; Pennsylvania, by three hundred dollars. The states used the money to hire substitutes and to care for the wounded and sick.

In February 1864, a new federal law provided alternative service for conscientious objectors. "Members of religious denominations who shall by oath or affirmation declare that they are conscientiously opposed to the bearing of arms" when drafted were assigned to organizations providing help to wounded soldiers or to freed slaves. Alternatively, they could make a commutation payment of three hundred dollars "to be applied to the benefit of the sick and wounded soldiers."[10]

Probably because all three sects condemned slavery, the internecine conflict put many church leaders in a quandary. Their hearts lay with the Union cause, yet they could not desert their peace testimony. The Brethren's Annual Meeting of 1863 asked, "How are we to deal with our brethren who have enlisted and gone to the army as soldiers or teamsters, or those who have been drafted, and are gone to the army?" The cautious answer: "We think it not expedient to consider (or discuss) these questions at this time."[11] Many Quaker meetings in the North expelled members for wearing the uniform, but others decided to forgo discipline, allowing those who had fought to free the slaves to retain membership in the Society.[12] Although all three churches worked with both governments throughout the war to gain greater recognition for conscientious objectors, there is no evidence that they ever coordinated their efforts.

Ironically, two of the most fateful battles of the Civil War raged around Brethren properties. The humble Mumma meetinghouse of the Manor congregation near Sharpsburg, Maryland, was pockmarked with bullet holes as twenty-three thousand men on both sides fell across the fields of Antietam on September 17, 1862. Ten months later, the turning point of the war took place near and around the farm of Jacob Sherfy, a member of the Marsh Creek congregation of Brethren at Gettysburg, Pennsylvania. But again, after the cessation of hostilities, interest in nonresistance subsided; there was no longer a federal or a militia draft.

As the First World War engulfed Europe, a general pacifist sentiment ran deep across the United States. When President Woodrow Wilson's attempts to broker an honest "peace without victory" eventually crumbled under Allied financial and diplomatic pressure, protests rang out across the nation. Organizations such as the American Union against Militarism published public pleas for peace and gathered signatures on petitions. Branches of the Emergency Peace Federation sprang up everywhere and lobbied Congress and the media to support peace. Labor organizations in Seattle, Spokane, and Chicago officially opposed the war. California congressmen reported that most of the mail from their constituents opposed the conflict, and thousands of Americans daily bombarded President Wilson with telegrams, attempting to hold him to his election promise to keep the country out of war.[13]

Wilson fought back, ordering his staff of propaganda specialists to portray the "Huns" as unfeeling monsters who bayoneted infants. He also recruited clergymen and university officials to offer their moral and intellectual support for war. Congress got into the war spirit by passing the Sedition Act, which virtually silenced all opposition to the conflict—whether it originated from a soapbox, a pulpit, or a lectern. The president quickly won the support he desired as the vast majority of Americans seemed willing to accept war as inevitable and, more important, that the conflict could be won.[14]

Extremist hawks, encouraged by the silence of the moderates, lashed out at all who stood in their way. Hundreds of thousands of men enrolled in the American Vigilante Patrol and immediately branded all Socialists, members of the Industrial Workers of the World, Anarchists, and other leftists as villains and traitors. Overnight, scores of Socialist newspapers went bankrupt after the postmaster general pulled their second-class mailing privileges. Labor leader and former Socialist presidential candidate Eugene Victor Debs was jailed for making pacifist comments. Police and national guardsmen forcibly broke strikes. Authorities jailed more than fifty clergymen, as well as officers of the Jehovah's Witnesses. Zealous patriots terrorized "slackers" who refused to buy war bonds, and neighbors suspected of harboring pro-German sympathies were forced to kiss the flag. Others were tarred and feathered, beaten, and run out of town. In the small town of Collinsville, just east of St. Louis, a mob needed no more reason for lynching a man than that he spoke in a foreign accent. With the rising hysteria, the nationalists demanded even more stringent and repressive laws.

Rabid nationalists also attacked all things German, including Mennonite and Brethren churches. Town fathers quickly changed German-sounding city names, while restaurateurs transformed the lowly hamburger into the liberty sandwich and sauerkraut into liberty cabbage. Orchestra leaders avoided the symphonies of Beethoven and Mahler, while school authorities dropped German language classes. Mobs torched some churches of German-speaking peoples and also harassed church members. One Mennonite minister in Whitewater, Kansas, was able to turn the tables on tormentors who had invaded his home, by suggesting that they sing together the anthem "America." He led the singing of the first verse in a vigorous manner and proceeded to sing the following two verses. Members of the mob grew visibly embarrassed when it became evident that they did not know all the words.[15]

On May 18, 1917, Congress passed the Selective Service Act, which included an exemption from battle for members of well-recognized and already existing peace churches. But it also contained a caveat: "No person so exempted shall be exempted from service in any capacity that the President shall declare to be noncombatant." It took President Wilson almost a year to designate the noncombatant units. During the interim, the government ordered all drafted men, including conscientious objectors, into mobilization camps. Because the churches had been caught unprepared and because of the vague nature of the draft bill, Brethren and Mennonite church administrators counseled their men to enroll in the draft. But church leaders soon realized that the federal government had taken a major step backwards since the Civil War in dealing with conscientious objection. At some of the so-called concentration camps, conditions resembled those that had existed in the Confederacy. The situation was even worse for men who refused orders to work. They were court-martialed and sent to federal prisons.

The form of harassment inflicted on the conscientious objector varied in degree of humiliation and physical suffering. Some men were tossed in blankets, while others had to stand at attention for hours out in the open. Some masochistic officers, armed with brooms, scrubbed the conscientious objectors' skin raw as they stood under cold showers. Prodded by bayonets, other conscientious objectors had to endure beatings, mock executions, and long forced runs—or were forced to "baptize" themselves in the human waste of latrine pits.[16]

By October 1917, authorities had tried to rein in camp commanders by ordering them to isolate all conscientious objectors and treat them kindly and respectfully in an effort to win them over. When asked to do simple chores, many objectors complied, mainly out of boredom. In turn, commanders asked them to do more and more—hoping the men would eventually agree to accept full or noncombatant military service. A considerable number of men did bend under this policy.

In March 1918, President Wilson finally released the three classifications of noncombatancy—service in the medical, quartermaster, and engineering corps—all closely connected to combat. Many conscientious objectors were bitterly disappointed. Several hundred who refused to cooperate were automatically convicted under courts-martial. According to War Department figures, more than 64,000 men filed claims for noncombatant status under the Selective Service Act. Local draft boards recognized more than 56,000 claims, but medical examiners found only about 21,000 physically fit for military service. Some 16,000 of those eventually abandoned their conscientious objector status—leaving about 4,000 conscientious objectors. An unknown number of absolutists refused even to register or to appear for medical examinations. In the final tally, objectors were obviously not numerous—especially when compared to the 170,000 draft evaders and almost 3,000,000 men inducted into the armed forces.

Almost a third of the 4,000 objectors eventually entered noncombatant military service. In 1918, because of a labor shortage, the government offered the remaining conscientious objectors an alternative for service unrelated to the military—furloughs to perform farm labor or to work on Quaker war relief programs in France. The government offered no guarantee of pay, but conscientious objectors finally got the chance to engage in civil occupations and pursuits—albeit still under supervision of the armed forces.

War Department records show that of the 504 courts-martial, 17 conscientious objectors were condemned to death and 142 were sentenced to life imprisonment. The average sentence at hard labor in 345 cases totaled sixteen and a half years. Although no objector was officially executed, the roll of the Mennonite *Martyrs' Mirror*—a vast tome containing the names of those who had died for their faith throughout the centuries—did expand during the war years. Wardens at Alcatraz federal prison in California stripped almost all the clothing from four young Hutterite men who refused to don military uniforms and forced them to sleep on a cold concrete floor. They gave the prisoners a ration of half a glass of water per day for four and one-half days. They also beat the men, who were kept in solitary confinement for four months and permitted one hour of exercise per week. In November 1918, authorities placed the men in chains and transferred them to the federal prison at Fort Leavenworth, Kansas, where they suffered more abuse. Joseph and Michael Hofer eventually died in prison. Prison authorities shipped their bodies home clothed in the uniforms that the brothers had refused to wear. When dragged before his own court-martial, Maurice Hess, an Old Order Brethren, declared, "We would, indeed, be hypocrates [*sic*] and base traitors to our profession if we should be unwilling to bear the taunts and jeers of a sinful world, and imprisonment, and torture, and death, rather than to participate in war and military service."[17]

Some argue that Wilson, the first president to have to deal with conscientious objectors under conscription, had no choice. The fervent hawks who dominated public opinion would not tolerate kid-glove treatment for those unwilling to fight. Humanitarian groups, moreover, made no efforts to denounce the despicable treatment or to enlighten the country about the religious tradition of nonresistance.[18] In short, the U.S. government and the American public still did not know what to do with the nation's nonresistant patriots.

Church leaders blamed themselves for the low percentage of conscientious objectors who remained true to their beliefs throughout the ordeal. The Brethren failed to realize that the peace principle had not been passed on to its young people. For years, no church institution had been in place to encourage the young to discuss nonresistance, allowing them to think through the problems of war. Consequently, those who were conscripted failed to resist the psychological and physical pressure applied by military officials.[19] Many Mennonites also agreed with this thesis about their own draftees.

Not until 1933 did the government grant the last of the court-martialed objectors a full and free pardon. Some conscientious objectors hardly had time to catch a breath of fresh air before the winds of war began to blow again.

During the twenty-odd years of peace between the two world wars, the vicious suppression of freedom of speech subsided, but intolerance toward those who refused to wholeheartedly support and promote the virtues of capitalism and industrialism continued to haunt the nation. The popular press promoted what were called anti-Communist crusades, and authorities continued to imprison labor organizers. Members of the historic peace churches, especially traditionally agrarian Mennonites and Brethren who had moved into urban areas, realized that fewer and fewer of their neighbors considered conscientious objection an integral part of religious freedom. For the first time, all three historic peace churches (anticipating another war) cooperated to promote the idea of nonresistance as an inalienable right—despite the fact that, ironically, the American public once again seemed set on peace.

Within a charged atmosphere of national isolationism championed by the likes of aviation hero Charles Lindbergh, a universal peace effort with roots in Great Britain slowly spread across the United States. An antiwar pledge, first circulated at England's Oxford University, surfaced on U.S. campuses and within local Socialist organizations. In 1935, 175,000 American students boycotted classes for a one-day antiwar strike to sign the Oxford Pledge. Still, despite pressure from the isolationists, President Franklin D. Roosevelt pressed for large increases in U.S. defense expenditures.

Meanwhile, at a fall meeting in Newton, Kansas, in 1935 the three sects agreed to form a Joint Committee of the Historic Peace Churches to promote a program that would provide conscientious objectors with furloughs from the military for alternative service beyond military influence or control, spiritual care for the men in these camps, and financial support for the dependents of conscientious objectors.[20] Differences among the churches immediately became apparent. Friends wanted any official policy to include support for absolutist objectors who would refuse to even register for a draft. Both Mennonites and Brethren disagreed, insisting that the government had the right to expect all men to register.

On February 12, 1937, President Roosevelt granted the committee members a sitting. At the White House, they presented a statement putting forth the idea that draft boards should route conscientious objectors directly to a civilian board that would judge their sincerity. Those qualifying for deferments would work in programs set up and managed by the peace churches. The programs would include relief of war sufferers and refugees and of evacuated civilian populations; reconstruction of war-stricken areas; and resettlement of refugees. Other projects would cover reclamation of forests in the United States and elsewhere; relief and reconstruction work in local communities; medical and health services in connection with any of these projects; and farm labor.

"The types of projects we are suggesting are closely related to tasks in which we have been long engaged in times of peace," the committee pointed out. "We would be willing to undertake an extension of these tasks up to the limit of our abilities." The members also stressed that they were "concerned that any arrangements . . . would also be extended to all conscientious objectors who act from similar convictions, whatever their affiliation."[21]

Three years later, the draft legislation introduced into Congress, known as the Burke-Wadsworth Bill, mentioned nothing about alternative civilian service for conscientious objectors and instead proposed designating them for noncombatant service within the army. In other words, Congress wanted to revert to the troublesome World War I arrangement.[22] Church lobbyists scrambled into action, pleading for a more liberal bill, determined that some of their requests were not to be denied.

The ensuing Burke-Wadsworth Selective Service Act of 1940 created the first peacetime conscription in U.S. history. Although the three churches did not receive everything they had asked for, the act was far superior to anything their ancestors had seen since settling in Pennsylvania. Although the law contained no provision for absolutists, it did offer religious conscientious objectors alternative service outside the military in "work of national importance under civilian direction." The law also presented a broader definition for objection—one based upon religious training and belief—which opened the door to those who did not belong to the historic peace churches. A third unique offering allowed the draftee to file an appeal in the event the local Selective Service board refused him conscientious objector status. And finally, a provision removed the control of alternative work from the armed forces and gave it to civilians.

The Selective Service identified a dozen types of conscientious objectors but for the most part recognized only religious

and, to a limited degree, moral objectors. According to guide-
lines published by the Department of Justice, the religious
objector believed in "a personal Creator whose immortal laws
forbid the killing of human beings, particularly as set forth in
the Commandment: Thou Shalt Not Kill." The moral or ethical objector considered war to be

> inconsistent with his moral philosophy and humanitari-
> anism which is independent of religious beliefs, except
> as it may be predicated upon a belief in a brotherhood
> of man. . . . His conscience is bound by a moral law,
> which enjoins him from having to do with so destructive
> and futile a force as war, which evidences a breakdown
> of reason by substituting force. In fact, most of this type
> of objector denies a belief in a deity except insofar as
> there may be a moral force in the universe. It is his view
> that mankind is sufficient to itself, that it owes no obli-
> gation to any power except humankind, and that it may
> achieve perfection in and of itself without the interposi-
> tion of any deity or supernatural power.[23]

According to the government psychologists, those two
belief systems were legitimate. But men who couched their
petitions in other terms often faced rejection. Those considered unworthy of the conscientious objector deferment
included the economic, political, and philosophical objectors. Also unacceptable were the sociological objector, who
based his objections "upon a theory that war has no place in
his own particular ordering of society," and the international-
ist objector, who would destroy or abolish "all international
boundaries and sovereignty, racial and trade lines, and consider the world one big family of peoples devoid of war." Sym-
pathetic draft boards often encouraged other types of
objectors to express their beliefs in a manner that fit within

the religious or moral categories. Unsympathetic boards often denied a 4-E exemption to legitimate conscientious objectors, prompting appeals to the Selective Service.

The weakest arguments before the draft boards were those of the neurotic objector, who had "a phobia of war's atrocities, a mental and physical fear and abhorrence of killing or maiming"; the naturalistic objector, who abhorred blood; and the professional pacifist, whom government psychologists branded as one who "wants to enjoy all the protections of the Government, but is unwilling to bear any of the responsibilities of citizenship in this respect."

And finally came the Jehovah's Witness, who would pick and choose the wars he participated in. The Jehovah's Witness objected to "all man-made wars and Governments, but says he is not a conscientious objector to all wars, since he would fight and kill in defense of the Theocracy, his property and his brethren."[24] Most Jehovah's Witnesses refused to apply for 4-E status. Instead, since the church considers each convert a minister of the gospel, most witnesses insisted on ministerial deferrals—which the government refused. Although scores of Jehovah's Witnesses did enter CPS, about five thousand ended up serving prison terms.

Although the Selective Service bill originally stated that the alternative service would fall under civilian supervision, this never happened. The churches first proposed to General Lewis B. Hershey—key administrator of the Selective Service agency—plans for three kinds of camps: those run and financed solely by the government; those run cooperatively by a peace church and the government, with the church administering the camp and the government responsible for the work project and maintenance; and those financed and run solely by the church. The president, thinking that the conscientious objectors were getting off too lightly, took violent exception to the proposal. Hershey then asked the peace churches if they would be willing to administer all of the camps for conscientious objectors, bearing all the costs except for the transport of drafted men and the direction of the actual work projects. The only other alternative was to seek congressional appropriations for the camps to be run solely by the government. The peace churches agreed to try to administer and finance the camps for a six-month trial period.

At first the Selective Service planned to hold the men at least one year, maybe eighteen months. But once the war began, the rules changed and the men stayed in CPS camps for the duration. The government also altered the terms of financing the camps. The three peace churches not only ended up writing the country a blank check to care for the men, but in the end they had no say in the quality of work assigned to the volunteers. "In short, the churches provided a home for the men so they would be available to work without pay on government projects," observed historian Richard C. Anderson.[25]

The absolutists who refused to enroll in CPS accused the churches of selling out and becoming agents of the state to protect their own from harm. Their individual protests, for the most part, led to federal prosecution and lengthy prison sentences.

Once the CPS program was under way, the government set up the camps, and the churches informed the men where to report. According to Gregg Phifer, a CPS smoke jumper who later became a professor at Florida State University in Tallahassee, the CPS base camps followed the pattern of the Civilian Conservation Corps, which had been abandoned once the war effort started pulling in the available manpower of the country and the weapons production lines of the military-industrial complex popped into gear.

"Following CCC meant that CPS assignees served the Forest Service, the National Park Service, or Soil Conservation," Phifer observed. "Early camps were all under the auspices of one of the historic peace churches. Much to the dismay of many Catholic bishops, a Catholic camp opened in New England. And the Methodists, my denomination, established a detached service unit at Duke University. The military ran the Three Cs, but Selective Service and the National Service Board for Religious Objectors [NSBRO] formed an uneasy partnership to administer CPS."

During the later years of the program, at the urging of many CPSers who had tired of work of what some called "national impotence," NSBRO developed special projects that involved more direct human assistance. More than two thousand CPSers volunteered to work in forty-one under-staffed psychiatric facilities and seventeen training schools for those who were considered mentally handicapped. Objectors in these units blew the whistle on the rampant negligence and brutality within the mental hospital system. Experts in the field credit the CPSers with stimulating whole-scale national reform of this system.

Others volunteered as "human guinea pigs" for medical experiments. The most widely known project involved an experiment monitoring near-starvation conditions, which was conducted by scientists at the University of Minnesota. Gregg Phifer explained that one of his friends "volunteered for the so-called starvation unit, living on extremely low calorie meals to let scientists study conditions they expected to find in post-war Europe." The research proved to be of great assistance in planning the rehabilitation of war sufferers after the armistice. Other CPS men, including four hundred Brethren, were assigned to agricultural projects such as dairy testing or farm-work under the Emergency Farm Labor program.

Quite a few CPSers wanted desperately to serve overseas in the tradition of the British Friends Ambulance Unit. Eleanor Roosevelt favored the idea and persuaded her husband to endorse it. With Selective Service approval, the first contingent of men shipped out to China in 1943. However, right-wing columnist Westbrook Pegler got wind of the project and publicly condemned it. Reacting to vehement public protests, the U.S. Congress attached a rider to an appropriations bill for the War Department that forbade any CPSer from serving outside the country. The shipload of workers bound for China, by then rounding the Cape of Good Hope, was called back to port.

Eventually the Selective Service set up a few government camps that had no religious affiliation. These camps catered to agnostics, atheists, and absolutists, as well as troublemakers expelled from religious camps.

"Although the law was not as liberal as the peace groups had hoped for, it was certainly more reasonable and considerate of conscientious objectors than it would have been had the churches and other organizations not worked so constantly with the government," observed historian Rufus Bowman.[26]

From 1940 to 1947, more than seventy-two thousand draft registrants filed for conscientious objection status. Not all were accepted. Of the twelve million men drafted during World War II, the Selective Service granted conscientious objector status to about twelve thousand, classifying them as 4-E. These men served in Civilian Public Service. The Selective Service granted 1-A-O status to another twenty-five thousand men who agreed to sign up with the military but only for noncombatant duties. No one knows how many other men ignored the draft call altogether, but the Selective Service reported more than six thousand convictions for violations of the act. About nine times more objectors were sent to prison during the Second World War than during the First World War; in proportion to the larger number of draftees for World War II, there were still two to three times more prisoners in the later conflict on a relative basis.[27]

Most men assigned to CPS received two dollars and fifty cents a month for their services. Politicians rationalized that the virtual work-without-pay balanced the sacrifice of the men in uniform. General Hershey was convinced that if CPS men were paid, "it would destroy the best public relations."[28]

Eventually, the CPSers represented 230 different churches, the vast majority coming from the historic peace churches and the Methodists. Other individuals occasionally applied from more obscure denominations such as the African Methodist Episcopal Church, Church of the Open Door, Hepzibah Faith, Christian Spiritual Jumpers, Schwenkfelders, Black Moslems, and Zoroastrians. With the courts eventually ruling that agnostics with no particular church connection could oppose war "on a general humanitarian concept which is essentially religious in character,"[29] about 450 men accepted into CPS claimed no church affiliation.

Of the CPSers representing the three peace churches, about 6,000 were Mennonites. The Church of the Brethren followed with more than 1,300, while the Society of Friends numbered 951.

On the surface the government may seem to have come a long way in providing a sufficient alternative for most conscientious objectors—but problems arose as the war dragged on. As many men grew bored with the meaningless labor, activists accused the church administrators of the camps of becoming part of the military establishment.[30] In March 1946, the American Friends Service Committee withdrew from camp administration months after hundreds of radical conscientious objectors walked out of the camps to sit out the duration of the war in prison, while others, who remained, engaged in work slowdowns, strikes, and other forms of Gandhi-like nonviolent protest.[31] Most of the dissenters resided at the nondenominational camps.

Despite the advances in accommodating nonresistors, most draft-age members of the three peace churches chose to enlist in the armed services. Mennonite church officials estimated that about 40 percent of the men eligible to be drafted became soldiers, while about 15 percent chose noncombatant work and the rest were assigned to CPS camps.[32] It was the sole historic peace church that could boast that the majority of its members chose some form of alternative service. As for those Mennonites who did enlist in the military, the GI never knew what kind of chastisement he might receive from his individual congregation. At the time there were thirteen different ribs under the Mennonite umbrella, and they all took different approaches to the problem. Some churches that threatened to revoke membership to GIs when the war began, backed off as they witnessed the expansion of the trend to enlist. Other churches pronounced that those in regular military service or defense work had severed their relationship with their church. The General Mennonite Conference Church, one of the major divisions, tried to provide grounds for bringing the men back into the churches without condoning their error. All together, the Mennonites lost nine hundred members because of the nonresistance issue—a major loss for a church with only fifty thousand total congregants.

Walter Reimer, born in Goessel, Kansas, had attended the local Alexanderwohl Mennonite Church. Both he and his older brother were drafted. While his brother enlisted in the army, Walter became a conscientious objector and eventually a smoke jumper. "This was typical in my church," he wrote. "About fifty percent [went] to CPS."

In the Brethren sects, about 90 percent of military-age men chose to accept the uniform, with only about fourteen hundred of those opting for noncombatant service within the military. In all, fewer than 20 percent of those members drafted followed the church's peace position.[33] Although the church officially counseled young men to take advantage of CPS, it also recognized conscientious objectors as citizens of the state who had a responsibility for serving their country in harmony with their conscience.[34]

A rift occurred as well in the Quaker church. An unsubstantiated report circulated after the war estimated that more than 50 percent of the male Friends of draft age served in the military.[35]

During the war, Dr. Rufus D. Bowman, president of Bethany Biblical Seminary, surveyed 161 Brethren churches, asking why Brethren boys enlisted in the armed services. The young men responded with several reasons: duty to country, social pressure, the economic problem, inadequate peace teaching, the feeling that the war was forced upon them, indifference to the church, and lack of sympathy with the conscientious objector position.[36] Bowman concluded that the Church of the Brethren had "moved some distance from its historical peace convictions" despite its official peace stance during World War II.

These facts illustrate the difficulties that young men faced in declaring conscientious objection during the "good war." The social pressures urging conformity often overwhelmed them. That same pressure would remain for another twenty-odd years.

In 1951, during the Korean War, Congress restricted the definition of conscientious objector to one whose military objection came from a belief in a Supreme Being. This qualification served to weed out objectors primarily motivated by moral or humanitarian concerns. As a result, the vast majority of objectors during the entire cold war era came from the three historic peace churches.

The Universal Military Training and Service Act of 1951 directed duly classified conscientious objectors into "such civilian work contributing to the maintenance of the national health, safety, or interest as the local board may deem appropriate."[37] President Harry S Truman laid out the arrangements a year later, directing the Selective Service to assign objectors to positions in government or nongovernment agencies providing health, welfare, charitable, educational, or scientific services. Some positions paid a wage, while others demanded strictly volunteer work. Conscientious objectors (or I-Ws, as they came to be called in accordance with their classification) could not work in their home communities, but they did have some say in choosing the type of work they wanted. They could also volunteer for an assignment before receiving a draft notice. The biggest change was that church administrators—just as they had requested—were not involved at all.

Historian Perry Bush described the I-W program as a great improvement over CPS, especially in the freedom of choice, more meaningful assignments, and steady pay. Since only members of the peace churches qualified, the Selective Service no longer had to deal with many dissenters or troublemakers. Moreover, since the conscientious objectors were mostly out of sight, they were also out of mind as far as the public was concerned.[38]

By 1955, a total of 4,500 men had enrolled as I-Ws—more than two-thirds of them were Mennonite. From 1952 to 1967, the Selective Service reported that of the estimated 11,500 conscientious objectors of that era, 14 percent belonged to the Church of the Brethren, about 4 percent to the Society of Friends, and about 67 percent to the different Mennonite groups.[39]

In the mid-1960s, as the United States shipped more and more ground troops into Vietnam, the Supreme Court broadened the definition of conscientious objector. The 1964 Seeger ruling opened the door for conscientious objectors from other congregations outside the three peace churches, and in 1970, the Welsh ruling opened I-W service to secular objectors who morally opposed war. At that point the floodgates burst open, and for the first time young men belonging to the historic peace churches became a pronounced minority among conscientious objectors. Between

1965 and 1970, more than 170,000 drafted men obtained conscientious objector classification—so many that the beleaguered Selective Service could not arrange alternative jobs for up to half of them. In 1972, the year before the draft ended, the Selective Service classified more registrants as conscientious objectors than it inducted into the military. Many other men refused to register for the draft or to cooperate in other ways with the Selective Service.

By the 1970s, American society seemed to have become more tolerant of dissidents and people of conscience. Many Americans also changed their attitude toward war. Although the majority of Americans voted to support the continuation of the Vietnam War in 1972 when they reelected the hawkish President Richard M. Nixon over his dovish Democratic opponent Senator George McGovern, few in society seemed to think that war in Vietnam was a good idea—rather, it seemed a conflict that could not be abandoned without some sort of resolution.

The Vietnam War drastically divided the nation, just as the war in Iraq did in 2004. After Vietnam, however, the armed forces of the nation had turned to an all-volunteer basis, and the draft had become a moot point. Young men still had to register for the draft but did not face being called up. Consequently, they had no need to declare conscientious objection or not. Only time will tell whether the nation's young men—and maybe young women—will ever have to make that decision or what the social pressures will be like if they do.

CHAPTER TWO

The Historic Peace Churches

The three historic peace churches that united to lobby for reforming the treatment of conscientious objectors during World War II shared many religious beliefs, but they also differed in many aspects—especially in dogma and ritual. Most important, though, they all agreed that men and women should never do harm to others (physically, emotionally, socially, or economically) or retaliate with violence and aggression when attacked. This doctrine of nonresistance is what bound them together.

MENNONITE

For Clarence Tieszen, who grew up in a Mennonite community in eastern Montana, each parachute jump became a distinct adventure. One very hot afternoon, Tieszen was fire boss on a two-man stick (the number of parachutists who dropped on a fire at one time). With no open meadow offering a gentle landing spot, he guided his chute toward the timber and draped his canopy over the tip of a tall tree. After sliding down to the end of his let-down rope, he still faced a long drop to the ground. At first he tried to swing himself to the trunk to grab a branch and climb down, but each pendulum-like movement caused the chute to slip a little. However, the greater fear of burning alive prompted Tieszen to keep trying. He recalled,

> I had to do something, I couldn't wait for my partner to come; he could also be in trouble. In desperation I tried swinging into the tree again and the chute held and I got down. When I got to the fire my partner had [it] almost surrounded with a fireline. That was great, but I was somewhat miffed that he hadn't first come to check and see if I was hurt or why I wasn't at the fire, especially when the fire wasn't going anywhere fast. When I asked him, he replied with, "Yes, I was about to go look for you, but thought I should first put a line around the fire."
> The fire boss didn't get first consideration on that fire.

In 1916, the Tieszens had migrated from a developed farming community in southern Minnesota to eastern Montana's sagebrush-covered plains that were inhabited by coyotes, jackrabbits, and American Indians. Clarence was born six years later, the oldest of a half-dozen children. He said of his parents that "they must have had a lot of faith and a great spirit of adventure to venture twenty-five miles [from the nearest town] out on the unknown prairies in horse and wagon to stake out their future." At Clarence's birth, the Tieszens lived in a building that served as both barn and home, with a wall separating the living area from the animal stalls.

But the family was not completely isolated. The Lustre Mennonite Community quickly took root in the area as others migrated into Montana to homestead. "Their goal was to establish a Christian community and live the Mennonite tradition they inherited," Tieszen wrote. "They were quite successful with that, living their beliefs and allowing little influence from the world contrary to their convictions. Non-violence and pacifism was taught, and, if persecuted because of their religious beliefs, to turn the other cheek." In typical fashion, the Mennonites insulated their community center far from cities and major highways. It had "no corner drug store." All social activities centered on family, church, and the schools—which eventually consolidated into an academy. The community survived without electricity until the 1940s.

"Growing up in this kind of sheltered community left me quite ignorant about the immorality and lawlessness in this world," Tieszen wrote. At CPS camp, he continued, "I was the only one there from my home area and suddenly having to live and work with complete strangers in different surroundings was a lonely and shocking beginning."

Roy Wenger, the director of the smoke jumpers' CPS camp, was born into a Mennonite family in Ohio. He remembered old stories that were "passed down from my grandfathers and through my father and mother about restrictions and repressiveness in the old country—in Alsace and Switzerland—concerning military conscription during the Napoleonic wars. There were stories about leaving those countries to find places where military service was not required. The church community from its beginnings was opposed to war as an institution—opposed to all wars—because no one should train for or carry out acts of violence threatening the lives of others."

In sixteenth-century Germany and the Netherlands, officials of the state-sponsored Catholic and Protestant Reformed churches hunted down, tortured, and brutally murdered thousands of early-day Mennonites (then called Anabaptists, or rebaptizers, for their belief in adult baptism). Consequently, the sect became a martyr church—much like the original Christian church during the first four hundred years of its existence. Personal suffering for the Mennonites became a badge of distinction, a qualification of membership. They even recorded the names and lives of thousands of their ancestors who had been murdered, in a 1,582-page volume entitled *The Martyrs' Mirror.* The tome measures ten inches wide by fifteen inches long and is five inches thick.

The *Mirror* stood as testimony that the Mennonite church was not for the faint of heart or for those who interpreted the teachings of Christ to fit their own lifestyles. Mennonites accepted that the demanding ethic of Christian love and suffering superseded all other human law and tradition, even if the consequences included death and severe persecution. As a result, Mennonites kept their noses out of politics (although they did occasionally vote), avoided joining secret societies (such as the Masons), refused to take oaths, and avoided lawsuits.[1] Although they functioned within the world, they formed a community with distinct boundaries. For all intents and purposes, their king and kingdom waited beyond this world.

As happens in most religious sects, the Mennonite church fragmented over various issues and practices. At the start of World War II, thirteen different Mennonite sects—such as the Amish, Hutterite, Mennonite Church, and General Conference Mennonite Church—existed in the United States. Despite church differences, many Mennonite parents assiduously taught nonresistance to their children.

Luke Birkey, a CPS smoke jumper, was born on a farm near Airlie, Oregon. His mother, Sarah, was a schoolteacher, and his father, Joseph, farmed in Oregon and Montana. His four grandparents, all members of the Mennonite Church, "were more comfortable with the German language . . . than English." As a small boy, Birkey learned that his religion set him apart from the other children: "I recall once we moved into a new community and early in the school year several bullies felt they needed to beat us up, and did. This experience was discussed in our family. My mother then made a batch of candy and we were instructed to take it to school and share it with our tormentors. We did. As time went on these individuals became our best friends."

By mostly residing in isolated agrarian communities for their first two hundred years in America, Mennonites easily maintained the line of demarcation between their religious world and the social and political world of the nonbelievers. But after the First World War, many Mennonites migrated to urban areas, attended college, and pursued professional careers, prompting their assimilation into mainstream society.[2]

There was also a subtle shift, begun in the late 1800s, in their religious makeup. No longer persecuted and murdered for their beliefs, the more liberal Mennonites began to shade their religious outlook with a gentler, more pietistic, evangelical hue. The churches developed Sunday schools, foreign and domestic missions, and institutions of higher living. They became more involved in politics—especially in the campaign for the prohibition of alcohol in the 1920s. Consequently, by the time World War II rolled around, young Mennonite men such as Wenger, Birkey, and Tieszen had a lot more to mull over when facing the draft than did their American ancestors back in the days of the Revolutionary War and Civil War.

QUAKER

Rupert H. Stanley and Helen McCorckle married a year after graduating from Monmouth College in Indiana; they then sailed from San Francisco on the *Manchuria* with sixty-four other missionaries, many of whom were young Quaker couples like themselves. Their goal: to spread the Word of God in China. Rupert, a YMCA secretary, worked primarily with college students at various Chinese universities. On April 19, 1919, Helen gave birth to her third son, Philip, in the city of Kiafeng, in northwestern China's Honan Province.

Even though thirty years had passed since the founding of the Chinese Republic, the Stanleys soon discovered that China was still politically unstable, with local warlords continually battling for territory. Not far from the Stanley home, various factions fought bloody battles in the fields and woods near the local grade school that Phil eventually attended. When the troops left the battlefields, Phil and his young cohorts rummaged for shell casings and artillery duds in the weeds and brought the trophies home to show off to schoolmates and parents. "I remember a half dozen missionaries and their children sitting in our living room passing a dud aerial bomb from hand to hand with surpassing innocence and curiosity," Stanley said. As local wars escalated, zealous foot soldiers sometimes aimed their loaded rifles at the foreigners "with a finger on the trigger."

Phil became conditioned to feeling part of a minority. Not quite an outcast in China, nonetheless he learned what it was like to live outside the mainstream of society. "The vast majority of Chinese were very friendly and mainly curious because they had never seen a white before. Because all whites looked alike, they could tell who was Russian, who not, by the size of their hats." This experience as an outsider later helped him decide to speak out against a popular war after he grew to be a young man.

By 1927, the danger in China had escalated, and the YMCA brought the missionaries home. Phil was eight at the time, brother Jim, ten, and Rupert, twelve. After a brief stay at their old home territory in Indianapolis, Indiana, Phil's parents accepted positions in Pennsylvania to teach at Westtown School, a Quaker boarding school. Later, when his parents moved to New York City to attend Columbia University, Phil was enrolled in a private school founded by Felix Adler and run by his Society for Ethical Culture. A feeling of alienation lingered in Phil's mind, even in the land of his countrymen: "We found that we still belonged to a small minority after returning to the states because world travel at the time was pretty unusual. Being born out of the country was even more unusual. We learned to avoid any mention of our origins just to avoid the tedious questions."

The Stanleys also differed from most Americans in their choice of religion. According to the publication *Religious Bodies—1936*, 717 Quaker churches (with a total of almost 94,000 members) existed in the United States that year. Other Americans seldom understood the unique way of worship at Quaker meetings.

As a young man, Phil Stanley would have arrived a little early for Sunday service at the meetinghouse to find a seat before the appointed hour when silence would ensue—a time of meditation to rinse the mind of prejudices and grievances. The stillness also helped melt the various social statuses and physical distinctions of the gathered. After a while, someone might speak, and the meeting would begin to take one of three directions. Random observations on some mild moral issue could lead to more silence. Or the words of one Friend could inspire another to speak in the same vein, culminating in a group sermon. Another time, uninspired words might lead to an intellectual argument better suited for the lecture room—and the meeting could go dead, which was not uncommon.

However, if "released through the indefinably right words of a particular speaker or more usually though a sudden crystallization within the silence itself," then the meeting could lead to a spiritual breakthrough as the group contributions helped individuals recognize their own Inner Light and, consequently, "reflect God's spirit." The unity among the assembled might last only a minute, or longer, but it could seem timeless. It is this group, or corporate, experience for which Quakers strive.[3]

Few Quakers have private raptures, and there are no great Quaker contemplatives. Instead, the Friends use the meeting as a method to induce "the Light of God to flood into the conscious mind." When a meeting is really fruitful, each participant feels His presence within. But one scholar has noted, "as with all methods it is open to failure for a hundred and one reasons."[4] The Inner Light, the Guide, the Good Angel, the Atman, the Seed, the Witness, and That of God in every man—several different terms define the Quaker connection with God.

This revolutionary type of worship germinated in England toward the end of the 1640s, at the time when Parliament was pitted against the king and the Puritan movement against the state-supported Church of England. During the previous century, London had become a hotbed for the cross-fertilization of many religious ideas. This atmosphere prepared the ground for George Fox, who started preaching a new type of "older" worship in 1647. He preached that all believers in Christ, as in the days before the established church, possessed the knowledge and authority to be "spiritual planters, and spiritual waterers."[5]

Disheartened by the attempts of kings and priests to uphold their own power by controlling the spiritual life of the common man, Fox disrupted church services, vilified the "steeple houses," and preached to multitudes in meadows. Fox held silent meetings of worship, encouraged women to minister alongside men, and enjoined his followers to lead outward lives of simplicity and neighborly affection. Fox did not believe that individuals were inherently sinful and corrupt. Nor did he consider the Bible the final word on religious truth. He considered Jesus a perfect human being—one who had listened to the Voice Within. If others followed Christ's example, Fox reasoned, then they also could attain spiritual perfection.

Fox also adopted simplicity in speech and dress and refused to swear judicial oaths. Those who followed his example never doffed a hat to anyone, believing in equality between man and woman, servant and master, old and young—and, eventually, slave and master. Socially, Fox offered the same protests against the ruling establishment that were commonly voiced at that time by artisans, tradesmen, and small farmers—the "disillusioned decent poor."[6] Fox discerned that the laws protecting property were expanding, while those protecting human rights were becoming ever more constricted. He advised overhauling the legal system so that the laws of the land, written in layman's English, would fit into a pocket-size book. He wanted to rid the country of priests and lawyers. He insisted on freedom of speech, assembly, and worship. But Fox never preached political revolution. He and his followers believed that the discovery of peace within each man or woman will lead to the pursuit of peace without.

Although Fox visited America for a short period, he left the planting of the Quaker seed in the soil of the New World to William Penn, who received the land grant of Pennsylvania as repayment of a royal debt owed his father. Penn hoped to form an ideal commonwealth based on Quaker principles of reconciliation and peace that would stand as an shining example to the rest of the Christian world.[7]

That social experiment came to an end during the years leading up to the American Revolution. Unlike the Mennonites and the Brethren, the Quakers had always been deeply involved in society, especially in the fields of trade, merchandising, and manufacturing. Quaker businessmen were famous for their honesty. From World War I on, the Friends also reached out to many dispossessed and poor through the American Friends Service Committee. They also proactively solicited public support in behalf of equality for women and minorities, of fair labor practices, and for peace.

Despite a strong and consistent peace testimony declared by Quaker meetings throughout their American experience, some Quakers have always chosen to fight for their country. By World War I, the church had stopped expelling members who joined the armed services. With such a history and background, it was no surprise that Phil Stanley would agonize over his decision to become a conscientious objector. But he had also been traumatized by the loss of his mother; doubt and confusion paralyzed his mind when Helen Stanley fell dead one morning while greeting parishioners after a service. She was forty-three.

"Her death left me, thirteen at the time, with serious misgivings about Divine Justice," Stanley wrote. "I can attest to the fact that a thirteen-year-old boy needs a mother." Moreover, the winds of war in Germany coincided with "strange new urges in my body, a new stepmother, poorly understood grievance procedures and a perennial shortage of money." Despite the internal and external pressures, Stanley managed to finish high school and was accepted into Oberlin College, but he dropped out his sophomore year. When brought face to face with the draft in 1942, the regimen and narrow focus of the military at first attracted him, but in the end, Stanley stuck with the teachings of his youth. He requested a 4-E classification as a conscientious objector and was assigned to a Civilian Public Service camp at Patapsco, New Jersey.

Stanley's moral and philosophical dilemma seems to have been typical for Quakers. It was reported that more Quakers enlisted in the armed services than enrolled in CPS during the Second World War. This is not a very strong acknowledgment of the traditional Quaker corporate view, which still officially backed nonresistance to violence and war. Still, other Friends joined CPS, and a few took the more extreme absolutist stance by refusing to even recognize conscription. Many Quakers also studied the teachings of Gandhi and began using techniques, which the Hindu spiritual leader had exemplified for various purposes, to pressure for social change. In this respect, the Inner Light seems to have been interpreted differently by very many young men.

BRETHREN

Clarence E. Quay from Chester County, Pennsylvania, grew up a member of the Church of the Brethren, often called Dunkers because of their tradition of baptism by immersion. His was a tight-knit agricultural community where neighboring families often helped one another with seasonal chores, such as sausage making. "I remember that a large copper kettle used to cook the sausage was borrowed from a neighbor," Quay recalled. "A tripod was set up to hold the dead hog for butchering, a table or two was put up to cut the meat and wrap it in packages, and a fire was started to heat the copper kettle for making sausage."[8]

When Quay was five or six years old, he sat on the fence watching his father and some neighbors prepare to kill a hog. After Quay's father isolated the desired animal, a neighbor offered him a .22-caliber rifle to finish it off. But the senior Quay shook his head and handed back the weapon. The neighbor shot the hog, and then Quay's father helped pull the carcass onto the tripod, where he cleaned and butchered it. Young Clarence Quay grew up hunting deer and rabbit, but as a teenager he began thinking about his father's refusal to shoot the hog. The subtle lesson stuck with him throughout his lifetime. "I am not sure how much this experience has affected my faith in not taking the life of a person," he wrote, "but the fact that I remembered it has something to say about the affect [*sic*] it has had on me."

As a smoke jumper, Quay surprised himself by not hesitating at all on his first jump, which proceeded smoothly. On a later occasion, however, he found himself in a dangerous predicament. He recalled,

> My seventh jump was scary. I was in the door of the plane ready to jump when I noticed that the strap of my pant leg, which is normally around under the shoe, was not fastened and had made a lap around the step of the Travelaire plane on which I had my foot. Suddenly the back of my mouth got dry and I could not talk. I got the attention of the spotter and pointed to the step of the plane. He saw the predicament I was in and signaled the pilot to make another circle while he got my leg back in the plane and fastened the strap properly.

Quay's family belonged to the Parker Ford Church of the Brethren in Pennsylvania. When Quay was in high school, he wrote an essay on the financial costs of World War I; he titled it "The Price of War." During the research for this paper, he discovered how profitable war could be: "Before the war the average yearly profits of the Central Leather Company was $13 million. In 1916 Central returned a profit of $15.5 million. The international Nickel Company showed an increase from a mere average of $4 million a year to $73 million a year." This knowledge of corporate profiteering influenced Quay's decision to become a conscientious objector as much as his church doctrine did. He asked later, "Why should I risk my life so that a few others can make huge profits? To say nothing of the destruction of life and property."

Still, he found the decision difficult:

> It was not the patriotic thing to do. You are expected to support your country and do your part to win the war against the Japanese who attacked us at Pearl Harbor. I was willing to do my part, but that did not include killing the enemy. My parents said the decision was up to me. I felt I had the support of the church, but not of the community, and I did not know about relatives of the family and I did not know about my friends. But I made the decision not to participate in the military. . . . My pastor was very helpful in assisting me [to] fill out the various forms for 4-E classification and even went with me to the local draft board.

The Brethren sect came to life in Germany at Schwarzenau in the early 1700s. Its founder, Alexander Mack, was a leading Pietist from the area around Heidelberg. Pietism was a movement among Protestants that emphasized the believer's personal behavior and spiritual consciousness rather than church doctrine. As the group studied the life and teachings of Jesus Christ, Mack noted that the Gospel of Matthew urged followers of Christ to settle disputes "in the church"—so he decided to break with the Reformed Church and establish the new sect. In August 1708, five men and three women assembled near a stream. The other men chose straws to see who would first baptize Mack—with triple immersion. Mack then baptized the others. They never revealed the identity of the first baptizer so that his name could never be associated with that of the sect.

The group immediately began to expand, with most of its adherents emigrating to Pennsylvania by the mid-1700s. After the trials and tribulations of the American Revolution, the Brethren (following tradition) fled to safer havens. This time, they migrated south and west into the frontier. Those who remained in Pennsylvania moved to new counties.[9] Much like the Mennonites, the Brethren slowly emerged from their self-imposed isolation after the Civil War and became more involved in society by printing a church newspaper and establishing Sunday schools, colleges, and missions. As church doctrine became less legalistic, officials began to tolerate and respect differing views by individual members. Brethren young people attended public schools and colleges and joined life in the larger community. Again like the Mennonite church, the Brethren fractured into a handful of different sects adhering to slightly different doctrines.

World War I stimulated the Brethren to reevaluate their peace position. The church developed strong programs for children, young people, and adults—even setting up summer camps. Young Brethren attended college in greater numbers and entered professional fields. More students earned higher degrees. As a strong missionary enthusiasm evolved, sparking a growth of interest in relief and reconstruction projects, the church formed the Brethren Service Committee. The Brethren also pressured more for political action and began to address the growing problems between labor and management. "The Brethren looked out of itself, overcame in a large degree its inferiority complex and focused its attention upon the needs of the world," observed historian Rufus D. Bowman.[10]

The publication *Religious Bodies—1936* reported almost fourteen hundred Brethren churches in the United States, with a total membership of 180,000 members, before the Second World War—making the Brethren the largest of the historic peace churches. In 1940, the church reaffirmed that "we continue to advise our young men that noncombatant service within the army is inconsistent with the teachings of the Bible and the Church of the Brethren. Further, that it cannot be reconciled with our historic peace position."[11]

Still, at the time Clarence E. Quay faced the draft, many young Brethren men agonized over what road to take. The deficiencies seemed to rest at the local congregation level. Before the war, pastors had received scant training about the importance of conferring with young men about nonresistance so that their convictions could mature.[12]

PEACE TESTIMONY AND WARTIME ACCULTURATION

Within all three historic peace churches at the time of the outbreak of the Second World War, the peace testimony seemed to be taken for granted. Church officials expected their young men to automatically refuse the uniform and were startled when many chose otherwise. In reality, the choices for young members of these churches had become more clouded ever since the American Revolution and, especially south of the Mason-Dixon line, the Civil War. With acculturation almost complete by the 1940s, they found it harder than ever to strictly follow the peaceful teachings of Christ—especially with friends, schoolmates, teachers, colleagues, neighbors, and, in some instances, relatives carefully watching and judging.

CHAPTER THREE

Yellowbellies

"What would you do if a German came up to you and stuck a bayonet in your stomach?" A drunken teenager spat this question into the face of Gilbert Weldy, a CPS smoke jumper stationed at McCall, Idaho. During the Second World War, the town housed only seven hundred people: mostly loggers, mill workers, and their families, who supported seven bars that lined the dusty main street. During the summer, the population expanded as tourists from Boise and Nampa flocked to the nearby lake and surrounding mountains.

The confrontation occurred in the Dog House, one of the more respectable bars in town, according to Weldy. Underage drinkers accessed the bar through an alley entrance that opened into a back room filled with chairs and tables. A jukebox against a wall inspired sporadic dancing. Once a year the local sheriff raided the joint for illegal gambling and fined the owner one hundred dollars. "It was considered a sort of tax," Weldy explained. When the CPS smoke jumpers stationed at the satellite or spike camp, with its wilderness landing strip, "got lonely for a little social life," they often joined the gang at the Dog House.

On this occasion, the Dog House hummed with activity, and Weldy bumped into two local youths celebrating their last night of freedom before leaving for Navy boot camp. Weldy had played basketball with both youths during the winter, but on this occasion they decided to harass him. He recalled,

> They were drinking and beginning to feel a little belligerent. One of them, Ray Watkins by name, chose me to be the object of his last night's fun. He challenged me with this question: "Hey, why aren't you in uniform?" The question wasn't a new one by any means, but from Ray it was a challenge, because he knew my status.
>
> I answered, "Ray, you know why I'm not in uniform."
>
> From this point on his purpose was evident; he wanted to make trouble. He continued, "Yeah, but I want to hear you tell me."
>
> I told him, "I'm not in uniform because I'm a conscientious objector."

Watkins persisted in demanding that Weldy explain why he was a conscientious objector.

"Well, that's a long story," Weldy answered. "But if you want to hear it we'll go somewhere and talk about it."

Instead, Watkins insisted that the two talk it out in the bar where everyone could hear. By that time a group of excited high schoolers and recent graduates, anticipating fisticuffs, had gathered round the two young men; Watkins had a reputation as a good fighter. Weldy proceeded to try to explain his beliefs. He later observed,

> I'm sure that some of it sounded pretty empty in that situation. It even sounded flat to me. Ray didn't allow me

to continue in any detail, but he kept throwing questions that were not only repetitious but absurd. The argument continued and I fortified my case with all the logic I could muster, and as I explained more of what I believed, I realized that much of it was not actually real to me. Much of it wasn't sounding too convincing at that moment. I knew that very soon Ray was going to be at the fighting stage of the argument, so I tried to make a few quick decisions. The alternatives were really very few, because I had already committed myself on certain courses of pacifist action before the whole group.[1]

Gilbert Weldy was not the only CPSer forced to defend his beliefs as he stood with arms by his side, fists unclenched and his jaw a wide-open invitation to a sucker punch. No matter how hard CPSers tried to stay out of the spotlight and melt into the background, their personal passiveness often fanned the suppressed aggression of a substratum of society into open hostility.

Once the Japanese had bombed Pearl Harbor on December 17, 1941, few Americans opposed the country's participation in the fracas. Not only did the Japanese sneak-attack the U.S. naval base, but Adolf Hitler had already run rampant across Europe, forcing the English army to scurry out of France and retreat across the English Channel from Dunkirk. Although Hitler's plan to exterminate the Jews and other minorities had not yet materialized, he still managed to project a menacing persona. Meanwhile, in Africa, Mussolini and his Italian troops ran roughshod over parts of that continent. What American in his right mind would not join the effort to rid the world of these madmen and barbarians? When President Franklin D. Roosevelt asked Congress to approve the declaration of war, only Congresswoman Jeannette Rankin of Montana voted to stay out of the conflict.

It was thought to be a just war and became a popular war. Young men streamed to recruiters to volunteer for service, while others quickly tied up loose ends, knowing the draft would soon beckon. Citizens donated home appliances and tools as scrap metal to be melted down for the construction of airplanes, warships, and artillery. In many backyards, women, children, and old men planted victory gardens to help with food shortages. People at home for the most part willingly sacrificed so their soldiers could fight on.

Battlefield deaths soon touched every extended family. Young men who walked the streets without a uniform had better be prepared to explain themselves. Why weren't they making the supreme sacrifice for their country?

"It's a humbling experience to suddenly discover that you're way out of line with everyone else," said Mennonite Roy Wenger, the civilian director of the smoke jumpers' camp. "All COs had to develop thick skin. What else can you do when an entire community turns against you?"

Once they cast the die, the conscientious objectors entered a much-reviled class of society. As young men, many just turning eighteen, they were part of the reviving spirit of America. Along with their families, they had survived the Great Depression and Dust Bowl years of the 1930s. They had learned to sacrifice and develop a good work ethic. Many of their childhood experiences mirrored those of Clarence W. Dirks, whose Mennonite ancestors had emigrated from Holland to Poland and then on to Russia by the 1800s. In the middle of that century, they sailed to the United States in search of religious freedom. Dirks' father eventually settled a farm in western Kansas, and in the 1920s, he and his wife began a family that would expand to include a dozen children—nine born in Kansas. Clarence, born in 1923, was the oldest.

"I remember very little until 1929, when the Depression hit," he wrote. "I was in my first year of school at the time, having begun without being able to speak a word of English." The collapse of the economy forced the family to move to western Kansas, an area that seemed like the middle of nowhere. Dirks observed,

> I remember moving with a wagon and a team of horses. It seems that things were no better here, since I recall spending time in a storm cellar because of tornadoes, and sticking our heads out of that cave from time to time to see what was going on—and what might be blowing away.
>
> I remember walking to school against the cold north wind. I'd get there and my ears and hands would be frozen. The teacher would get a big pan full of snow to thaw us out, rubbing our hands and ears with it before she'd let us near the old coal-burning stove.

The family held on until 1937, even without being able to grow a cash crop. The weather continued to plague them, as Dirks recalled: "Dust almost every day, wet blankets hung over doorways and windows to keep out the worst of it." But the Dirks family finally gave up on Kansas. After selling almost everything they owned, Dirks' father, with sixty-nine dollars in his pocket, began driving the family to northern Idaho. All eleven family members rode aboard a 1935 truck. Father, mother, and babies sat up front in the cab, while the rest, according to Clarence, "assorted ourselves among the furniture and other possessions we were able to bring with us. Dad had made a canopy to cover us and the load." Beneath the truck squawked a handful of chickens in a crate that was lashed to the frame. "You've heard of the Okies leaving Oklahoma for California?" recalled Dirks. "That was us."

As they rolled across the plains of eastern Colorado, the rising Rocky Mountains held Dirks spellbound. By the time the family reached the Continental Divide, the truck brakes had deteriorated so badly that Dirks' father used the hand-operated emergency brake to keep from driving over the cliffs. Finally in Idaho, Dirks proclaimed, "The country looked so beautiful to us, after the wind and dust of western Kansas. How green it was; all those trees, so gorgeous."

The trip cost twenty-nine dollars and ten cents. When Dirks' father got his first job as a construction worker, he boasted, "I am earning fifty-five cents an hour—just think of it, almost a penny a minute."

It was a sign that life could only get better for Americans. Most thought that opportunities were bound to increase for the younger generation, particularly when wartime industrialization began to revitalize the moribund economy. The country would certainly rebound. Victory at war would assure that. Postwar America would offer room for advancement—if one survived the carnage. But those who did not help out with the war effort might find themselves left out in the cold.

Any conscientious objector who had worked for the federal government automatically lost his Civil Service status when he entered CPS. Some state legislatures unsuccessfully tried to ban conscientious objectors from public employment. And the state of Montana suggested that Congress pass a law that would deprive any CPSer the right "to own or acquire any real property within the confines of the United States, beyond a limited amount." As an obvious swipe at the communal Hutterites, Montanans also asked Congress to ban any group holding conscientious objection as a principle from acquiring "any further tracts of land in this country." The memorial also asked Congress to repeal all income tax exemptions extended to pacifist groups that were also religious groups. Much to its credit, Congress never acted on the Montana memorial or other proposed acts that would penalize conscientious objectors after the war—but the threat was always there.

The day before receiving their draft notices, the CPSers had been part of this country's future. By the next day, many were outcasts. Polite society referred to the young men as "conchies," conscientious objectors, pacifists. Others branded them "yellowbellies" and were not shy about confronting them in public as if they were traitors. Many conscientious objectors humbly endured outright hostility; a few suffered injuries from physical attacks.

An especially unpleasant incident happened in 1944 to six Mennonites who boarded a bus headed for Fort Leavenworth for preinduction physical examinations. When one lad brazenly reacted to bitter joking about Mennonites by referring to those in the military as "nothing but murderers," another youth punched him in the face. The verbal abuse intensified as others joined in—slapping, punching, and kicking the dissenters. Meanwhile, the bus driver egged on the so-called patriots. The three Mennonites wearing beards lost them to a razor-wielding antagonist, while the others received rough haircuts. As the Mennonites prayed and cried, their antagonists forced them to take off their pants. When they refused to perform homosexual acts, they were beaten with their own belts. In the end, such conflicts often proved to be the greatest test of an individual's pacifist convictions.

For smoke jumper Roy L. Piepenburg, the harassment began before he graduated from high school. Just before the war began, his parents left an old established Protestant church to join the Society of Friends. His mother, a part-time journalist and social reformer, explained to her three sons that, as a family, they had become Quakers by "convincement." A few years later, Piepenburg, in the middle of his senior year, registered for the draft. He requested and received a 4-E classification for conscientious objector. Soon after, his life began to change. He later wrote,

When I refused to purchase defense or war stamps in my home room, I was somewhat ostracized. When military recruiting officers came around, I was obliged to sit in the orientation sessions. My peers were always puzzled by my apparent lack of interest in "signing up." The social pressure that I experienced caused me to waiver between getting assigned to a CPS camp and entering the Army as a noncombatant, most likely in the Medical Corps. Finally, to escape the stigma of being different, I quit high school and headed back to the village where I had grown up. In a few days my parents located me and counseled me to return to high school.

Harassment by his peers may have damaged Piepenburg psychologically, but more traumatic experiences, instigated by government officials, awaited many other conscientious objectors. In *Peace Was in Their Hearts*, Richard C. Anderson describes some of the stock antagonistic questions that draft boards asked:

> One of the most common was, "What would you do if someone broke into your home and was about to rape your sister/wife/mother/grandmother? Would you just stand there and do nothing?" This question was seen as a shrewd way of entrapping the unwary CO. If he would use force in protecting a loved one, he would not be sincere in opposing war. Or, alternatively, if he would do nothing to protect his family, he could be labeled a corrupt deviant.
>
> Many young objectors were intimidated by these types of questions. They would not have the presence of mind to ask their interrogators how such a hypothetical situation compared to a battlefield where men are expected to kill other young people whose only crime is

that they live in a different country. Or, to ask how the threatened rape scenario related to the bombing of cities and the killing of civilians.[2]

Then came the humiliation meted out at the draft physical. Smoke jumper Ivan E. Holdeman hailed from a small settlement of Mennonites near the wheat-farming community of Greensburg, Kansas. In high school, he became an integral part of school life, even becoming the first member of his church to play on the football team. He also acted in school plays and later flourished socially in college. Ivan's fall from social acceptance occurred abruptly, after he enrolled as a CPSer. After he was drafted during his junior year in college in 1944, federal officials soon made clear to him that, as a conchie, he was a second-class citizen and open to all types of prejudice and harassment. Holdeman recalled,

The worst day of my life was when I was called to Fort Leavenworth, Kansas, for my physical examination. I went there with a busload of young recruits from Newton, Kansas.

I was the only recruit who had had two years of college, and therefore, did not have to take the IQ test or the "idiot test," as it was called by the military personnel at the time. This situation jumped me ahead of all persons who were on the bus with me, a circumstance that I was very thankful for later on.

In due course we were told to strip to the buff. Our clothes were checked in and we were given a leather bag to hold our valuables. This bag was then hung around our necks. In this state of nudity, we went from doctor to doctor who checked out our physical condition.

At the first station I gave my papers to a doctor's assistant who looked at the document and said to the M.D.

in a loud aside whisper: "Here's another one of those goddamn c.o.s." Whereupon the doctor cussed and swore at me and, in a very loud voice, observed that my belly was yellow, and made other disparaging remarks about the nature of my character. This was the first station, and for the rest of the day every time I put my papers before a new examiner I expected a repeat.

This became the longest day of my life.

Another CPS smoke jumper, Homer Rice, suffered similar humiliation during his draft physical. Born November 25, 1925, in Columbiana, Ohio, Homer was one of eleven children. There apparently was always a bit of rebellion in the Rice family. His father disobeyed the directives of the local Mennonite preacher by playing softball with his children after church on Sundays. "If the preacher had [as] large a family as we, he'd see things differently," Leo F. Rice explained to his son. Homer loved school, sports, and making new friends. He also liked to garner attention by playing the class clown:

> My earliest recollection at school was near the first day or so. The teacher, Miss Albright, began to teach us a song that went like this. "Bow, wow, wow. Whose dog art thou? Little Tommy Tinker's dog. Bow, wow, wow."
>
> I had a sudden inspiration to change the lyrics on the third line to "Little Tommy Stinker's dog."
>
> The teacher had no sense of humor whatsoever and rapped me on the head with a yard stick. The rest of the class however was on my side. They gave me an "A" with their gleeful laughter.

While in high school, Homer registered for the draft at Harper, Kansas, in Harvey County. But his documents were transferred to a draft board in an area that had no Mennonite

community, and the board denied his request for 4-E classification. Several months later, Homer appeared for a preinduction physical at Fort Leavenworth, Kansas, assuming that
his 4-E classification had been approved. It proved to be one
time in his life when he wished he weren't the center of attention. He later wrote,

> At the very end of the physical, when I was standing
> before the final officer with my papers, he says to me
> which do you want? Army or Navy? Seeing the 1-A clas-
> sification on my papers, I said to him neither one. I
> want a 4-E. He began to shout and swear extremely vile
> language insomuch that in this huge building hundreds
> of typewriters stopped and silence reigned except for
> this officer chewing me out for being a blankety blank
> yellow so and so. I like attention but this was a little
> much for a naive farm boy like me.

Life in CPS camps was relatively secure and peaceful. Since
the peace churches ran most of the camps, they usually
catered to men of one particular denomination. Consequently, the camps often became extensions of sheltered, isolated communities—especially for the Mennonite farmboys.
But beyond camp limits, the locals often declared open season on the conscientious objectors.

Smoke jumper Clarence E. Quay did not expect to be
treated like a hero when he became an objector, but he also
had not expected to be physically attacked for his beliefs. The
son of a steel worker, Quay was born August 11, 1916, about fifteen miles from Valley Forge in Chester County, Pennsylvania.
His mother labored in a knitting mill. While a senior in high
school, he lived and worked on a farm, doing chores before
and after school. "To say the least, taking a conscientious
objector position was not at all popular," he wrote. "There was

a song, 'Praise the Lord and Pass the Ammunition,' which was popular at the time. Those who were opposed to the war effort, for whatever reason, were called cowards, yellowbellies, and having a yellow streak running down our backs." One evening, while stationed at Lyndhurst CPS Camp No. 29, Quay, with a few other fellows, walked down the road that led toward town. A group of youths that had gathered on the county road started throwing stones at the men. "I don't remember anything being said, just the stones coming at us," Quay recalled.

Some communities would not tolerate CPS camps, while others welcomed the free labor that the men performed, often within the community itself. Farmers especially benefited from projects of "national importance" when they needed help planting or harvesting their crops. Still, some CPS camps, such as that in Coschocton, Ohio, often proved to be political hot potatoes. Some citizens thought that the camps should be run like prisons, with no amenities for the men and no movement outside the camp gates allowed. They often took offense if the CPSers dared to look at the young ladies in town or if they tried to spread their pacifist message.

In mid-1942, the CPS camp in Coschocton housed about three hundred men, according to T. Richard Flaharty (a native of Chicago), who was stationed there before transferring to the smoke jumpers' camp in Montana. Isolated about ten miles from town, the men made best with what they had, organizing a library, a co-op candy store, a recreation hall with a stage, a woodwork shop, a tennis court, and a baseball diamond—which they dubbed Fracture Field because of the proliferation of gopher holes. A dozen musicians and a male chorus "spasmodically" presented concerts. When nothing else was going on, the men studied or participated in discussion groups. The Society of Friends often sponsored speakers. But the "happy community life" was short-lived.

"A congressman of the Coschocton area who had earlier taken credit for providing all of this cheap labor began to get complaints from the locals about those yellowbellies who were coming into town, attending their churches and ogling the local belles," Flaharty recalled. "This congressman did a quick switch and began to build a new reputation for being the man who rid the area of this yellow menace. In short, the camp was soon reduced to fifty men."

Oftentimes, townspeople harassed a conscientious objector's family, as well. Wives, when they followed a spouse to camp, were especially vulnerable. Murray Braden, the son of Methodist missionaries who worked in Santiago, Chile, at the time of his birth, encountered very little direct harassment during his stay in CPS. But his wife, Geraldine, was less fortunate. The Bradens married in July 1943, after Geraldine graduated from Northwestern University. She moved to New-comerstown, Ohio, a small town about fifteen miles from Camp Coshocton, and landed a job as a roving music teacher for the school system. She drove many miles over dirt roads to reach the isolated schools. When some local citizens discovered that she was the wife of a conscientious objector, they tried to get her fired. "But the district superintendent told them that her work was quite satisfactory," Murray Braden wrote, "and he could fire her only if they were willing to come up with her salary for the rest of the year. Geraldine also learned that the county sheriff had spent several evenings watching the house in which she had rented a room, hoping to catch me visiting there—AWOL from camp."

A few years later, when Geraldine moved to Missoula, Montana, to be near the smoke jumpers' camp, she landed a job as a clerk in an insurance agency. When the agent discovered that her husband was a conchie, he taunted her by insulting Murray. The agent stopped short of firing her, but Geraldine soon found another job to escape the harassment.

Conscientious objectors often faced the greatest degree of harassment while traveling between camps or when returning from furloughs. Strangers could spit on them, punch them, or insult them, knowing that they probably would never see the conscientious objector again and that their victim would never be able to identify them—even if law enforcement authorities wanted to prosecute. Roy Piepenburg had two close brushes while traveling to and from a camp in Trenton, North Dakota, before he became a smoke jumper. "En route home by bus I was confronted by returning servicemen who demanded to know why I was not in uniform," he wrote. "When they found out I was a 'conchie' they threatened to put me off the bus." The other episode caught him completely off guard and was more dangerous:

> I became worried when I heard of rumblings in some congregations, because the pastor extended open arms to "conchies" from Trenton (North Dakota). That same antagonism was felt directly by me one evening when I returned to camp on a Great Northern Railway train. When the train reached Trenton, it merely slowed down and the conductor contemptuously pushed me from the platform between two cars. After I got to my feet, I knew for the first time in my life what it meant to be an outcast.

Train conductors seemed a natural nemesis of conscientious objectors, and since trains at the time offered the only form of speedy national transportation, conchies could not avoid them. While traveling through Wyoming, Ivan Holdeman had a run-in with a conductor who seemed to feel it his patriotic duty to harass shy farmboys from rural Kansas. After inspecting the tickets of the CPSers, the conductor asked, in what Holdeman described as a very loud voice,

"Conscientious objectors, eh? Religious or political?"

"Religious," we replied.

"What church you belong to?"

"Mennonite," we answered.

"Mennonite, hell, you sure don't look like it," he shouted, making sure the entire car were [sic] aware of who we were.

This train ride was so long and tiring that I thought that when I got to camp I'd never want to leave until the war was over.

Signs in shops and restaurants proclaiming, "We reserve the right to deny anyone service," certainly applied to conscientious objectors at the time. The Selective Service paid for transportation for the men to and from camps. For meals, officials doled out meal tickets that restaurants could redeem at the local banks. Just as food stamps mark those on welfare, the meal tickets often revealed the inconspicuous conscientious objector to prying eyes. When Ivan Holdeman was drafted in January 1945, he boarded a train at Hutchinson, Kansas, where he met two other draftees traveling to a camp at Belton, Montana, just outside Glacier National Park. At Denver, Colorado, they had an eight-hour layover while changing trains. Holdeman observed, "I remember trying to use our government issued meal tickets in a restaurant near the railroad stations. Some of the restaurants refused to honor these meal tickets because of the CO status. As I look at it now, we should not have allowed them to check our tickets ahead of time—we should have just had our meal first and then presented our tickets."

Not only strangers looked down on the CPSers. The war strained many families too, including that of Maynard W. Shetler, introduced at the beginning of this book. Shetler and his brother were the only two on his father's side of the family who applied for exemption from the army and navy. "The Shetlers were a militant clan," he observed.

The CPS men usually turned the other cheek when verbally insulted or physically attacked. But doing so was a struggle in itself. Few outside the peace churches acknowledged the intellectual courage required to stand up against the rest of society while maintaining one's ideals. Moreover, many men brought up in the peace churches knew the legends of ancestors who had sacrificed their lives for their beliefs. Like many soldiers, the CPSers yearned to be heroes. Courage was part of their heritage. That is why smoke jumping caught the imagination of many CPSers. It took guts to parachute out of an airplane to fight forest fires in inaccessible, rugged mountains. This was a chance to prove their mettle. No men were assigned to the smoke jumpers' camp; they all volunteered. Many answered the call from camps around the country.

James Brunk, at eighteen years old, first heard of smoke jumping while stationed at a CPS camp in Denison, Iowa, where he unhappily worked on a soil conservation project. A coworker named Harvey Weirich had already spent a summer smoke jumping. Hearing of Weirich's adventures, Brunk believed that smoke jumping was for him: "I thought that if I could get into the smoke jumpers there would be enough danger involved that people might realize that I was serious about my stand against war and was not just a 'yellowbelly.'"

Other conscientious objectors, such as Willard D. Handrich of Fairview, Michigan, approached smoke jumping as a way to alleviate a guilty conscience because many of his Mennonite neighbors had sons who had been wounded or killed in the armed forces. "I felt a lot of pressure. So when the second call came for volunteer smoke jumpers, for CPS men, I volunteered."

Lee Hebel of Liverpool, Pennsylvania, also recognized that smoke jumping would offer an opportunity to escape harassment from the public. Hebel wrote, "Jumping on fires gave us status. Besides, I suppose we all felt more secure from criticism and prejudice. It would be difficult to judge a smoke jumper cowardly or yellow; and just maybe, some of us had something to prove to ourselves."

For others, such as David Kauffman of Whitefish, Montana, smoke jumping offered the prospects of fun and adventure. He observed, "I enjoyed the notoriety and glory that went with being a parachuting fire fighter."

Floating down from a plane lasted only about two minutes at the most, often followed by twelve- or sixteen-hour days devoted to digging fire lines or searching for hot spots over a charred landscape. After extinguishing the fire, the men often faced hikes of ten to fifty miles back to the nearest road and then a ride in the open bed of a truck back to town. The romance faded quickly, but still most CPSers remained enthusiastic about smoke jumping. Like jumpers today, they basked in the mystique of the job.

But smoke jumping offered much more.

The smoke jumpers' camp resembled that of the military in many respects. Men bonded. They learned to depend on each other, to sacrifice for one another. They became part of something bigger than the individual. Earning the right to float two minutes through the air past majestic mountain peaks instilled a sense of pride that all the men shared.

A disenchanted CPSer, Lee Miller, from a Mennonite community in Freeman and Marion, South Dakota, felt his spirits rejuvenate once he signed up to become a CPS smoke jumper. His experience brought him a self-confidence that lasted a lifetime:

> I was feeling a big let down [at a camp in Terry, Montana,] . . . and went through a fairly serious feeling of doubt about the whole CO position. All those millions

of young men were defending our country. Were they all wrong, and we right?

Then I got the call from the smoke jumpers. I recognized immediately that these were some really special people, and through the years I've realized more and more how special they really were. The Mennonite CO camps were really just an extension of the community I grew up in, but here in the smoke jumpers unit was a whole new perspective. Many of these guys had actually made their decision to be pacifists in the face of opposition from their family, friends, and community. I was impressed.

Of course, the bond that drew us together was mainly our convictions, but there was more. We all, I think, wanted to prove to ourselves as well as to society, that we were not yellowbellies. This seemed a chance to do that. I certainly felt more confident about my stand than ever before—and that feeling has stayed with me ever since.

Although a few men heard choruses of "yellowbelly" shouted from the streets during their Missoula years, most local residents respected the hardworking CPS jumpers. Montanans knew that forest fires could kill people and destroy homes, as well as the trees that local industries depended on. In addition, many local loggers personally knew what it took to fight fire. Logging crews were required to carry firefighting tools whenever they worked the woods during fire season, and Forest Service officials often recruited help from local communities during emergencies. In fact, they often hit the bars to round up able-bodied men.

But once in a while a CPSer inadvertently crossed socially acceptable lines, especially those concerning young women. Talk too long to the girlfriend of a local youth or, worse yet, to the girlfriend of a GI fighting overseas, and repercussions soon followed. But at times, the young jumpers could not

resist striking up a conversation with a member of the opposite sex. William P. Weber, who was stationed in Missoula during the summer of 1944, often went roller-skating at a rink a
few blocks from the smoke jumper barracks near the airport
in town. One evening he met a lovely, dark-haired girl and
escorted her around the rink a number of times. At closing
time, he offered to walk her home, and he later described
what happened as a result of his chivalry:

> The moonlight on her hair, her perfume blending with
> the smells of fall and her soft warm hand in mine
> tended to negate any apprehension I might have had of
> a car following behind us.
>
> Arriving at her parents' house, she thanked me for
> walking her home, gave me a quick hug and kiss and
> she was gone.
>
> It was now after midnight, the moon hung low in the
> western sky and it was two long miles back to Missoula. I
> was already tired from skating and the walk out there.
> But I had no choice.
>
> Hardly more than a half mile from this lovely girl's
> home, I saw the lights of a car racing toward me. As I
> jumped off the road and across the ditch, it went roar-
> ing past, the occupants shouting "yellow belly, draft
> dodger, get out of town," and many other obscenities.
>
> Recovering my composure, I climbed out of the ditch
> and back on the edge of the highway. I had only gone a
> short distance when the car came roaring back, again
> forcing me off the road with many of the same words of
> greeting as the first encounter.
>
> By now, I knew these fellows meant business. The girl
> I walked home must be the girlfriend of one of them,
> and it was obvious they were unhappy with my entry into
> the picture.

The remaining mile and a half was a nightmare, they continued to come at me at a high rate of speed and I expected that if they could not hit me with the car that they would stop the car and beat me up. Luckily, this did not occur and after what seemed like forever, I was back in Missoula. I had survived.

I have had some scary things happen in my life, nearly drowned, nearly got electrocuted, that first parachute jump, a pistol held to my head by a drunken MP. But never, never have I been so terrified as I was that night.[3]

Although the men were frequently confronted by those who pushed them to defend their convictions with more than words, they seldom failed to maintain a stance of nonresistance. Defending themselves with physical force was unacceptable. At the beginning of this chapter, we left Gilbert Weldy in a confrontation with the drunken Roy Watkins. The affable CPSer attempted to deflect the impending aggression with humor. But Weldy understood "that the reputation of the camp was at stake and that I would be a traitor to our cause if I did not hold fast to the things I had claimed to believe in. For that reason I claim no merit for what I did, because I certainly had misgivings."

The antagonistic teenager then demanded to know how Weldy would react after Watkins smacked him in the face. The pack of teenagers surrounding the two closed in like wolves ready for the kill.

"I don't think that I would do anything," Weldy replied, resigned to his fate.

"You mean to tell me that you would stand right there and let me smack you in the face, and you wouldn't do a thing?"

"What should I do? Hit you back? I have nothing against you, and I'd a lot rather be your friend. If we fight, there'll be nothing but rotten feeling. Besides, you aren't going to change my mind by hitting me, and I certainly wouldn't change yours if I beat up on you."

"Beat up on me? Boy, you don't have to worry about that," Watkins gloated. "I can't believe that you'd stand right there and let me hit you."

"Ray, you've been drinking, and I would be taking advantage of you to fight you now. If you like to fight so well, we have some gloves out at camp, and I'd be glad to go a few rounds with you just in fun, but not like this."

Again Watkins could not believe his ears.

"Well, there is only one way you'll ever find out," Weldy added. By this time, he was resigned to getting pummeled, and he stuck his hands deep in his pockets.

"Stand back, everyone; this is going to be a pleasure," Watkins said, moving the crowd back for more room. As he cocked his fist he asked, "Do you mean that you won't do a thing?"

"That's right; I don't have anything against you."

Much to Weldy's relief, his antagonist eventually abandoned the confrontation. As Weldy walked home that evening, several of the locals congratulated him on his cool demeanor and reassured him that they would have intervened if the verbal confrontation had turned violent. The incident left him "pleased and strangely exhilarated."

The following day, on the street, he ran into Watkins, who greeted him with a smile and asked, "No hard feelings about last night?" Weldy assured the teenager that he harbored no resentment. Forty years later, the former CPSer observed, "I had been in a situation where there had been only one way out, so I claim no virtue for my behavior. In the same fix again I might do something different and shame myself and my cause, but this one time convinced me about this thing called pacifism. That is, merely, it works."[4]

CHAPTER FOUR

Hard Choices

The decision to become a conscientious objector was not something to approach lightly. Boys raised in the peace churches could not use religion simply as an excuse to stay out of the armed services. As evidenced by the deep commitment to nonviolence that many of the conscientious objectors retained throughout their lives, they understood at the time that their decisions would constitute lifelong commitments.

Nor were all conscientious objectors raised in the peace churches. Wilmer Carlsen found the path toward pacifism circuitous and confusing. A high school graduate from Harlan, Iowa, Carlsen left the family farm in the midst of the Great Depression with war the furthest thing from his mind. At the time, failed Wall Street investors were jumping off skyscrapers in New York City. Unemployed workers stood on big-city street corners selling apples for five cents apiece. Thousands of men hopped freight trains to follow rumors of opportunity in the West. Carlsen, eager to relieve his family of a mouth to feed, joined them. One evening, his parents drove him and his brother into town and then waved good-bye as the two boys scrambled into a boxcar on a freight headed for Minneapolis and points west.

Down the line, the train reached its destination, and the boys located another westbound train. After his brother successfully scrambled aboard the moving boxcar, Wilmer slipped and fell. By the time he recovered, the train had gained speed. He despondently waved good-bye to his brother as the train rounded a curve.

Wilmer's spirits quickly revived. The mysterious West awaited. Companion or no companion, he would find adventure, see strange sights, and meet interesting people—maybe even make a little money in the process. Later, Wilmer climbed aboard a slow-moving freight on the same track, resigned that he would not see his brother for some time.

The next day, as the train rolled through Laurel, Montana, Wilmer woke up and sat in the open boxcar door enjoying the sunshine. In the distance, he spotted a man walking down the highway that paralleled the tracks. As the train neared, he recognized a familiar hitch to the gait, a gentle stoop to the shoulders. Wilmer jumped to his feet, shouting and waving to his brother. A short distance down the line he jumped off. After a happy reunion, the boys headed for the potato harvest in western Montana.

By the time the Carlsen brothers reached the Bitterroot Valley, crews had already started the harvest, so the boys backtracked to Missoula to hop the Milwaukee, Chicago, and St. Paul Railroad to Seattle. For their first trip through the seven-mile-long Cascade tunnel between Wenatchee, Washington, and Seattle they climbed into an open coal car. They were fortunate in their choice of railroads; if they had chosen the Northern Pacific they would have been smoked out, but the Milwaukee ran off electricity through the mountains, the power partially generated by the engines as they rolled downhill.

In Seattle, the unemployment lines stretched for blocks. Undaunted, the boys took some advice and traveled back through the tunnel on the Milwaukee line to find work in the apple orchards near Omak, Washington. There they earned twenty-five cents an hour and slept on straw in a shed. When the season ended, they returned to Seattle, sleeping in a flophouse where dormitory beds rented for ten cents a night. "I think there were fifty or more men staying in one room," Carlsen recalled. "Also we had meals on Skid Row at ten to fifteen cents per, depending on whether one wanted to pig out or not."

When they could find no work in Seattle, the boys proceeded down the West Coast, once again by freight. In Canby, Oregon, they stopped and inquired about a cheap place to stay. A night watchman led them to the local jail, let them in, and then locked them up. He did not return until nine the next morning to liberate them. "If we had known he was going to lock us up in there we would have brought in more wood to keep the fire going," Carlsen said. "As it was, we were just as cold inside as we would have been outside."[1]

By November 1936, the boys had crossed into northern California, stopping long enough to earn some money pulling weeds and sawing firewood near Stockton, California. They camped in hobo jungles outside town but usually ate meals in a skid row café operated by a Japanese couple. Carlsen was nineteen years old at the time.

The boys eventually ended up in the Pasadena area and hooked up with an uncle and aunt who operated a fruit stand. Wilmer helped out at the stand, and he baled hay and plowed fields for neighboring farmers while his brother took a job at the American Potash and Chemical Company at Trona, California. With steady work, the future looked good. About the only worry on Carlsen's mind was falling in love with a woman for the first time. Then came the draft. Not having been raised in a peace church, Carlsen had never thought about how killing another man would affect him. Soon he found himself thinking about it a lot.

"In early winter I started plowing the selected fields with a small Farmall tractor and that gave me the opportunity to argue with myself about everything and still follow the furrow," he wrote. "The mental activity must not have adversely affected my job performance for my boss said to me that I was the only man that he had ever hired who could plow a straight furrow." In the end, after miles of guiding the tractor up and down the fields, Carlsen decided to register as a conscientious objector: "The Authority could shoot me if they willed, but I would not shoot another man because of an order to do so." The social repercussions were immediate. "As a result of the stance that I had taken, two of my uncles considered me a disgrace to the family. Also, all the men that I had become acquainted with were entering the Armed Services. That made it all a traumatic and lonely experience." Still, Carlsen never wavered from his decision. To this day he remains a staunch pacifist.

Carlsen arrived at the smoke jumpers' CPS camp in 1943 and stayed on for three seasons. One day he participated in an exhibition jump for some Forest Service brass from Washington, D.C. He recalled,

> The jumping area was one of the Remount pastures west of the camp. A few others had jumped before Harry Burks and I were to take our turn. The Travelaire was the plane being used, the drift chute had been dropped, and the spot we were to leave the plane had been selected. Only one jumper left the plane per pass, and Harry was the first one. He came down close to the spot. During the time that the plane made its circle for the next pass, the wind had started blowing. I jumped at

the selected spot and soon after the chute opened I discovered that I was sailing crosscountry so fast that I doubted slipping the chute would have been of much help. The wind was blowing toward camp so I just turned one hundred and eighty degrees and went as far as I could—over the hill, over a gully, and half way up the next slope—out of sight. The other jumpers were usually eager to help stretch out the chute, chain up the lines and stuff it in the bag. This time I got to do it myself. To the top of the hill and I was in camp.

Early manhood can be a time of blossoming love and fledgling ideas, a time when boys move beyond the phase of observation and begin to analyze and think for themselves and to form opinions. In a normal life, there is room for mistakes. Young men take up causes, become disenchanted, look for something new. But in 1939, society forced these young conscientious objectors to make a choice that would stick with them all their lives. Carlsen did his soul-searching in virtual isolation, bouncing his options off the drone of the tractor engine. He was not the only one suddenly confronted with this moral issue with no one to turn to for guidance. Theodore Norman Pfeifer found himself in much the same situation. Pfeifer was raised in a small Christian and Missionary Alliance Church in New York, which did not advocate the teachings of nonresistance as the historic peace churches did. The concept was also foreign to his family and friends. His upbringing seemed nothing out of the ordinary:

> During the summer, Sunday was the day to go to church. There were times we went to church camp where there was special preaching and singing and all kinds of special meetings on many different topics. This was a time when many people would can all different

types of food. We would at times go and pick huckleberries on a Sunday afternoon. The following week my
mother would put these in jars for the winter. We would
at times pick apples for the same reason. This was not all
work—we would go to the beach and again would visit
friends. Then we would stay at home if this seemed to
be the thing to do.

When he became of age, Pfeifer naively informed his draft
board that he did not believe in war. He received a classification of 4E. "Not knowing what this meant," he recalled, "I
began inquiring what it was. Then I found that I was a CO.
This still meant nothing to me. Where I was living, to my
knowledge, there were no such people as Quakers, Mennonites, or Brethren. While studying history I had read of William
Penn and the Quakers, but that was history. The Friends sent
me a letter stating I was to be sent to one of their camps in
Royalston, Massachusetts, and what I should bring with me."

Other young men, caught off guard as well, suddenly had
to reassess their belief system—or quickly develop one. An
eighteen-year-old Calvin Hilty expected to be deferred from
the draft because he worked on the family farm near Fortuna,
Missouri, so he was unprepared when a member of the draft
board informed him that his number had been posted at the
courthouse. "It was serious thinking for me," he recalled. "I
had been baptized when I was in my early teens but I'm afraid
I had never given my [Mennonite] faith very serious
thought." While stationed at a CPS camp in California, Hilty
went on furlough to attend the funeral of his good friend
David Kauffman, who had been killed while training as a navy
pilot. "It was hard to go and see his parents but they were glad
to see me and even offered me some of [David's] clothes."

At the time of Calvin's birth, his father belonged to the
largest recorded family at that time, according to *Ripley's*

Believe It or Not: the family counted 168 first cousins. Calvin was the oldest of eight siblings. He sacrificed an opportunity to work his way through the University of Missouri to keep the family farm going. When he volunteered for CPS, the Hilty clan came down to the depot to send him off. The train conductor singled him out and asked where he was headed.

"To Dennison, Iowa," Hilty replied. "I've been drafted."

"Well, that's funny, there isn't any Army base there," the conductor said.

"Well, that's where I'm going," Hilty answered and left it at that.

When Hilty first heard that the Forest Service was recruiting smoke jumpers from the CPS camps, he decided that he "had it real easy as a telephone operator and was ready for something else." Hilty was unnerved as he boarded the Ford Trimotor for his initial practice jump. He gained some confidence when trainer Frank Derry encouraged him by saying, "I can tell by the looks in your eyes you can do it." Hilty recalled, "When it was my turn I was determined to do it like the rest of the fellows. I was all but out of it on that first jump but as the chute popped open I was king of all that I viewed below. What a feeling of achievement. I spent two years with the Cave Junction group and it was an experience that gave us a feeling that we were not afraid to take a chance to make a contribution to our country."

Many others brought up in the pacifist tradition also faced internal struggles when it came to requesting exemption from military service. Bradshaw Snipes was a ninth-generation Quaker whose maternal ancestors had sailed to America with William Penn in 1682. Throughout his youth, Snipes had listened to renowned speakers at the Friends meeting in Fallsington, Pennsylvania, discourse on such topics as the plight of American Indians, prison reform, and "efforts to try to get the Nazis to permit Jews to emigrate from Germany." He also attended weekend work camps in Philadelphia, where he helped paint homes of the poor. "At these times there were after supper discussions with black families," he recalled.

In 1939, Snipes joined other Boy Scouts from across the country at the New York World's Fair. "Part of the fun was to parade in unison and shout slogans. My mother and father came to the fair one day and saw our activities and were disappointed. They said we were doing the same as the Hitler youth." Snipes later attended a Friends work camp in Maine, where he helped fishermen build a cooperative cold-storage locker.

When confronted by the draft, he sought the astute counsel of his family. His parents recognized the repercussions that the decision could have on his future life, and his father "was quite persuasive in suggesting that [my brothers and I] would have a better future if we went into the military service, and we would have the benefit of GI tuition payments when we came home." But Snipes' mother encouraged him to request conscientious objector status. He noted, "Both parents said they would support us whatever our decisions were. Sam, Tom and I all took the CO stand, and our father and sister, who was in college, had to bear up to some pretty harsh criticism."

As a smoke jumper, Snipes suffered from airsickness but thrilled "in jumping, looking over the territory on the way down, and being on a real fire jump." In 1944, he joined seven other jumpers on a fire call near Bell Lake on the Montana-Idaho line in the Bitterroot Mountains west of Hamilton, Montana. Snipes remembered that jump well:

> After two or three passes, as others jumped, my crab salad supper was churning ever so greatly in my stomach. That friendly tap on the shoulder sent me forward and somewhat head first. The crab salad came up and partly blocked my vision as it caught in the wire mask. I could

tell that I was clearing the lake, and it appeared I was clearing some big trees, when all of a sudden my feet landed on a tree top, which then broke off. I was falling backwards very fast and I was prepared to write the post card real fast. Fortunately the chute caught air again as I prepared to do a backward somersault over a log.

Some men, however, did not have to think twice about requesting 4-E status. Many—including Laurel Sargent of Ness County, Kansas—carried on a family tradition by refusing induction into the military. Sargent's father had served a short period in the army in 1918 as a Methodist conscientious objector. Sargent recalled,

> My father had no CO background and only earned this classification after refusing the rifle that was issued him on induction. Because of his business training and his ability to type, he served his time in the office. This firm belief in the futility of war was a mainstay throughout his life and he and my mother, and later, stepmother, passed this strong belief on to myself, my stepbrother and the rest of the family. Sometime after the war, in the 1920s, the whole family became Mennonite and we have supported the First Mennonite church in Ransom since that time.

Sargent described his first fire jump as an "abject disaster." He and Diz Lehman flew to the fire northeast of McCall, Idaho, in a Travelaire with Forest Service crew chief Johnny Johnson. The fire smoldered in an area full of dead trees. Sargent later noted,

> Diz reached the ground and I reached the snags—not one but three. After crashing down through the dead

wood, I dangled about fifty feet up from the ground. Every move brought a snapping of the deadwood. After a Herculean effort, I managed to rope down. Our equipment landed nearby and after pounding the blaze for a couple of days, we decided it was time to retrieve my chute. With deep apprehension I struggled up the tree and attempted to clear the chute. My trembling seemed only to fasten it tighter. I was scared—some little voice at those times always said, "Go on, do it," and I usually did. Anyhow, I chickened out, slid down the snag, taking off equal bits of bark and skin.

After much consultation, Diz and I decided to chop down the trees, lean them together, and pull them up the slope. We did accomplish the first two steps. We gave a mighty heave and the trees that had leaned together leaned the wrong way, hit, bounced and slid down the hill for two hundred feet, more or less. We gathered up the tattered shreds of the chute, put it in a bag, poured our last water on the ashes, and headed for the road which was about two or three miles away. The shocking news when I reached McCall was that a parachute was worth one hundred and twenty-five dollars, and a message that the chute will be sent to Missoula and "You're never supposed to drop a snag with your parachute entangled in the top—let alone three snags."

As time passed no severance papers with a ticket back to Fort Collins came for Laurel Sargent and I began to breathe easier. Diz said he figured the Forest Service people were probably over on the road watching with glasses all the time.

Ralph C. Belzer (a Jehovah's Witness from Glasgow, Montana) also had no problem accepting his church doctrine. He based his decision to go to a CPS camp "on my religious beliefs that a true Christian cannot involve themselves in any world government conflict. The Bible tells us that Christ's heavenly government will soon remove all of this world's governments and replace them with His own government where peace will abide."

But for Clarence W. Dirks (a Mennonite from Durham, Kansas), the choice to maintain his religious heritage was not as clear-cut. "My draft notice created a turmoil within me. Which way to go? Stay with my upbringing as a pacifist, or go along with our government? I decided to go with my family's identity, although I stayed in this mental whirlpool throughout the war years."

Ivan E. Holdeman, the Mennonite who was verbally abused during his draft physical, also did not lightly make the decision to stick with pacifism. Born on February 14, 1923, Ivan moved with his farming family from Hesston, Kansas, to Rich Hill, Missouri, during his first year of life. But after being flooded out of the bottomland property three out of four years, the Holdemans moved again to Greensburg, Kansas. "I remember father saying he would rather dry out than drown out," Holdeman recalled.

During the depression, the family lost the farm when his father had to sell the cattle because of protracted drought. They then moved into Greensburg, a wheat-farming community, where Ivan eventually thrived in high school, playing football and earning money for his books and clothes by herding cattle for a neighbor for twenty-five cents a day. In 1943 he graduated from Hesston College. For a while, he received an agricultural deferment from the draft while working for a farmer. But after eighteen months, the draft board had a change of heart, forcing Holdeman to put his religious convictions before his sense of civic duty. He observed,

I had all the feelings of patriotism that our nationalistic society had given to its new generation. The feeling that each citizen must be willing to sacrifice himself for society in whatever capacity that society asked the person to serve. On the other hand, my home and church had passed on to me the conviction that one should not do violence to one's fellow human beings no matter what the provocation might be. Joining the armed forces was, in fact, submitting myself to an organization whose primary function was to do violence.

By joining I gave up my individual right of deciding what cause I would give my life for. The decision would be made by the machine not by the person whose life was at stake. My family and church values in my case won the day, and I opted to follow my religious convictions rather than my patriotic feelings. This inner conflict has been a part of my life's experience to this day. I expect that this will always be so.

Lee Miller, a Mennonite, struggled with the same dilemma. The attack on Pearl Harbor triggered in him, as in many Americans, the natural instinct to retaliate. "We were having classes at the church for young men like myself, explaining the Mennonite belief of non-resistance. I think it was hard for all of us in the class to think in terms of non-resistance. It just didn't seem natural for energetic young boys not to resist."

Later, as a smoke jumper, Miller quickly adjusted to his new job. "My training at Ninemile went well, and my first jump was rather automatic. It seems I wasn't aware of what was happening until my fifth jump. After that it was all downhill. It became easier each time. I don't remember any close calls and no injuries."

Other patriotic-minded young men, such as Lee Hebel (a farmboy from Pennsylvania), found solace in the fact that they would be doing something to help their country while in CPS. Although Hebel was a Lutheran, his stance mirrored the classic Mennonite doctrine of living astride two separate worlds—church and the state. "I began to think seriously about God's will for my life and the Christian ministry," he wrote. "I was trying to be a follower of Jesus Christ and could not reconcile war and killing with the Master's example and teachings. Therefore, I registered as opposed to war. I felt that God was to be obeyed above country, and yet acknowledged that our government had some stake in my life. Civilian Public Service rather than jail seemed right for me."

Ralph Ziegler—a direct descendant of Brethren leader Peter Becker, who arrived in Pennsylvania in 1719—found spiritual guidance in a movie. A friend who had flown army airplanes during World War I took him to the Wright Air Force Museum in Ohio, hoping to convince Ziegler to become a flyboy. "But everything I saw was repelling," he wrote. Not long before the visit to the museum, Ziegler saw the antiwar film *All's Quiet on the Western Front*. He observed, "That impressed me with how foolish war is."

Although the young men stood against war, some aspects of the military—especially airplanes—fascinated them. In 1927, when Charles Lindbergh flew the first solo flight across the Atlantic, airplane pilots became the idols of American youth. Mennonite and Quaker boys fell under the spell as well. Whereas civilian aviation was still in its fledgling stage, the military used airplanes to their full potential: transporting troops, surveying behind enemy lines, dropping paratroopers and bombs. Flying for the army and the navy meant free training and access to the best flying machines—a dream for many adventurous young Americans, including Merlo M. Zimmerman, a Mennonite. Merlo recognized that he was giving up a good opportunity to become a professional pilot when he chose Civilian Public Service over military service. "After quite an internal struggle," he noted, "I came to the conclusion that I could not disregard my convictions which were based on my understanding of scripture and the teachings of my church."

David Flaccus, a Quaker, also ignored a strong attraction to the skies when he decided to join CPS. "A good Quaker friend at the same time chose to join the Naval Air Service," he wrote. "I was taking some flying lessons at the time and had just soloed, giving up about seventeen solo hours. My friend went on into the Navy, learned to fly, and became a carrier pilot, spending the war in the Pacific."

When the issues became too confusing, some men turned to mentors for guidance. John Ainsworth sought help from a church minister to formulate his convictions, even though he did not belong to a peace church. After graduating from the University of Southern California in 1940 with an engineering degree, he worked for Westinghouse in East Pittsburgh, attending a Methodist church in Wilkinsburg. "The minister was interested in peace activities," Ainsworth said. "I thought his ideas of how Christians should be were pretty much right. I do not think the congregation thought the same way. A conservative dissenting group had withdrawn from the church, displeased with the content or style of preaching." After consulting with the minister, Ainsworth requested a 4-E classification from his draft board. After the war, he recalled some memorable plane flights he took while a smoke jumper:

One was leaving Missoula on a very hot day and heading north when the pilot allowed the thermals to lift the plane much higher than normal to where the air was very cold. Another was a long trip, stopping at Spokane to refuel then flying north over the Pend d'Oreille and Columbia rivers where they join. One river is blue and the other green. Two of us then jumped on a small fire near the Canadian border. A third flight went to Pot Mountain in Idaho's Clearwater Forest where a dry lightning storm had started a fire. Pot Mountain had good visibility for watching another electrical storm. The ground cables [of the lookout] hummed just before distant lightning strikes.

A man of the cloth also helped mold the beliefs of Dick Flaharty of Chicago. Flaharty described the minister at the Humboldt Methodist Church as "a militant pacifist, a real fighter for social justice." This minister, Reverend Bailey Waltmire, had once run for city alderman in Chicago on the Socialist-Labor Party ticket. Ultimately his politics seemed too provocative, and the local bishop transferred him to the ultraconservative community of Libertyville, Illinois. The reverend still influenced "a number of us. We had learned about Jesus, Kagawa, Gandhi, social action, the evils of prejudice, the power of nonviolence, and I was one of several who got acquainted with the World Peace Commission of the Methodist Church. There were twenty-six young people who were called into service from our church in World War II; twenty went into the military service and six of us into CPS as COs."

Another place of influence was the YMCA. Murray Braden, the son of Methodist missionaries, began attending YMCA programs at Northwestern College, becoming president of the student organization during his senior year. He recalled that Claude C. (Buck) Shotts had a profound effect on many of the students at the university. He described Shotts as "a pacifist, and a very persuasive one." Braden worked with the Northwestern Peace Action Committee, sponsored by the YMCA and YWCA. He observed one particularly notable event: "In the spring of 1939 I was the presider at a student strike against war (we cut classes to attend) held on the meadow in front of the library, at which something like seven hundred students took the Oxford Oath to refuse to participate in war outside the continental United States."

For some men with special qualifications, the declaration against war was so important personally that they refused to enroll in less-invasive and less-demanding assignments in lieu of CPS duty. Murray Braden, being enrolled in a theological seminary, could have opted for a ministerial exemption. But he refused it. "I was not intending to become a minister," he recalled. "My objection was not to national service, but to military service. Further, I felt it was important to demonstrate that though I was a pacifist, I was not attempting to avoid service to our country."

When the draft board called Bill Bristol, he registered and applied for 4-E status. However, his older brother, Jim, went even further; although a Lutheran minister of a church in Camden, New Jersey, Jim refused the automatic deferral and spent more than a year in federal prison. Bill Bristol had no problem registering for the draft and even indicated that he would be willing to join the army medical corps. "However," he noted, "since regulations at that time did not guarantee medical corps assignment to those with 1-A-O noncombatant classification, I was granted the 4-E."

With three years of graduate study at the University of Pennsylvania already under his belt, Bristol approached smoke jumping with less enthusiasm than did some of the younger jumpers; perhaps he had outgrown the youthful proclivity toward a sense of invincibility. Bristol recalled,

> I was one of about ten jumpers who made up a unit at Twisp in northern Washington. On my first fire jump, in the Wenatchee National Forest, I made a bad landing on an incline, suffering a sprain fracture in one of my ankles. The fire was already a mile or two long when a number of us arrived on the scene, and before long we were followed in by an all black army unit of probably two hundred paratroopers. I hobbled around and operated a

radio. Later, with my ankle taped up, I made two jumps on much smaller fires with just one other fellow in each case. Being in CPS Camp 103 was a great experience, but I must confess I was not as gung-ho about jumping as some of the others in our unit. I wasn't disappointed when we didn't jump, and I found as much satisfaction in fighting fires reached by ground transportation as in working on those reached by air.

As several of these life stories indicate, choosing conscientious objector status was not merely a choice for the moment. Remaining stateside during the war, no matter what a man's religious convictions were, could carry a lifelong social stigma. At that time, the men did not know what type of prejudice they might face after the war. Would they find jobs, get bank loans, be accepted by returning veterans?

The conscientious objectors thus faced a moral dilemma imposed on people throughout time: remain absolutely true to one's individual beliefs, or temper one's beliefs in a pragmatic way to reflect the mores of society in general? For the CPSer, it became apparent that his first priority was his spiritual life, regardless of whether he would be able to flourish socially and economically after making that decision.

Roy Wenger, an older CPSer, had already established some worthy professional credentials by the time the draft board summoned him. After teaching eight years at Cuyahoga Falls High School about twenty miles south of Cleveland, he was invited to become a research assistant in the Bureau of Educational Research at Ohio State University. His doctoral work centered on educational media. He later wrote,

> My mentor and close friend was Dr. Edgar Dale, brilliant, witty and an intellectual model whom I tried to emulate. Dale was a member of the American Civil Lib-

erties Union, then led by pacifist Roger Baldwin. We bantered back and forth about military service versus the new Civilian Public Service as my draft number came ever closer to the top of the list. When I told Edgar Dale I was going to choose CPS he looked me straight in the eye and quietly said, "It will ruin your career."

I replied: "None of us really know whether it will ruin my career, and we hope that will not happen." I was thinking of my three exemplars [Jesse Smucker—a fifth grade teacher; Jacob Meyer—a faculty member of Western Reserve University; and Newton D. Baker—a member of the Cleveland Council on World Affairs], all of whom had creative careers in spite of, or maybe because of, their World War One service as COs. I also suggested to my father that if he had a choice, he should hold on to the farm until after the war [in case I couldn't find work].

These were difficult choices in difficult times.

During the course of their ensuing lives, few of the CPS smoke jumpers changed their convictions. But as the years passed, some men—such as Asa Mundell, the son of a parson from Pindstaff, Illinois—came to more clearly understand the motivation that had kept them out of the popular war. Mundell observed,

> I often wonder what I might have done, and been like had I entered the armed brigades, instead of going into CPS. I have finally figured out one of the most basic reasons I had, but at the time could not know, why I did not go into the military in 1942. It was my growing abhorrence of the idea of regimentation, and simply being just one of a mass of dumb bodies without a personal

voice of my own or personal control. It also had to do with war as a non-principle, and a mad machine.

It was not a matter of discipline-hating, but of just being a nonentity, and smothered in a sea of khaki-colored automatons. I was not taken in by all of the war propaganda. As I continued to seek more reason and spirit for my attitude and reasons for objecting, I realized that my own religious upbringing and my seeking the way of Jesus, was actually the greater basis for my convictions. I had only heard of peace movements and the FOR [Fellowship of Reconciliation], and such from my brother, and other college friends. Strangely, my introduction to them and their strong pronouncements against war made it easy for me to make the decision for CPS. Interestingly enough, not one of them ever made the commitment for CPS. They just became ministers, and rode through the war preaching pious garbage and going on through college and seminary. But, they did their good work too. And they encouraged me in my stand.

CHAPTER FIVE

Birth of Smoke Jumping

On July 12, 1940, more than a year before the entry of the United States into the Second World War, Earl Cooley and Rufus Robinson parachuted from a small plane over Martin Creek on the Nez Perce National Forest, to become the first men in history to ever jump a wildfire. Earlier that day, around three o'clock in the afternoon, pilot Dick Johnson, of the Johnson Flying Service in Missoula, had landed his single-engine Travelaire at Moose Creek to pick up the firefighters. Robinson, Cooley, and project foreman Merle Lundigan had loaded the tools and supplies onto the plane, with Lundigan going along to kick out supplies.

As the plane took off, Robinson (a few years older than Cooley) folded his tall, thin frame onto a box near the fuselage opening where the door had been removed, while Cooley crouched on the floor. When they arrived over the scene, both men poked their heads out the door to observe the patch of flaming trees in the timbered gulch below. As high winds buffeted the plane, the men discussed aborting the trip. "We were rocking and bouncing from one side of the

plane to the other, with no safety bar across the doorway,"
Cooley recalled. "The strong winds and downdrafts made it
difficult to control the plane and get low enough to pick a satisfactory jump spot."

As the plane circled several times, the men decided upon an
open green slide area as their landing spot, about a quarter
mile above the fire. A small test chute revealed a drift of about a
half mile, indicating at least a thirty-mile-per-hour wind.

Rufus Robinson, pulling rank, decided to jump first. He
crouched in the doorway as Johnson maneuvered the plane
into position. When Johnson cut the motor, Robinson bailed
out and yanked his ripcord. The Eagle canopy blossomed
above him without a hitch. But Robinson struggled with the
wind the whole way down, overshooting the landing spot by
fifteen hundred feet and sailing over two small ridges before
landing in a small outcropping of rocks on top of a third
ridge. Despite the minor glitches, he sounded enthusiastic as
he radioed back that he was O.K.

Then Cooley took center stage and almost ended the
smoke jumper program before it even began:

> I was sitting on the box by the door, with my hand on
> the ripcord, ready to get out on the step, when we hit an
> extremely bad air pocket. The drop threw me com-
> pletely off the box; I felt my back hit the top of the fuse-
> lage. After the impact was over and I opened my eyes, I
> found Merle Lundigan with his back also on the top of
> the plane, facing me in mid air. After the plane stabi-
> lized, I struggled back to the box. I found that I had
> pulled my ripcord out of the housing but fortunately
> had not cracked my backpack.[1]

As Johnson circled again and maneuvered over the jump
spot, Cooley placed one foot on the step outside the door and

then signaled the pilot to cut the motor. Cooley dropped away from the plane, while Lundigan and Johnson waited to see the canopy blossom—but nothing happened. They held their breath as Cooley seemed to be plummeting toward certain death.

Earl Cooley had been born a flatlander on a homestead on the prairie, about forty miles northeast of Hardin, Montana, where his father planted about twelve hundred acres of bottomland in alfalfa along Sarpy Creek, and the same amount in wild hay. The elder Cooley also ran the post office, which housed the area's only telephone. During the First World War, the Cooleys had often acted as bearers of bad news whenever the War Department phoned to report the death of a young neighbor on the battlefields of Europe.

But even in bad times, the living had been good. "A man could put food on the table, find a wagonload of coal, and hope that times would be better for the kids—so long as he had a little ranch," Cooley noted.[2] By 1919, though, times had changed. During the next six years, about twenty thousand farms went bankrupt. Cooley's father sold the ranch to cover the losses for the bank, and the family moved to a little spread near Corvallis in the mountains of western Montana.

Young Earl rode in a boxcar with his grandfather, the two guarding the family possessions. Along the way, three tramps (one a black man) climbed through the car's open door, professing that they meant no harm. But the Cooleys sat at the opposite end of the boxcar, suspiciously eying the intruders. When the train stopped in Helena, the drifters helped feed and water the Cooleys' livestock before embarking to seek their fortune. At that point, young Earl learned something about human nature: "Our fears subsided when we found that they were victims of hard times just like we were. They, too, were looking for a place where they could make a new start."[3]

Cooley matured doing ranch work in the Bitterroot Valley

at a dollar a day in the summer and fifteen a month plus board in the winter. However, the work had little appeal for him. Realizing that his interests lay in the forests with hunting, fishing, and trapping, he hired on with the Forest Service as a fire guard and lookout at Moose Creek. In those days there were two ways of fighting fires. After spotting a nearby lightning strike, a lookout would shoulder his shovel or pulaski and hike to the fire and put it out. If the fire burned too far from the lookout's location, a team of firefighters would walk to the site, hoping to arrive before the fire grew too large for them to contain. When a large fire erupted, crews of men marched into the area, followed by mule teams, dispatched from the Ninemile Remount Depot, carrying supplies.

In 1937, Cooley went on his first smoke-chaser fire. That expedition remains an interesting contrast to the smoke jumper program that developed a few years later. He described that experience prosaically:

> We were hauled to the mouth of Boulder Creek, given fire packs, and were told the fire was in the head of Canyon Creek on the west side of the Bitterroot-Idaho Range, about sixteen and a half miles away. We left the end of the road shortly after noon and started over the divide. When we reached the top of the divide, we saw the smoke about two and a half miles away. We started toward it but darkness overtook us just a short distance from the fire. We thought we heard someone working on the fire. It was Bob Brennan, who had just come over from Mount George Lookout, from the Idaho side. The next morning we put out the fire with snow and started the long hike back to road camp.[4]

Cooley helped build logging roads, drove a dump truck, maintained trails, worked as a lookout, and helped construct the fire towers. During winters he attended the forestry school at Montana State University in Missoula.

That was an interesting time to work for the Forest Service, especially in fire protection. The agency began expanding its firefighting capabilities shortly after the devastating fires of 1910, when hundreds of fiery maelstroms blew together to char three million acres of timber in Idaho and Montana, destroying entire towns in their paths. Until that time, Native Americans and landowners had routinely set low-intensity fires to burn litter and underbrush from the forest floor to help prevent large fires. When the Forest Service adapted an industrial timber management program, it outlawed the light-burning practice.[5]

After the First World War, the agency began experimenting with new technology to extinguish fires, focusing on dropping supplies from airplanes and on water bombing. Also, Chief Forester Henry S. Graves asked the chief of the Army Air Corps to provide flyovers in areas of certain western states to detect wildfires.[6] That request led to a California fire patrol—in which Colonel H. H. "Hap" Arnold, commander of the U.S. Army Air Corps during the Second World War, started his aviation career. By 1925, the aerial-detection program had expanded to other states, with the Fire Patrol of Spokane regularly cruising the skies of eastern Washington, Idaho, and western Montana. During the next decade, the scope of the project expanded to include aerial photography and cargo dropping. In 1926, a spotter in a plane pushed out packages of food, tools, and mail to firefighters battling a blaze on the Chelan National Forest in Washington. Figuring out how to package the drops took a while. Tightly packed containers often broke apart on impact, while loosely packed containers—holding mess outfits, fire tools, and bedding—offered more air resistance and landed more gently.

In 1933, Forester Howard Flint, a pioneer in aerial activities in the Northern Rocky Mountain Region, tied parachutes to some cargo drops. Two years later, the Forest Service obtained some condemned army chutes for supply drops; these worked even better. Personnel in Washington state also experimented with tying seventeen-foot shrouds to the corners of burlap parachutes to deliver their payloads, for the most part, intact. Similar experiments followed on the Colorado National Forest in Arizona during the 1937 forest-fire season. Two years later, airplanes routinely delivered food and supplies via parachute to isolated firefighters.

During the same decade, some visionaries in the Forest Service experimented with dropping water or fire-retardant chemicals from airplanes. In 1938, the service purchased its first plane—a commercial-type high-wing, five-seater Stinson aircraft—and retrofitted it for fire-control research. The plane was assigned to the California Region. Around the same time, in Missoula, Montana, Bob Johnson installed one-hundred-gallon tanks and trapdoors in a Ford Trimotor and experimented with water drops in the Blue Mountain area south of town. Unfortunately, the experiments proved unsuccessful. By 1939, the Forest Service had abandoned its water-bomb tests, realizing that the available planes and research resources would get them nowhere. But if a plane couldn't drop water on fires, why not drop men?

Ever since Leonardo da Vinci had first drawn a parachute design, men had experimented with the device from balloons and high places, sometimes successfully, other times not. By the First World War, engineering daredevils had all but figured out the functional features needed for successful parachuting. In 1916, Herbert L. Adams of Somerville, Massachusetts, designed a chute that he claimed could be steered by pulling on the shroud lines. A few years later, Englishman John William Cawdery sewed together a chute that was steered by means of guide lines attached to lateral flaps. Other technicians added their own twists to the parachute design so that as World War II approached, a man jumping out of a plane had a good chance of safely reaching earth via parachute. T. V. Peason of the Forest Service's Intermountain Region first proposed delivering firefighters via parachute in 1934. Peason conducted a few tests using dummies, but his superiors considered the scheme too hazardous. Most administrators considered the idea a "hare-brained scheme" and regarded parachutists as "crackpots, publicity-loving daredevils, or just plain crazy." But by 1939, others had picked up Peason's torch.

That year, the service transferred the Aerial Experimental Project from California to the North Pacific Region, with David P. Godwin in charge. Working with Regional Forester Lage Wenstedt and Harold King (the Forest Service pilot), Godwin abandoned the water-bombing tests and transferred that program's funds to a parachute-jumping experiment. Godwin designated airports near Winthrop, Washington, in the Chelan National Forest and Seeley Lake, northeast of Missoula, as the main bases. Other supporters backing the program included Otto Lindh, chief of fire control for the region; T. Albert Davies, a technician in the regional office; and Walter Anderson, fire assistant in the Chelan National Forest.

Eagle Parachute Company of Lancaster, Pennsylvania, won the contract to provide parachutes, protective suits, and the services of professional riggers and jumpers. The first experimental jumps took place near the Winthrop base from October 5 to November 15, 1939. Joining Eagle's head parachutist Frank Derry and assistant Glenn Smith were Frank's two brothers, Chet and Virgil, as well as Richard Tuttle and Allen Honey. After a number of tests with a 28-foot-diameter condemned military silk canopy with a 150-pound sand dummy attached to it, the men boarded the Stinson. After being joined by some Forest Service employees, the group made about sixty-five live jumps. The Derry brothers discussed technique and equipment after each jump.

The jumpers used an Eagle 30-foot backpack and a 27-foot emergency chest pack, both attached to the harness with quick-attachment fittings. For protection from tree butts, branch stubs, and rough terrain, they wore a two-piece padded felt suit, a football helmet with wire-mesh face mask, athletic supporter, ankle braces and back-abdominal braces, stout gloves, and heavy logger boots. The chest pack proved a great help in protecting jumpers from injuries when they slammed into limbs and tree trunks. The experimental jumps proved that smoke jumpers could land safely in all kinds of green timber common to the national forests, at elevations ranging from 2,000 to 6,800 feet.[7]

The professional jumpers noted ways to improve the airplane for jumping. A special handle bolted just outside the door enabled the jumper to steady himself. A metal step outside the plane below the doorway gave him a perch from which to drop.

The first two men to parachute to forest terrain—as opposed to jumps onto airport landing strips or open, level meadows—were Glenn Smith and Francis Lufkin. At the time, Lufkin, with no previous parachuting experience, was a forest guard at Chelan National Forest. Later he became a professional smoke jumper in charge of the Forest Service's parachute training center near Winthrop. Following that jump, the squad of men repeatedly landed without serious injury in mountain meadows, on open ridge tops, and onto steep, boulder-strewn slopes. The project chief's report suggested that jumpers avoid "snag areas, areas of down timber, lodgepole deadenings, extremely steep slopes, deep canyons, and areas of rock cliffs or ledges."[8]

The following season, Region One and Region Six organized small crews, with Region Six recruiting many of the men who had made the experimental jumps the previous fall. There was no shortage of volunteers. Ages ranged from twenty-one to thirty-five, with a weight ceiling of 190 pounds. The new jobs paid $193 for the summer and provided board for two and one-half months. The Johnson Flying Service won the contract for delivering the jumpers.

Region One selected Leonard Hamilton, from the Lolo Forest; James Alexander, from the Cabinet Forest; Dick Lynch, from the Flathead; Jim Waite, from the Clearwater; Rufus Robinson, from the Nez Perce; Bill Bolen, from the Kootenai; and Earl Cooley, from the Bitterroot. After taking the standard ROTC cadet physical exam, Leonard Hamilton had to drop out of the program because of an enlarged heart. Later in the program, Bill Bolen also dropped out.

The Region One crew moved to Seeley Lake for training. There they immediately constructed the first Forest Service parachute loft by placing two fourteen-by-nineteen-foot tents end to end on wooden platforms. They also set up three wall tents for living quarters. "The job was finished about 3 p.m. and the crew then began their first jumping lesson," Cooley recalled. "The instructor hung a parachute in a tree, called the crew together and said: 'This is the apex, these are the risers, these are the secondary lines, and the colored ones are the guide lines. Tomorrow we are going to jump.' That was the extent of our training."[9]

That June, four U.S. Army staff officers visited the parachute-training camp at Seeley Lake. One of them, Major William Cary Lee, later incorporated smoke jumper techniques and ideas into the first paratroop training at Fort Benning, Georgia. Major Lee subsequently commanded the 101st Airborne Division, which was instrumental in the Normandy invasion. Doctors L. P. Martin and Amos Little also trained with the jumpers so that they could quickly reach injured or helpless individuals in the backcountry. Martin later set up an advanced course in first-aid technique for the jumper squads, while Little was credited with fifty-one rescue jumps from 1943 to 1946, some of them to aid injured smoke jumpers.

With the usual tenseness of a rookie, Cooley survived his training jumps. On July 10, the crew broke camp and assembled at the Moose Creek airstrip, where they built the first permanent parachute loft, which included a tower tall enough for hanging a thirty-foot chute. Then they waited for a smoke report from the Fire Desk at the regional headquarters in Missoula. That call came a few days later on July 12, 1940.

After Rufus Robinson had safely landed on the ground, he looked up to see Earl Cooley plummeting toward earth, Cooley's chute streaming behind him. Robinson tensed, expecting the worst. Cooley later described his descent in his autobiography, *Trimotor and Trail*: "I struggled to free my shroud lines, which were a twisted mass on the back of my neck. I unsnapped the buckles on the big collar of my jump suit and tried to see what I could do with my chute. I was getting the lines straightened when my chute slipped into a streamer that was letting me down at almost maximum speed. I could feel the wind on my face. The unopened parachute streamer was just enough to hold me upright."

When Cooley bent his head down to look for his emergency chute handle, he freed the knot in his chute risers that had bunched behind his neck. As they loosened, the risers unwound and spun him around until his main chute fully inflated. By that time, he was only a few hundred feet from the tops of dry lodgepole pines, drifting along at fifteen to twenty miles per hour. "I saw one big, green spot," he recalled, "and guided my chute to it, trying to avoid hazards on the ground. Almost before I knew it, I was hanging in a huge spruce, grabbing for limbs. I hit this tree about a hundred feet up at such speed that I went through the branches and broke them off, but my chute clung to the side of the tree. I was still swinging, my heart pounding—I was still alive." Sensing that his chute did not have a good hold on the tree, Cooley elected to climb down the trunk to the ground.

Later, when he returned to retrieve the chute, a light shake of the rope brought the canopy falling onto some snags. The parachute project almost died in infancy, Cooley testified: "If our spotter, Merle Lundigan, had not caught himself in the door; if my parachute had not fully opened as I neared the ground, there would have been one and possibly two fatalities on this first fire jump. In all likelihood the controversial idea of parachuting men to remote fires would have been abandoned."[10]

Despite that flirtation with death, the smoke jumper program showed much promise. After the inaugural season, Forest Service officials transferred the project to Region One, of which Missoula was the geographical center. The operation expanded to three eight-man squads, plus riggers, squad leaders, and administrators. All the men reported for training at Seeley Lake.

Region One boasted eight million acres of roadless area at that time. In addition, Missoula was home to the Johnson Flying Service. Bob Johnson and the U.S. Forest Service were a perfect match. Johnson's round, chubby face and thin, greased-back hair revealed his conservative nature—despite his reputation as the best mountain pilot in the northern Rockies. Although he flew in weather conditions that others avoided and into tight spots where few would venture, Johnson did so only after thorough calculations. His careful bent ensured success when dropping smoke jumpers at low altitudes to fires smoking in tight canyons and near ridges of craggy cliffs where winds swooped, churned, died down, and spiraled with changing temperatures throughout the day.

Originally begun as a small passenger and tourist outfit, Johnson Flying Service took off as a legitimate business in 1929 when Bob opened a branch in Boise, Idaho, and inaugurated a year-round mail service covering more than twenty thousand square miles of rugged mountain terrain. On the circuit, Bob flew a 330-horsepower single-engine Travelaire, bolstered with a supercharger. The plane carried no instruments other than altimeter, airspeed indicator, bank and turn indicator, and motor gauges. With the first snow, Johnson rigged the Travelaire with skis. He used no compass or map. Instead he memorized each individual canyon, river, and ridge top that led to an isolated ranch or mining or timber camp.

Bob's reputation grew as he consistently took off in foul weather that grounded other pilots—and safely returned. Late in 1930, the Forest Service asked if he would be interested in flying firefighters and supplies into backcountry airstrips that the agency was considering building. Bob Johnson accepted the challenge. The following summer, Forest Service officials held a small send-off party as Johnson and his copilot—his brother, Dick Johnson—prepared to take off from Missoula for the Moose Creek landing strip, deep within what is now the River of No Return Wilderness in Idaho. They presented Bob with a topographical map that agency cartographers had painstakingly crafted for weeks. Bob handed it to his brother, who, before boarding the plane, handed it back to the Forest Service officials.

Bob Johnson approached flying with a scientific bent. Before attempting to land heavy loads at the short backcountry airstrips, he carefully figured out how many feet of runway he needed for landing and takeoffs while ferrying certain weight loads. One reporter from the *Daily Missoulian* who dropped by Hale Airfield in Missoula, where the county fairgrounds now sit, was baffled by what he saw. The journalist apparently had thought he would get a story out of Johnson that day, but instead he reported to his editor, "We've been out here two hours already, and all you see is Dick pacing up and down with flags, and Bob going up and down, up and down. Bob takes off lots of times, but he don't do nothing. All he does is make a real sharp bank. Then he circles and sets her down and then Dick throws some sandbags inside, and he takes off again."[11]

Twenty-six men assembled during the spring of 1941, with many of the same faces from the previous summer. Only one jumper from the original experiment did not return. Jumpers were dispatched from Missoula to other regions when needed. Squad leaders Francis Lufkin and George Honey led the contingent stationed at the Ninemile Remount Depot, with Chet Derry and Glenn Smith as riggers. Dick Lynch went to Big Prairie in the Flathead National Forest, with Jim Waite as parachute rigger. And Earl Cooley was assigned to Moose Creek as parachute rigger, with Rufus Robinson as squad leader. For the most part, rainy weather doused the fire season in Region One that summer; Robinson and his men spent most of the time building a recreation hall at the Moose Creek airport and working in the parachute loft.

Late July produced a flurry of lightning activity in the Pacific Northwest, and the jumpers handled or helped man nine fires, saving the Forest Service an estimated $30,000. Also, for the first time, a large group of smoke jumpers was dispatched to a fire that had run away from the initial attackers. Three squads jumped the threatening fifteen-acre blaze burning in extremely heavy fuels. They successfully held the fire in check until more reinforcements arrived on foot.

The most important technical advancement of the season was the creation of the static line release, developed by Frank and Chet Derry. Jumpers hooked the static line to their ripcord and clipped the other end to a wire running overhead through the frame of the plane. The first static line they experimented with, according to Cooley, was "a fifteen-foot mule halter rope that I'd found in the corral." The device eliminated the need for a jumper to manually pull the rip-cord, reducing the level of prejump jitters.

A few months after the season ended, as administrators planned for another smoke-jumping season, the Japanese attacked Pearl Harbor and the United States went to war. "Just when parachuting men to fires had proved practical, we were hit by shortages of men and equipment," Cooley recalled.[12]

Nevertheless, when the next spring arrived, four squads of men mustered for work. One squad was stationed at each of four locations: Big Prairie Ranger Station, Moose Creek, Ninemile, and Seeley Lake. But of the thirty-three recruits, only five had previously jumped. To make matters worse, by then, parachutes had become scarce. "We managed to obtain military chutes rejected because of minor flaws," Cooley noted.

That year, Frank and Chet Derry made a breakthrough in parachute design by perfecting a slotted chute that could be easily opened and maneuvered. The new design also pro-vided a slower descent. With the slotted Derry chute, jumpers could turn and use a small amount of forward speed to make headway at right angles to the wind. They could also turn into a strong wind to prevent drifting past their mark. Or they could ride a gust and stretch a glide so that a dying wind wouldn't drop them short of the mark.

Cooley, then thirty-two and married with two children, got a military deferment after a Forest Service official informed his draft board that Cooley was "an essential man and occu-pies a key position with the Forest Service." Cooley decided not to enlist in the armed services, believing his work with the agency was of national importance. After the war, some of the pioneer jumpers who had enlisted in the military targeted Cooley as a slacker.

By early September, the ranks of the smoke jumpers had diminished as more and more men had left for the service. Those who remained gathered on the critical forests with high fire danger. "For about a week men jumped to fires as rapidly as chutes could be retrieved and repacked," Cooley recalled.

The financial figures proved the value of smoke jumping. In 1942, the jumpers controlled thirty-one fires on their own and assisted on four others. Estimated savings more than doubled over the previous year, to about $60,000. But the program seemed headed for mothballs, at least for the duration of the war—until conscientious objector Phil Stanley (the Quaker who had been born in China) came up with a brilliant idea.

Stanley—stationed at a CPS camp in Coleville, California at the time—had become disenchanted with Civilian Public Service, finding "most of the projects worthless. Rather than work of national importance," he noted, "we called most projects 'work of national impotence.'"[13] At Coleville, he listened with rapt attention as Ray Brieding, the engineer of the Mono National Forest, described the intriguing new method of fighting fires by landing parachutists near the scene.

"It occurred to me that CPS had more than enough ablebodied men who would probably volunteer for the duty, so I started a two-pronged letter-writing campaign," Stanley said. "One was addressed to Region One Fire Control. The other was to my brother, Jim, in Washington, D.C., who was on detached service with the National Service Board for Religious Objectors to write and edit 'The Reporter.' I asked him to alert the Service committees to the possibilities in the event the Forest Service became interested."

On October 12, 1942, Stanley wrote to Axel Lindh, then head of fire control for Region One:

It occurred to me some three months ago that you might need men for your parachute fire-fighting corps, either for experimental purposes or to do the actual fire fighting. . . .

You have probably heard a great deal of CPS both pro and con, but a few pertinent facts might be welcome. We are all drafted men, pretty well fit physically, self-supporting, and have had a moderate amount of fire fighting (mostly in the East.) The fires we have been on were probably nothing like ones that require parachute tactics and we would probably need more training both physically and tactically. . . .

If there is the slightest possibility of your being able to use us, we would appreciate more information concerning requirements, the type of forests adaptable to this technique, location of the training school, and any details that you consider useful. Of course, if you can use us, the project will have to be okayed by Selective Service and the Friends' Service Committee in Philadelphia. . . .

We are very anxious to get into this type of fire fighting, and I think it is safe to say that our enthusiasm has passed the fascination stage. So we would greatly appreciate a favorable answer.

Much to his surprise, Phil Stanley got his wish. Lindh petitioned the Selective Service and the National Service Board for Religious Objectors to have smoke jumping approved as a CPS assignment. He wrote to Stanley: "So far as the Forest Service officials here in this region are concerned, we will be mighty glad to recruit parachute fire fighting candidates from the CPS camps."[14]

On February 12, 1943, executive camp directors of CPS agencies met to write a memorandum of agreement between the National Service Board and the Department of Agriculture, the agency that oversees the Forest Service. They agreed that sixty men were to be chosen, with more to be selected later when more funding became available. Each agency of the three peace churches would submit names of thirty-five interested applicants. On March 8, 1943, the National Service Board of Directors approved the plans for a parachute firefighting unit. A few days later, the Forest Service agreed to provide maintenance, cots, blankets, and sleeping bags for the men. They also agreed to house the civilian director, Roy Wenger, and his wife, Florence (as camp nutritionist), plus an assistant, a nurse, and six cooks. After training, the cooks would disperse to the various spike camps. At first the national board agreed to feed the men.

Word of Camp 103 quickly spread throughout the CPS system. Officials instructed the men to send their applications to the church agencies. More than three hundred responded, with 118 applications forwarded on to the Forest Service. The applicants included physical examination reports and recommendations from camp superintendents. On April 19, at Ninemile, Roy Wenger, Earl Cooley, and others sifted through the applications, choosing twenty men each from the Brethren, Friends, and Mennonite camps. One government official remarked that all the applicants could have been used if equipment had been available for them. Forest Service officials invited the men to camp with the understanding that they could send any man back to his original camp if he proved unsatisfactory. At the same time, the men maintained the privilege of returning to their camps if the work did not suit them. Five men from each of the three church agencies reported to the camp in early May for two weeks of intensive training in parachute rigging.

All other CPS camps paid their men two dollars and fifty cents a month. At CPS Camp No. 103, Forest Service officials doubled the pay, but it was not really a raise. They encouraged the men to use the extra money to buy health insurance, since the Forest Service refused to cover them. Few of the men followed that advice. Those who were hurt on the job were left to their own resources once the fire season ended.

To sustain the project, the War Department released some parachute cloth. To overcome other shortages, supervisors, such as Cooley, used their depression years' experience to improvise.

As the first day of training camp approached, the Forest Service staff—including Cooley—expected the worst. They may have had good reason to be wary, depending on which of the many rumors about CPS camps had circulated to them.

Some were even true. If there was anything uniform about conscientious objectors, it was that there was no uniformity to them.

Even within the brotherhood of a religion, the individual views of service and responsibility often widely varied. While some men willingly surrendered their freedom as a symbolic sacrifice to their country, others believed that the government was holding them in a type of slavery. As some approached their assignments with pride, others grumbled. They did not like being told where to work and when to work. The lack of income jeopardized the welfare of their dependents. Some men disliked the isolation and the primitive nature of their quarters. Moreover, the "work of national impotence" gnawed at the psyches of many educated and highly skilled workers. The American Friends Service Committee eventually condemned most of the Park Service tasks, forestry work, and some of the soil conservation programs as "of minor significance under present conditions and incapable of utilizing effectively the men which have been placed at their disposal."[15] Also, some conscientious objectors could not accept any aspect of CPS. These absolutists felt compelled to breach

law and regulations as a matter of principle. Absolutism
became something of a sect within CPS.

As has been touched on earlier, the Selective Service
opened a number of government-run CPS camps to mollify
those conchies who held no church affiliation, as well as to
take the pressure off of church administrators who did not
want to deal with disgruntled agnostics or atheists. Moreover,
most of the CPS misfits—men labeled as convicts or
invalids—were assigned to these camps. While there, a good
percentage of the absolutists refused to cooperate with
administrators, taking part in work slowdowns or sticking to
their sick bunks in an all-out attack on the system of conscription. Observers at government-run CPS camps such as
Mancos and Lapine estimated that less than half the men
turned in a reasonable day's work. "These men calculated to
nullify all efforts to operate the government camp program
and deliberately goaded government officials to even more
repressive actions."[16]

Some sporadic trouble also occurred at church camps
where a number of individuals shifted their emphasis from
orthodox service to passive resistance or outright rebellion.
At one Mennonite camp, for example, two men tarred and
feathered the director. When disgruntled CPSer David Met-
calf walked out of Camp 46 in Big Flats, New York, on December 28, 1943, he summed up his disillusionment with the CPS
system in this way:

> It encourages hypocrisy, wishful thinking, "gold brick-
> ing," hypochondria, self-deception, submissiveness, lazi-
> ness, idle grumbling, selfishness, sheepish citizenship,
> and countless confusions and stupefactions of the mind.
>
> It discourages honesty, forthrightness, responsibility,
> courage, initiative, independence, constructive think-
> ing, strength of character, and mental health in general.

As a factor on the American scene it is making good
dupes for some possible future fascism; it is making
poor citizens for democracy. . . . It is a polite and gen-
tlemanly version of what we have been hearing of
forced labor elsewhere in the world. . . . Acquiescence
in it is not consistent with my understanding of pacifism.[17]

Cooley had obviously heard a number of disparaging
reports, for he noted, "We thought these men would be hard
to handle, independent, and real renegades." Indeed, he
became so disgruntled that he confessed, "When I first heard
we were hiring conscientious objectors, I considered joining
the Army."[18]

CHAPTER SIX

Boot Camp

Missoula, a town of 24,000 residents in the early
1940s, sat nestled at the hub of five valleys. Mount
Sentinel and Mount Jumbo, the latter named
because some say it resembled a reclining elephant, formed
the eastern backdrop for the town. Grass still covers most of
their rounded flanks, with ponderosa pine and Douglas fir
topping the summits and fingering down the draws. Then as
now, the favorite hiking path in Missoula zigzagged a third of
the way up Mount Sentinel from the Montana State University
campus, now called the University of Montana. At the time,
piles of white-painted rocks formed the shape of a giant "M."
(The current "M" is made of concrete.) The expansive Grass
Valley unrolled west of town, while the Bitterroot Valley lay
perpendicular to the south.

The Clark Fork River coursed between the two mountains
through the narrow Hellgate Canyon, named by French
Canadian fur traders who survived ambushes by the Blackfeet; getting past the Indians, they said, was like going
through the gates of Hell. A few miles east, up the canyon and

away from town, the Blackfoot River merged with the Clark Fork behind the Mill Town Dam. Downstream, west of town, the Bitterroot River contributed even more water to the Clark Fork. As it still does, the Clark Fork separated the downtown business area from cozy neighborhoods. The tallest structure downtown remains the Wilma Building, named after the rich, opera-loving lady who built it. The eight-story buff-colored brick building, which houses a lavish, chandelier-lighted grand theater, was the town's artistic center back then. Like the nearby mountain, the Wilma, looming above the river at the northern end of the Higgins Street Bridge, acted as a sentinel of sorts for downtown.

In 1942, Missoula underwent a rash of fires. A New Year's Day blaze destroyed or damaged several downtown businesses on Higgins Avenue. A month later, a fire destroyed a warehouse at Swanberg Lumber Company. One of the fire engines deployed to the scene carried back a hot ember to the Orchard Homes volunteer fire department, which went up in flames during the night.

Two years after the war started, twenty-five hundred Missoulians had signed up with the army or navy. One hundred and sixty-six of them would die by the end of the conflict. The half million residents of Montana led the nation in supporting the war effort through bond drives, scrap metal collection, and enlistment rates. Only one state had a higher percentage of its population killed in battles of the Second World War.

The CPS smoke jumpers were not the only outcasts in town. Twelve hundred Italian citizens, most of them merchant seamen, were detained by the U.S. Immigration and Naturalization Service at Fort Missoula, which had once been an army frontier post. Many of the Italians had been crewing on the luxury liner *Conte Biancamano* during a South American cruise. Some of the sailors sabotaged the ship's engines as it passed through the Panama Canal to prevent the British navy from seizing the vessel.

The barbed-wire fences of Fort Missoula also detained about 650 Americans of Japanese descent who had been forced from their homes along the West Coast shortly after the attack on Pearl Harbor. A Korean American who had arrived in Missoula on the same train with the first Japanese detainees had been beaten up at the station because he looked Japanese. The man had been planning to enlist in the army.[1]

In downtown Missoula, free citizens shopped at the Red and White Food Stores, Stop N' Shop at Pattee Street and East Broadway, or SuperSave on Alder, and they watched movies at the Wilma, Rio, and Rialto theaters.

During the 1940s, Missoula often resembled a dreary industrial town, especially during the winter months. Smoke from residential woodstoves and giant drying kilns at the riverside lumberyards accumulated in the valley, creating smog and low-lying clouds. Winter inversions locked in the pollution against the mountains for weeks on end. But when spring winds cleansed the atmosphere and wildflowers blossomed on the hillside meadows, the town looked like paradise—especially to the wondering eyes of conscientious objectors from the flatlands. Along the banks of the Clark Fork River in Hellgate Canyon, truck farmers grew enough fresh produce to take care of 80 percent of the town's daily needs. And many citizens grew vegetables in backyard plots and adorned their front lawns with flowerbeds, earning the town the nickname of "Garden City." Jumper Warren Shaw wrote, "I had never seen the mountains before and I recall thinking that Missoula was the prettiest city that I had ever seen."

Shaw grew up in the farming community of Geary in western Oklahoma. He saw his first large airplane bigger than a Piper Cub during a senior class trip in 1940 to New Orleans. It turned out to be a DC-3, which would become a staple in the smoke jumper unit after the war. Before the war, Shaw worked at a CCC camp, surveying terraces, ponds, and shelter belts on agricultural land. He then procured a civilian position with the U.S. Army Corps of Engineers to work on new dam sites on the Arkansas and Grand rivers in eastern Oklahoma. Drafted in 1942, he joined his brother at a Brethren CPS camp for the Soil Conservation Service. "I continued as a survey crew member, doing the same as before being drafted," he wrote. "The only difference was the landscape was much different from western Oklahoma—lots of trees and swamps and very little breeze. I had been used to lots of wind on the plains of Oklahoma."

Shaw later applied to be a smoke jumper and was accepted. Late in the 1943 smoke-jumping season, he dropped to a small fire located about forty miles north of Moose Creek. He described his experiences following that jump:

> We thought that we could have it out in an hour or so, but in the afternoon, the wind got up and the fire got out of control. We fought fire all day Saturday, all night and all day Sunday night. We were so tired during that time that part of the time I had to crawl on all fours to fight to keep from losing complete control. Sunday night we stretched a rope between two trees and made a lean-to out of our tarp, where we bedded down. Monday morning there was about eighteen inches of snow on the ground. We had done such a good job putting the fire out that Monday morning we had to search the burned over area to find something to warm our K rations.
>
> After spending all day Monday falling [sic] all the trees that had been touched by fire, we staggered about three miles through the snow to a one-room Forest Service shack, beside a small lake where the plane was to pick us up. In the meantime, a couple of our other

jumpers who had jumped on a nearby fire, and our packer had arrived at this cabin on Sunday. Unbeknownst to any of us, there were three elk hunters already there and they had killed their elk and were stranded as their plane couldn't get in to pick them up due to weather. Not only were they stranded, they had smoked all their cigarettes on Saturday, and they just couldn't believe that five different people came in on three different days, none of whom smoked. They were out of food, and we didn't have any either, so we made stew out of a young elk that they had killed and we lived on elk stew for three days, with seven of us in a one room shack, three of whom were nicotine crazed. Our plane was able to get in for us on Thursday.

But the best scenery was yet to come for Shaw and the other rookie CPSers who disembarked from the train in 1943 at one of Missoula's two depots, the Northern Pacific or the Milwaukee, Chicago, and St. Paul—each rolling in and out on tracks located on opposite banks of the Clark Fork River. (Consequently the depots stood at opposite ends of downtown on Higgins Avenue.) Forest Service officials had set up the first smoke jumper training camp at the Seeley Lake Ranger Station, about seventy miles northeast of Missoula. (The next summer, they relocated the training site to Camp Menard, a former CCC work station located about a mile north of the Ninemile Remount Depot at Huson, Montana.) The smoke jumper volunteers either rode in the back of a stake-bed Forest Service truck or took the Seeley Lake stage along Highway 200 to the camp. A dirt road at the time, Highway 200 paralleled the Blackfoot River, gradually climbing toward the Continental Divide. About fifteen miles from Missoula, the forested hills opened up into a wide mountain

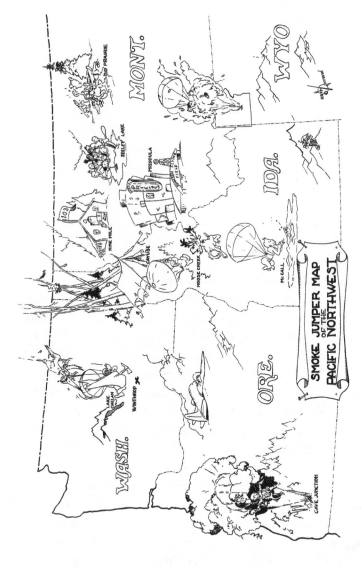

Map 2. From a booklet entitled *Smoke Jumper*, published in 1944 by the Civilian Public Service Camp 103 and written and compiled by Greg Phifer.

valley at the town of Potomac. Here, during the short, cool summers, most farmers grew only grass. The soon-to-be smoke jumpers could look out of their vehicles and watch cowboys push cattle herds down dirt roads or admire the modest log cabins that dotted the landscape.

Once through the valley, the highway again gradually climbed through mixed conifer forests of lodgepole and ponderosa pine, western larch, and Douglas fir. Deer grazed by the roadside, and occasionally a herd of elk made a frantic dash before the approaching vehicle. Farther east, the road crossed the Blackfoot River, and then the Clearwater River, which joined the Blackfoot about a mile to the south, out of sight of the highway. A short distance later, at Clearwater Junction, the vehicles headed north into a rugged country of cold water and majestic mountains—one of the last parts of Montana to be settled.

The lakes in the Seeley-Swan Valley sit like a chain of pearls: Salmon, Swan, Seeley, Rainey, Ira, Lindbergh. Clear, deep, and cold, the lakes were already attracting many summer visitors at that time. Aviator Charles Lindbergh had taken time off from a cross-country tour to camp at Elbow Lake, which he had admired from the air; Montanans later renamed the lake in his honor, and some of his descendants relocated to the area. The towering mountains that formed the backdrop for the lakes added to the area's charm. To the east loomed the midriff of the Rocky Mountains, with hundreds of square miles of roadless, rugged wilderness valleys stretching east to where the carpet of the Northern Plains began to unroll. But from Seeley Lake, the CPSers could only admire the wall of limestone that shut in the valley with a dike of rock. To the west they saw more of the same—the jagged, glacier-covered peaks of the Mission Mountains stood as mammoth protectors of the Flathead Indian Reservation. Grizzly bears still roamed this wild country.

At Camp Paxson, a Boy Scout camp, fifteen small cabins surrounded a large lodge and a well-equipped washhouse. One-hundred-foot-high tamaracks (or western larch), with trunks as big around as cathedral columns, created a parklike setting. Like many of his compatriots, Warren Shaw grew ecstatic when he first glimpsed the scene. The camp had been designed to please adolescents, and of course, many CPSers, not far past their eighteenth birthdays, were still boys at heart. "When we arrived at Seeley Lake, it was a picture post card," Shaw recalled. "And Camp Paxson was beyond anything of my wildest dreams. Even the rich people in Oklahoma didn't have anything like this. I don't know even if my thoughts of Heaven were any prettier than this."

Floyd Yoder (born on a small farm near Kalona, Iowa), likewise fell under the charm of the grandiose landscape, as well as the rustic nature of the buildings. He observed, "The picturesque lake as a foreground and majestic snow capped mountains towering in the background made an inspiring site for our camp. Our quarters were log cabins neatly arranged in groups of four all of which went to make up a neat camp."

Sixty volunteers—twenty from each of the camps of the three peace churches—were chosen for the first smoke jumper training in 1943. Yoder recalled that "one requirement was to have approval from your parents, or wife, if married. I decided to give it a try and wrote to my parents. To my surprise they gave permission for me to sign up." Yoder, who had played football and basketball in high school, had hesitated in his decision to declare conscientious objector status because "community pressure to be a part of the great American war effort was strong." He finally leaned toward CPS after receiving a supportive letter from his brother, Lester, and he later noted, "I never did regret it."

After training at Seeley Lake, Yoder reported to the Redwood Ranger Station with nine other men. Because of the ample rainfall that season, his first jump was delayed until September 12. He described the experience:

> After locating the fire we circled around to find an open spot in which to jump—a little brush field about a half mile from the fire. . . . My partner jumped first and landed about two hundred feet from the field among some trees, but his signal was soon visible indicating that he was all right. We made another circle and dropped a test chute, my nerves becoming more tense each moment. We were now on the last circle coming over the spot and then that pat on the back and out I went sailing through space. A sudden jerk and the parachute was open. "Now hold that chute into the wind so you won't overshoot that brush field," I said to myself.
>
> However, I misjudged the wind speed and landed among some 150-foot Douglas fir trees about fifty yards from the brush field. . . . As I nestled down into the trees, part of the parachute broke the top, letting me down faster than usual. But the landing was all right.
>
> After getting our cargo and equipment we ate a K ration and started to the fire. Things looked quite simple from the air, but once we were down among the trees and brush it was more difficult than anticipated to find the fire. At ten o'clock that night we had the fire under control. By this time we were quite tired, hungry and especially thirsty.

Most of the recruits had no idea what they would be getting into, and some acted as naively as the country bumpkins they were. Dale Entwistle from Athens, Ohio, had been working at a camp in California when he was cleared to join the smoke jumpers. He rode into Missoula on the Northern Pacific early one April morning and was met at the station by Earl Cooley. He recalled, "I remember asking Earl, 'About how high do you bounce when you hit the ground [after parachuting]?' Earl got a good laugh out of that and it seemed to break the ice."

Entwistle later broke a bone in his foot during a landing, which put him out of commission for the season. Afraid that the injury would dim his chances of continuing with smoke jumping the next season, he cautiously asked Cooley if he had a chance of being signed up again. "Well," Earl said, "we've been feeding you all winter so I guess we'll have to get some use out of you this summer." Entwistle loved western Montana so much that after the war he got a job on the Northern Pacific and later the Milwaukee railroad. He lived in Missoula for twenty-five years.

Once all the volunteers had assembled at Seeley Lake, boot camp began in earnest. The first important obstacle they faced was overcoming the prejudice of the Forest Service workers. Earl Cooley, who had not quit his job as he had threatened, tried to keep an open mind. However, a number of other civilian personnel reacted in a hostile manner toward the CPSers from the beginning. Some did not want to eat in the cookhouse with the CPSers, reported Cooley: "They said that anyone who would eat at the same table with a conscientious objector was not very damn patriotic. Others felt that the CPS should be treated like dogs. One of the packers, shoeing horses, tried to catch a CPS recruit's head in a sliding door."[2]

As trouble brewed between the CPS crew and some Forest Service employees, one official drafted a letter to try to improve working relations. The letter contained many accusations and abusive opinions, according to Cooley, who threw the draft in the trash can. Cooley, it seemed, was gaining a different perspective of the men. Within a short time he had come to respect his new jumpers, never catching a glimpse of the alleged dissension rumored to be the norm at other camps. "We thought these men would be hard to handle, independent, and real renegades," he said. "But they were just the opposite. The Mennonites were almost all Midwest farm boys who had never been away from home. They were used to working hard from daylight to dark and could not understand the eight-hour work laws."

Instead of issuing a letter that would be sure to divide the camp, Cooley met with the chief of fire control, Clyde Webb, who was acting regional forester at the time, and Ed McKay, supervisor of the Remount Depot. Cooley and McKay agreed to work out the problem in the field, while Vic Carter handled the administrative angle. After a few weeks, the tension between the jumpers and the mule packers began to subside. "Before the CPS program broke up we had excellent working relations with all CPS units," Cooley reported.[3]

Nevertheless, subtle prejudice still surfaced from time to time. "Near the outset of our training program, Vic Carter, the head of the Parachute Fire Fighting Training Branch, came out to address us in the shadow of the giant ponderosa pines that flourished in the mountains," recalled Roy L. Piepenburg. "His verbal barb was quick in coming and it penetrated well. 'All right you fellows,' he said, 'you've come here with two strikes on you, so it's up to you to make good here.' Instantly, I wondered again how much more my civil liberties as an American citizen would be trampled on."

At Camp Paxson, first thing after breakfast, the men rowed a lifeboat to the training site at the Seeley Ranger Station. Some days the valley fog made navigating a real adventure, according to jumper Bryn Hammarstrom: "One cloudy morning we were not at the ranger station but elsewhere when the shore was reached." But more often than not, the men docked on time, ready to begin the long grind.

One of these trainees, Frank Neufeld, hailed from Buhler, Kansas, where his father worked as a blacksmith. After his family resettled in Parlier, California, his father died suddenly at the age of forty-one. He recalled, "Our family, now five, lived in a modest home. . . . I was a shy, awkward boy and spent eight ordinary years in grade school. In high school I took an interest in music [piano and trombone]. . . . I also discovered that I had some athletic ability and played center on the varsity basketball team and did a little pitching on the baseball squad." After graduating from high school, Neufeld worked for the J.C. Penney Company in nearby Reedley, California, where he won an award for selling the most shoes in the area. Neufeld's ancestors had fled Russia for religious reasons, and when he turned seventeen he joined the Mennonite Brethren Church of Reedley. "So when I signed up under the conscription law I declared myself a conscientious objector," he noted. After stints at CPS camps in Hood River, Oregon, and Camino, California, Neufeld applied for a position as a smoke jumper because he was "so impressed with the importance of the program and the caliber of the men."

At camp, Neufeld found the training period—of approximately ten days' duration—to be strenuous and torturous. Each morning started out with a brisk jog around the camp. Then came calisthenics, with exercises aimed at strengthening the legs, arms, and back. The obstacle course followed. In a pit beside the parachute loft, the squad leader showed the men a motley collection of ropes, ramps, stakes, and tables. The men had to navigate the impediments as fast as they could. Neufeld described this training course:

> One by one the men run up the first steeply inclined ramp, grip the edge, drop seven feet to the ground and roll, under the watchful eye of the squad leader. Ahead of them hung a rope to climb, from which they stepped to a wooden platform and turned a flip into a rope net.
> Then they ran along the two ankle strengtheners,

three planks arranged in concave and convex shapes. The horizontal ladder followed, familiar sight on play-grounds of school or beach.

Next, the neophytes ran uphill toward a series of alternate shallow holes. Then came the tight squeeze, a pair of corrugated tubes through one of which he must wiggle on elbows and knees.

One innocent appearing item in the middle of the obstacle course deserves special mention. Called the tank trap, it consisted of a number of paired stakes, each with a strap near the top. The candidate straps his legs to the stakes, folds his hands on his stomach, arches his back as far as he can and attempts a back bend.

A final obstacle course tantalizer was a twenty-five foot rope to be climbed arms only.

But the grind that sent Neufeld's tired body crawling into the sack by seven-thirty every evening was not over. Looming beyond the obstacle course waited the dreaded tower. About forty feet high, the tower stood near a telephone pole topped by a cross-arm. A rope that hung down through a pulley on the cross-arm was attached to the rings on a jumper's harness.

For the tower, wrote Alan Inglis, "we wore our canvas pants and a jacket with a very high back collar." Inglis lived in St. Louis when he volunteered for CPS. After the war, he gradu-ated from Yale Divinity School, got his pilot's license, and became the "flying pastor" for five little churches in North Dakota. Inglis went on, "After attaching the rope to the [para-chute] harness and putting on the football helmet with a wire cage across the front, we would jump off the tower. With arms folded, spine straight, we would look forward to the shock of coming to the end of our rope before having to hit the ground. There was no other shock absorber other than the stretch of the rope."

Few men enjoyed jumping from the tower. Some suffered minor back injuries, but most simply disliked being jolted to a dead stop in midair. Many wondered how much worse it would be when a parachute snapped open, since this simulation hurt so much. Later, after their first jump, they could make that comparison. "The shock of being stopped from hitting the ground by the rope and harness inches above the ground was far worse than the opening shock of any subsequent actual parachute jump," wrote Russell Palmer of Chester, Pennsylvania. "In fact my back was slightly injured by one of the tower jumps which put me out of commission for a few days." The trainers viewed the tower as a test of will as well as a physical exercise. "They told me, if a recruit can take this body kinker, he can jump a chute," Frank Neufeld recalled.

Also waiting on the training course stood a mockup of the fuselage of an airplane with an open door cut to the specific proportions of the door on the Ford Trimotor, the plane most employed for smoke jumping. A small metal step jutted from the fuselage just outside the door. "We stood with one foot on the step and learned to jump out at the pat on the back from the spotter," wrote Gregg Phifer, who was brought up as a Methodist in Cincinnati, Ohio. The drop was about six feet; when they hit the ground, the jumpers performed a tuck and roll by bending their knees, tucking their bodies, and performing a somersault. For tight spots, when trees or rocks might prohibit a tuck and roll, the trainers also taught the Allen roll, which "consisted of landing with the knees slightly bent, using the legs as shock absorbers, twisting so that one fell on his hip and then rolled over backwards across the opposite shoulder," as Alan Inglis recalled. "At best you could continue the roll so that as you rolled over on your shoulders, you could give a push with the hands, do a backward somersault and land on the feet. I doubt if I accomplished that final maneuver with all my equipment on very often despite my wrestling and tumbling practice."

Earl Cooley knew from experience that heavily forested areas sometimes offered few clearings for landings. When confronted with no obvious place to land, he directed the men to try to hook their chutes over a treetop. During training he made sure the men learned how to let themselves down to the ground when suspended in midair. To execute the maneuver, the men carried long let-down ropes in a large pocket sewn below the knee of their pants. Jumpers stationed in Montana carried 75-foot ropes, while those amid Oregon's taller trees carried ropes 125 feet long. During training the men practiced with shorter ropes, according to Alan Inglis:

> With the rope in the pocket we were hoisted up into the air with block and tackle. Then the job was to thread the rope through rings in the harness and tie it on to what would be the ring of the parachute. Then all we had to do was chin ourselves and hold ourselves up with one hand so we could unhook the parachute from the harness with the other. It had to be done twice. Once for each shoulder.
>
> I was glad I had practiced chinning myself in high school and could do it up to twenty times, but not with jumping equipment on. My memory is that I could do this let down in two minutes. Some were faster than that.

The men also carried red cloth streamers in the leg pocket; they used these streamers to signal the airplane pilot whether they had landed uninjured or not, "since we had no radio on a two-man jump," Inglis noted. Because the chutes cost about $125 apiece, the men also practiced retrieving hung-up chutes by climbing trees with the help of long, sharp spurs strapped around the ankles of their boots.

Cooley also made certain that his men knew their woodlore, especially map and compass reading and orienteering. Most times, the men would be dropped miles from the nearest road and would have to find their way to a rendezvous point where a Forest Service driver waited on a road. For Forest Service records, the men also needed to be able to estimate the size of fires, so they practiced eyeballing chunks of real estate and scientifically guesstimating the number of acres.

Lessons at safety classes, held during different times throughout the day, were repeated over and over like Bible lessons. Attack a fire from an anchor point and move up the flank from which the wind blows across the fire. Never dig line directly in the path of a fire until you are ready to pinch it off when there is no wind. Remember to keep one foot in the black; safety lies where the fuels have already been consumed. Locate safety zones in case you have to run from a crowning fire. Make sure everyone knows the escape routes to those safety zones. Always face uphill while resting on the fire line and watch for rolling rocks and logs. Steer clear of snags whose roots may have been burned out; those phantom killers may fall without warning.

And if trapped by fire, they were taught the best methods at that time of how to avoid becoming human toast, since metal-coated fire shelters were yet to be developed. "As I remember it, although we never practiced it, we knew of burning out the nearest clearing as the escape of last resort when trapped by a fire," recalled CPSer Wallace Littel. "We were told, if possible, to use our canvas jump jackets or tarpaulins to cover ourselves as further protection while the main fire passed." Littel ended up working on one dangerous fire that blew up like a firebomb in a gulch above the Salmon River:

> The fire was around six to eight acres and had ideal burning conditions, including a hot sunny day, lots of dry grass and undercover, and an upcanyon wind off the [river]. We had time to scout the fire out before it blew up and got away from us. Thus, we were able to stay away from the front and work down the flank to safety.

We were also able to radio Missoula for help and had
around twenty smoke jumpers on the fire by the end of
the afternoon.

As I recall it, the fire blew up to more than 1,000
acres in a short time and eventually to more than 3,000
acres. We had more than one hundred firefighters on it
before it was suppressed, including several planeloads
of black paratroopers from their base in Pendleton,
Oregon. They landed complete with cooks, which made
it the only fire I was ever on with good food.[4]

The men also learned how to check, fold, and repair parachutes. But their work still was not done. After the grueling
workouts, the terror of the tower, and the lectures at the
safety classes, came the most basic training of all—how to dig
fire line. As nowadays, the tool of choice for wildland firefighters in the northern Rockies at that time was the
pulaski—a two-headed instrument on a pick-size handle.
Edward Pulaski, one of the legends of Forest Service history,
had refined the hand tool.

Caught in the epicenter of an Idaho firestorm in 1910,
Pulaski led forty-four men to safety in an abandoned mine he
had once worked. A falling tree killed one straggler, but the
rest safely huddled in the dank tunnel. There they found a
seep, dampened their garments, and put wet cloths over their
mouths. As the flames flashed up to the mouth of the tunnel,
Pulaski hung wet horse blankets near the entrance. Winds,
probably up to one hundred miles per hour, pushed hot chok-
ing gases into the mine. As the trees outside crashed down like
matchsticks, the men awaited their doom. When the air in the
mine grew hot and thick with smoke, some men rose as if to
run, but Pulaski drew his pistol and promised to shoot the first
one who panicked. One by one, the firefighters, overcome
with smoke, sank into unconsciousness.

The next morning the men at the rear of the tunnel

revived first and then helped the others. Five men never got up. The first to see Pulaski's body, lying near the tunnel's entrance, pronounced him dead. "Like hell he is," Pulaski answered as he opened his eyes. Three years later, the amateur blacksmith refined the ax-hoe that bears his name.

By 1920, the pulaski had become the standard firefighting tool for wildland fires. An ax head sits on one side of the tool, a slightly curved hoelike head on the other. Not many instructions come with it: scrape and dig with the hoe and chop roots, trees, and brush with the ax head. While perfecting the art of jumping out of airplanes and landing safely took weeks, the men learned to swing the pulaski within seconds. Once dispatched to a fire, most men quickly grasped the irony of the name "smoke jumper." Parachute jumps lasted only about two minutes, but a wildland firefighter often found himself swinging a pulaski for up to sixteen hours a day.

But simply wielding the tool was not enough. A technique that required practice, conditioning, and team coordination was what turned a bunch of flailing ground pounders into a well-oiled fire-line digging crew. Back then the CPSers called the method the caterpillar technique, here described by Alan Inglis for an eight-man crew:

> The last man determined the speed of all eight men. . . . He would determine when the line was secure against fire and say something to the effect of "up." Then each man would drop what he was doing and start on what the man ahead had been doing. Of course, the lead man often did little more than determine the direction the line would take. I remember when being in the lead taking just one or two whacks with my ax and then moving up three or four feet. This technique made us the best fireline builders, though we also admired the professional Indian firefighters. They probably used a similar technique and were certainly as determined.

The tough training did not discourage the men. In fact, many rose to the challenge that would prove their mettle. Harold Toews had been working in a cafeteria in a CPS camp in Downey, Idaho, before transferring to Camp Huson at Ninemile, and he considered himself "extremely overweight." During training, Toews always lagged behind at the rear of the pack. Near the end of the week, a supervisor summoned him to the office and told him that he needed another week of training before taking his first jump. Toews wrote, "I begged him for one more chance. I would show him I could do it. He said he would see what my trainer would say. The next day I was at the head of the group and found it was no harder to run there. I climbed the trees with speed because I was so determined. My spurs took hold better and with that determination I passed the test and jumped Monday morning."

Bradshaw Snipes, who equated the preparation at camp to training for a football team, admitted that being a smoke jumper was one of the most thrilling times of his life. He detailed his accomplishments with pride: "Climbing a thirty-foot rope, learning to use tree spurs to retrieve a chute after the fire was out, dropping free fall from the tower to simulate a chute opening, as well as trail work and sawing trees were most satisfying."

Others, such as Richard Lehman of Lancaster, Pennsylvania, reveled in the feats that their young bodies could perform. Lehman noted, "Since I was blessed with a good healthy body by well-planned and prepared meals at home, I was able to perform the necessary activities at boot camp training. I especially like the backbends since this was the first time I did such a thing."

However, some were more realistic in assessing their experiences at boot camp. Ralph Miller probably best summed it up when he recalled, "The training center had a way of finding hidden muscles that the farm and dad's sawmill, the ax or anything else hadn't ever touched before. . . . But I survived."[5]

Although each CPS smoke jumper could be referred to as a trailblazer of sorts, one individual associated with the group cut a truly unique path. Florence Wenger, the camp dietitian and wife of the civilian camp director, Roy Wenger, almost became the first female smoke jumper, partaking in the entire jumper training alongside the men in 1943. The well-proportioned woman with sinewy muscles weighed 140 pounds and stood five feet four inches tall. At seven-thirty each morning she would appear dressed in trousers and with her long, brown hair gathered behind her head. She fell in with the men for calisthenics forty-five minutes later. "She would sweat, huff and puff sometimes," Roy Wenger recalled. "She was a basketball player and was physically fit. She didn't have any trouble with the obstacle course. The men all supported her"[6]—especially the Quakers, whose sect had preached equality for women since the 1600s.

Florence wrote in a short memoir that she joined the guys "to keep busy." By May, when the men pulled on the bulky jump suits to train in, Florence also suited up. She learned to step out of the mock-up Trimotor and tuck and roll as she landed. She survived the jolting drops from the tower. But she ran into a roadblock on her pathway to history. "I took the strenuous training and was ready for the practice jumps," she said, "but was not permitted to." No official seemed willing to take the responsibility of letting her go any further.

"She had no tradition to support her," her husband observed. "She had a written description of her role at the camp, and jumping was not in it. Someone in the line of authority needed to give her encouragement. No one felt able to do that. Each supervisor in turn said to himself, 'If injury should happen, do I want to accept responsibility?' . . . 'Let someone else carry the weight of the decision.' Her turn never came."[7]

In private, Florence expressed her disappointment, referring to the Forest Service brass as "a bunch of waffle-bottoms." Wenger admitted that "she probably thought I was a little reluctant too—which I was."

As it turned out, women would have to wait almost three more decades before even being allowed on the fire line. History never recorded the name of the first woman who earned a paycheck for fighting a forest fire, although she is reputed to have signed on with the Bureau of Land Management in Alaska in 1971. Nine years later, Deanne Shulman successfully completed smoke jumper training, but "waffle-bottoms" appear to have still controlled the agency at that time. Officials refused to admit Shulman into the unit, claiming that she did not weigh enough. Shulman sued in court and won, and in 1981 she got the chance to jump a fire. By the mid-1990s, 30 percent to 40 percent of all forest firefighters were women.

Before she died in 1989, Florence recalled, "I've always felt a bit cheated. I could have been the first woman smoke jumper. Alas. I was ahead of my time."

As training progressed in 1943, Earl Cooley and his staff had a chance to assess the men, if not the lone woman. They liked what they saw. "Ironically enough, we soon began receiving field reports that one jumper was equivalent to the typical eight-man crew of old men and young boys picked at random and walked to the fire," Cooley recalled. "The CPS jumpers were all young, husky and hand-picked."[8]

Years later, former Forest Service smoke jumper Hal Samsel told writer Norman Maclean what he thought about the CPSers for the book *Young Men and Fire*. "It turned out them sons-of-bitches was farm boys and, what's more, didn't believe in using machines no way—working was just for their hands and their horses, and them sons-of-bitches took them shovels and saws and pulaskis and put a hump in their backs and never straightened up until morning when they had a fireline around the whole damn fire. Them sons-of-bitches was the worlds' champion firefighters."[9]

But although things settled down at the main training camp (first at Seeley Lake, and the next season at Camp Menard), many men had to once again prove themselves after being dispatched to satellite camps located in remote areas. Oftentimes, the local Forest Service workers and civilians at these outposts seemed less enlightened than those stationed near Missoula. Elmer Newfeld was in the first group of six jumpers assigned to Twisp, an airfield located in a remote Washington forest. They were warned that they might get a rude welcome in "the hornet's nest." Newfeld wrote,

Our first job was to erect a bunkhouse and bathhouse. In charge was a man from the Forest Service by the name of Cleo Jet. He made no bones about the fact that he was going to give us a hard time. We were going to work, and produce lots of finished product by the end of the day. Cleo made a few attempts to ride us hard, but that slowed down. All of us conchies were used to work. We didn't take any breaks, and with very little guidance we could get the job done. Things seemed to go pretty good for the first week, at least I thought it did.

On Monday of our second week, right at noon, Cleo, with lunch bucket in hand, came to where I had just sat down to eat my lunch.

"Elmer, can I sit down here and eat my lunch with you?" he said.

"Sure," I said. "Sit down here, Cleo. Is there something we are not doing right?"

"No," said Cleo. "It's just that when you guys got here, I had made up my mind that I was sure going to give you yellowbellies a rough time. I was going to work the tail

end off you and then kick you down the road. Well, that
hasn't worked out. There is no way that I can keep up
with you personally when it comes to putting out work.
You don't make stupid mistakes, and at the end of a day
there's a lot of work done.

"So Elmer, let me shake your hand and say welcome
to our forest. And yellowbellies you're not. If you were,
you would not have chosen this field of work. There is
no way that I would jump out of a perfectly good airplane and depend on a little piece of silk to let me down
to the ground. So the hard feelings are gone, at least on
my part."[10]

Boot camp proved a critical period for smoke jumpers that
first season—and for all rookies in the seasons to come. The
CPSers not only passed the physical rigors of the program,
but they also, in most cases, broke through social barriers
erected by misunderstanding and stereotyping. Through
their respectful manners, gentle persuasion, hard work, and
dedication they won the respect of outsiders. They also grew
to understand one another better—those men within their
own ranks who attended different churches. They bonded
into a well-disciplined team with each individual learning to
count on the man standing beside him in a pinch, whether it
be sweating on the fire line or sitting on a cot ruminating
about the decision made to join CPS. But one event remained
for which no man, no matter how true a friend, could offer
assistance. For that first parachute jump, there was only one
place to mine for fortitude—deep within oneself.

CHAPTER SEVEN

Hit the Silk

Nick Helburn had flown in an aircraft only one time before arriving at CPS Camp No. 103: that was an eight-minute hop from Woods Hole, Massachusetts, to Martha's Vineyard, an island south of Cape Cod, and the plane was a light six-passenger Piper. When Helburn completed boot camp and prepared for his first training jump, he was amazed by the size of the Ford Trimotor—the Tin Goose—that waited on the airfield. "By comparison the Ford Trimotor looked enormous and much too heavy to get off the ground," he noted.

Since the beginning of production in 1925, the slightly rhomboid crackerbox-shaped Tin Goose had been a workhorse for the budding U.S. airlines and the military. Sheathed in corrugated aluminum, it carried one engine slung under each wing and one planted on its nose. Ford built almost two hundred Trimotors between 1925 and 1932. In January 1967, *Time* magazine reported that twenty-eight of the workhorses were still "flying between remote points around the globe."[1]

Helburn boarded the plane with seven other conscientious

objectors, facing each other, four men on a side, "trying not to look scared." The engines roared as the plane lumbered along the grass runway. The tail came up as it gained speed. The bumping of the tires suddenly stopped when the plane lifted off and slowly climbed. In the days before widespread civilian air travel, many men suffered more during their first plane ride than they did their first jump, as Gus Janzen witnessed: "I still have to laugh as I think about Ken Diller as we were getting ready to jump for the first time. His face was getting very pale. I asked Ken, 'Are you getting sick?' He replied, 'Man, I'm ready to get out of this airplane.'"

As the plane approached the jump area, two men got into position. Each hooked his static line onto the heavy wire that trailed along the ceiling of the plane, and then he draped the line over his shoulder. If he jumped with it under an arm, the jerking static line might pull the appendage out of the socket as it opened the chute. The first jumper crouched in the open doorway and stretched one foot outside onto a metal step, just as he had been trained on the mock-up plane in camp. Then he waited for the slap on the shoulder and the spotter's traditional wisecrack: "Watch the second step, it's a long one."

"I didn't really know what was ahead of me," Helburn recalled. He continued,

> We all had been very well conditioned. We had jumped forward so many hundreds of times from that crouching position with one foot outside the open door [of the mark-up model]. If it had been the Devil himself who gave me that rap on the shoulder, I think I would have jumped.
>
> I never asked what the others were thinking. This was silent, masked pretense. Each of us conjuring up his maximum machismo. All I could do was to say over and over to myself: "No one but a fool would go up in

an airplane with the idea of jumping out." Again and again and again I said it like an emergency mantra.

Next to Helburn sat Dexter McBride, the former city attorney of Norfolk, Virginia. Helburn noted that McBride was reading a small paperback book: *The Release of Nervous Tension.* The men's various mental preparations for that first jump must have worked, for Helburn reported, "When the time came, each of us hooked our static line on the cable above the open door, crouched down with one foot on the step outside, and with a tap on the shoulder stepped out into the unsupported open air."

In 1943, the men practiced jumping into open fields near Seeley Lake. The next year, the Forest Service moved the training facility to the old CCC barracks at Camp Menard near the Ninemile Remount Depot at Huson, Montana, about thirty miles west of Missoula. That first year at Ninemile, the Ford Tri-motors and Travelaires took off from a private airstrip on a local farm. When the farmer demanded more money the next season, the agency built its own strip in a meadow about a half mile west of the depot. The men landed in the nearby hayfields. But no matter where the training jumps occurred, the CPSers reached deep into their souls to confront the fear of falling.

William Weber was born shortly after the end of World War I on a farm near Kendall, Wisconsin, where his Methodist mother instructed him in a peaceful way of life. He too saw the depression take a toll on his parents' finances, but looking back, he found much for which to be thankful. He observed, "Neighbors shared the larger jobs on the farm such as threshing, silo filling, wood sawing. Those were festive affairs, with heavy laden dinner tables, where labor was exchanged for labor and there was no dollar amount attached to it."

Acquiring a conscientious objector classification did not

come easily for Weber. He wrote, "My draft board did not look favorably upon those who refused to participate in the draft. However, after a number of meetings with them and under intense questioning of me, they finally gave me the 4-E classification." One of Weber's brothers joined the Army Air Corps, while another received a farmworker's deferment.

Weber headed off for his first CPS camp before the United States entered the war, but he felt some apprehension, as his father had confessed that he "was not sure I was doing the right thing." After a summer of searching for Japanese incendiary bombs along the West Coast, Weber became a CPS smoke jumper. With some experience gained as a wildland firefighter at a California CPS camp, Weber knew the inherent dangers of the job. He wrote,

> I remember one fire where I had taken a truckload of firefighters and their crew leader out to build a fireline and on my way out of the fire area I could hear the frightening roar of the fire as it was coming down the canyon. The heat was so intense that fir trees would explode like fiery bombs. I just made it out of the fire area in time and learned the next day that the crew never did get a line built for a back fire, but spent most of the night trying to get away from the fire itself.

Weber was already familiar with near-fatal accidents even before he became a smoke jumper—almost drowning in California's Lake Tahoe and almost getting electrocuted while repairing a phone line. Still, he did not hesitate to stretch his foot outside the Ford Trimotor when the spotter gave the word to get ready:

> I really don't remember jumping, but the next thing I knew I was looking up, the plane was leaving, and

suddenly there was a jerk on my harness and the beautiful white parachute opened above me. What a feeling of ecstasy. It was almost like having gone through the valley of death and now I had reached heaven, hanging suspended above the world and not a sound. But then suddenly it was as if the earth was rushing toward me and the next thing I knew I was on the ground. Not exactly where I was supposed to land, but not too far astray.

For others, that first float back to earth was a little more traumatic. As Vern Hoffman floated the two thousand feet down toward the earth, he discovered that he had forgotten a lot of the lessons drilled into his head during the training sessions—including how to land correctly. "As a result," he wrote, "I hit the ground with no leg support, landing in a sitting down position. It was a fairly hard landing so I immediately felt sharp excruciating pain shoot up my back into my head. Fortunately, I was able to get up and walk away. I was so embarrassed at the poor landing that I didn't even report the accident to the infirmary and never told anyone about the two weeks of pounding headaches that followed."[2] Seventeen years later, Hoffman had surgery to repair a ruptured disc in his upper back and, still later, surgery to repair broken vertebrae in his lower back.

Each spring, man after man boarded the Ford Trimotor, attached his static line, waddled in his heavy suit to the open door, and jumped. Although no one turned back, none seemed to escape the momentary jitters. The training jumps continued for two weeks, each man jumping seven times, practicing from both types of planes—eight men in the Trimotor, two per flight in the Travelaire. Although the initial jumps ended quickly, trepidation sometimes lingered. "The first jump for me was easy," wrote Frank Neufeld, "but by the third and fourth it was a real challenge."

One nervous jumper mistakenly pulled the ripcord of his emergency chute and was ever after referred to as "Double-Bubble." But each successful jump built a man's confidence. Every time a jumper tucked and rolled and walked away with his silk stuffed back into the canvas bag, he inched that much closer to earning his parachute wings. And during each step along that process, he advanced further from the insult of "yellowbelly."

"On my second jump," Gregg Phifer wrote, "I rode the step waiting for the pat on the shoulder from the spotter before stepping off into space. Since I had nothing to match heights with, jumping soon became less scary than leaning over the railing of a tall building. I was lucky."

All the while, Frank Derry carefully watched over the men like a mother hen—"and sometimes he could be as fractious," reported CPS jumper Paul "Jerk" Jernigan. This CPSer also noted the "colorful language" of the former stunt man.

In 1943, Jernigan snapped on his static line amid "all the noise, fumes and prop wash" of the Trimotor, making sure that the line led over his left shoulder as Derry specified. When his time came to jump, he stretched his right foot out onto the step, doubled over, and began to pull himself through the cramped opening. What happened next, he recalled, was not in the training manual: "Suddenly, I was jerked back into the plane, someone holding me by the collar of my jump suit. Above the roar of the motor I heard some choice Frank Derry words, then felt a kick on my backside which got me out the door." Although completely baffled, Jernigan made a good landing near the target by the dirt airstrip. While rolling up his chute, the jumper who had followed him out landed and explained Derry's mysterious behavior. "The static line of my chute had unfolded from the back pack, fallen loose, and the blast from the propellers had looped it around my neck," Jernigan said. That evening

Frank Derry called an emergency safety meeting and talked long and loud about the necessary attention the jumpers must give their static lines. "All sixty of us knew why the meeting was held," Jernigan noted.

With the initial jumps over, most men loosened up. Hoots and hollers of delight soon echoed from the skies above Seeley Lake and Ninemile. "Palms dry this time, flight not bothersome," recalled Ray Hudson in a journal entry describing his second jump. Hudson, the son of a minister, was born in Madras, India, and did not live in the United States until his twelfth year. He graduated high school in Eureka, California, and earned a Bachelor of Arts degree from Berkeley before volunteering for CPS. "Still, quite a job to step out the door," he wrote. "I went right out after Louis Goossen. We both made good takeoffs, suffered no bad opening shock, hollered at each other on the way down. Louis hit within fifty feet of target. I, seventy-five feet. Had fun maneuvering chute."

Each jump provided valuable experience. On his second jump, Maynard Shetler learned an indispensable lesson about downdrafts during a jump when he was the second one out of the plane but the first to reach the ground. He recalled, "Normally the last man out is the last one down. I have a picture of that jump which my brother took. The parachute is only half open instead of fully inflated. I landed, digging post holes with my feet.

Alan Inglis liked to sing hymns to help himself keep calm during his jumps.

"What did you sing?" his parents once asked.

" 'He Leadeth Me,' " Inglis replied.

"That is a good family hymn," his father answered a bit sarcastically. "They sang it at both your grandparents' funerals."

During one jump, Inglis and several others tried harmonizing while floating close to one another, but the concert was not an acoustic success. "There is no reverberation or reflection of sound to enhance hearing," Inglis wrote. "The sound just disseminates through the air. After a few shouted notes, we gave up."

Despite the joy that the men soon found in parachuting, they realized that danger lurked with every jump and landing. Many men suffered injuries, mostly to ankles and backs. "Landed hard, pulled a muscle under the gastronoemius [sic], limped most of the day," reported Ray Hudson of his second jump. "Phil Stanley, Bryn Hammarstrom sprained ankles. Ad Carlson pulled something. Entwistle broke a bone in his foot."

Winton Stucky had worse luck. During a practice jump at Cave Junction, Oregon, he experienced a rough opening with one parachute and requested another for the next jump. Unfortunately, by the time he got around to procuring one, all the other chutes were taken, so he jumped with the same chute again. "This time it knocked him unconscious on the opening and he landed in a heap, fracturing one vertebrae, with the next one O.K., and the next one split," reported Earl Schmidt. "His son [told me later] that they kept him in the back of a pickup for two hours waiting to find out who would pay the medical bills. He was released with no benefits, with a broken back, and had to provide his own livelihood after the initial hospitalization."

Another lesson was quickly learned by all: jumping was full of variables that were beyond human control. Sheldon Mills sometimes found it as "easy as walking through a door. Other times you wonder why you are doing such a risky thing."

With a little experience, the novice sometimes became cocky. Alan Inglis wondered why they were told to jump feet first rather than head first, "like Superman." Inglis reasoned that by jumping head first he could follow the lead jumper more closely. So he tried it—once. He recalled, "I did follow the man in front very closely, so closely that I saw every crisscross of the streamer and chute come out of the pack. But it was very hard on one arm when my chute opened, wrenching it rather severely. So that is why you jumped feet first with arms crossed."

As some men returned to training camp for three consecutive seasons, Earl Cooley and Frank Derry taught them more advanced techniques, such as the slip jump. This technique required a jumper to pull himself up some shroud lines to collapse the opened chute to make it descend more rapidly. As he approached the ground, of course, he allowed it to open again. The maneuver could help a jumper reach a landing spot if he was being blown off course. Maynard Shetler tried it once. He described the results of this attempt:

> To collapse the parachute, I nearly touched silk but when allowing it to open again I found the load lines wrapped around my neck. I fought to get the lines off and did get them all off but one. Knowing I was hurtling toward the treetops, I had visions of the chute hanging up and snapping my neck. I took the hunting knife which we carried on our emergency chute and cut the line. Then I didn't know what to do with the knife. I didn't dare drop it because of the men below. I didn't know where they were as I was concentrating on the lines around my neck. I landed safely with knife in hand, feeling and looking very happy.
>
> At that moment a farmer and his son came through the woods. I asked them where the jumping field was. They grinned and said, "Most jumpers are coming down over in that direction."
>
> I was one-half mile from the field. Cutting a load line was taken seriously by the Forest Service personnel. I expected to be reprimanded for it but received none. Fellow jumpers reported the red line on my neck, which

lasted about three days, was evidence enough to con-
firm my story.

Also during training, the men practiced parachuting a full
fire camp just off the Ninemile airstrip. Everything that might
be needed on a fire—tools, water pumps, water bags, food,
cooking utensils—was packed and dropped from the Trimotor. Ralph Miller helped pack the eggs in cargo bags filled
with bread. "The eggs usually survived quite well, if a tree or
rock did not get in the way. But the bread was usually a mess,"
he reported.

During training jumps, many men flew in an airplane for
the first time. Consequently, many did not get to land in an
airplane until much later that year, either when a fire jump
was aborted or when they were ferried to another region.
Edwin A. Vail wrote that he did not experience a landing until
his tenth trip aloft. For some nervous men, that first landing
was as nerve-wracking as parachuting could be.

Sometimes Earl Cooley asked the men to demonstrate
parachuting for Forest Service officials and other important
personages. On one such occasion, Audine Coffin joined the
party and witnessed her husband, Joe, descending from the
heavens. As Joe floated toward the big red bull's-eye laid out
on the ground, the trainer talked him down with the help of a
bullhorn. "Down he came," recalled Audine. "The chute getting bigger and bigger, the instructions sounding louder and
louder until suddenly the instructor grabbed the speaker
horn and my arm, saying, 'Gotta move.' Down came Joe in
the center of the target and with a tuck and roll landed at our
feet. It was glorious."

Other than the hymn that Alan Inglis and his pals
attempted to harmonize as they drifted through the sky, no
smoke jumpers had ever thought of shouting a slogan as they
jumped out of the plane—like the army paratroopers' cry of

"Geronimo." That almost changed when a discharged para-
trooper, Dale Fickle, signed on as an instructor at the camp in
1945.

"Do paratroopers really yell Geronimo?" asked Tom Summers.

"Well, yeah," Fickle answered, "But not all the time. Do you
guys have a yell?"

That got Summers and some other CPSers thinking. Summers, a Protestant from Tennessee who grew up in San Diego,
California, based his nonresistance not on historic religious
convictions or on political bases but instead on a philosophical—rationale, which as he noted, "made it all the more
remarkable that . . . the San Diego draft board, without even a
hearing, granted me 4-E status." Summers, who considered
himself "a bookish young man," eventually recalled a term he
had come upon while reading that was more appropriate for
a CPS smoke jumper cry:

> The Geronimo cry of the paratroopers struck us as too
> self conscious, overly dramatic, and frankly, inappropri-
> ate. What did a 19th Century Apache chief have to do
> with World War II? Our directing thought for our cry
> was that it should be as irrelevant as that of the para-
> troopers but also self deprecating, as befitted draft
> dodgers, slackers, conchies, and yellow bellies.
>
> Where it came from, forty-seven years later, I cannot
> precisely recall, but I had encountered the term some-
> where in my reading as an English major. My Oxford
> English Dictionary tells me now that it appeared first in
> English in 1768, and I probably ran across it in Sir Wal-
> ter Scott's *The Heart of Midlothian.*
>
> In any case, "Gardyloo" was a Scottish corruption and
> a pseudo-French phrase, gare de l'eau—In effect,
> "Look out for the slop water." The cry is said by the dic-

tionary to have been a common warning cry among the housewives of 18th and 19th Century Edinburgh as they threw such waste into the streets.

Al and Warren and I were enchanted by the comparison and contrast of Geronimo and Gardyloo, and used it casually and laughingly on our remaining practice jumps, often to the mystification of the other five jumpers and of Dale Fickle as we left the Ford Trimotor. Standing in my corral today is a six-year old mule, foaled in 1987 from my wife's Morgan mare, and when the time came to name him, partly because of his sire's name, San-Loo, the most natural thing in the world was to call him Gardyloo. For what is more proletarian, misunderstood, rejected, and miscalculated than a mule— except perhaps, in the public mind, conscientious objectors to "The Good War."

Once the men had earned their parachute wings only one more test remained—jumping a real fire. Although to a man they were eager to get under way, nature sometimes did not match their enthusiasm. During some summers, it was a long, long wait before they were able to hit the silk again.[3]

CHAPTER EIGHT

The Long Wait

Sheldon M. Mills, son of a traveling evangelist, almost died before getting to his first fire by parachute. But he could not even recall that most memorable event of his life. He wrote, "My friends tell me I was helping remove fire danger by cutting down tall dead snags of pine trees. A part of one of the trees fell on my head, smashing the lower part of my jaw and knocking me unconscious. Phil Stanley and friends put me on a stretcher and carried me out of the woods, put me in a pickup truck and transported me thirty-six miles to a hospital, with Cathy Crocker, camp nurse, watching over me in the pickup." Mills lay unconscious for six days and then spent six weeks under the care of the nuns at Saint Patrick Hospital, where his "teeth were straightened and my jaw was wired straight (and shut.)"

Mills had spent his early childhood on a homestead in northern Montana, where his parents "tried to grow flax." When his mother became allergic to sagebrush, the family moved to Michigan. When Sheldon was eight years old, his family moved from Bath to Bellaire, Michigan. "This proved to be a fortunate move because the school at Bath was partially destroyed by a deranged custodian who bombed a big portion of it and then took his own life," Mills said. "Many schoolmates of mine were killed. This incident is considered to be the largest mass murder in the state of Michigan."

During summer vacations, Mills picked fruit, earning twenty-five cents for every two cases of cherries. After graduating from high school, he worked on a neighboring farm for a dollar a day, plus room and board. As the barefooted Mills hoed corn one day, a youth leader from the Methodist church and a student from Albion College stopped by. They asked Mills if he would rather attend college than hoe corn. Since "there didn't seem to be much future in hoeing corn for a living," Mills followed up on their proposal. At Albion College, Mills studied under Dr. Royal B. Hall, a member of the pacifistic Fellowship of Reconciliation. Since he did not belong to a recognized peace church, Mills had to prove his nonresistant convictions. When he addressed his draft board, he told them, "Either send me to a conscientious objector camp or to jail."

Not quite two months after being struck by the tree, Mills returned to Ninemile. Although his accident had not happened during a jump, he had grown cautious. At one point he asked the spotter on a flight to "let me jump first because I wasn't sure how quickly I could get out of the plane." Nonetheless, he made it.

But Mills had missed little when it came to jumping fires that summer. With the last of seven training jumps under their belts, the conscientious objectors officially became smoke jumpers, but they had yet to pass the test of fire. Eager as kids looking forward to snow at Christmastime, the men watched the sky for "money clouds"—big, anvil-shaped cumulus clouds that peppered the ridges with lightning. Some summers they waited and waited and waited—especially that first season of 1943, when they had trained at Seeley Lake. Deep snows slowly melted throughout the spring, dampening pine-needle-laden forest floors. Drenching rain accompanied the infrequent lightning storms. More often than not, metal-gray skies inexorably produced rain. The first fire jump did not occur until the end of July. By then, smoke jumping had lost its luster for some CPSers, including John H. Andes. Assigned to a spike camp, Andes could only "sit there in all the summer heat, not being permitted to go far from the phone. The only thing to do was to listen for it to ring." Discouraged and frustrated, Andes left the program to inspect dairy herds. "It was not what I went to smoke jumpers to do, but it was all a worthwhile experience."[1]

Like cowboys who hated to climb off the horse to work afoot, smoke jumpers often did not appreciate the more mundane tasks to which they were assigned. In late spring, some men planted tree seedlings at old logging sites. The planters staggered across steep slopes carrying mailbag-sized pouches filled with sixty pounds' worth of eighteen-inch seedlings. Wielding a hoedad—a short-handled digger with a narrow eighteen-inch-long blade angled at ninety degrees—the planters pulled open a hole in the tough, often rocky soil. With the other hand, they inserted a seedling, making sure its roots pointed straight down. If the foreman found any J-roots, it meant big trouble for the planter. After tamping down the earth with his foot, the planter would move a broken branch close to the tree to shade the tiny trunk. Four paces onward and the planter bent again to strike with his tool.

Dropping snags, as Sheldon Mills had done, was another important job at the time. Foresters then considered dead trees nothing more than hazards for humans. Several decades passed before foresters recognized that snags are the most important trees in the forest for wildlife. Woodpeckers and other birds seek the insects that invade the rotting wood. Many birds and small mammals live in the woodpecker holes. Bears often tear apart snags looking for insects to eat. Today, fire-fighters try to leave snags alone but avoid working around them whenever possible.

At some spike camps adjoining the wilderness airstrips, the men built parachute lofts, airplane hangers, and bunkhouses. Regional forest rangers also found a plethora of maintenance jobs for idle hands. CPSers made signs for trails and roads, repaired and built new fences, reshingled roofs, and painted buildings. They toiled as cooks and dishwashers, laundrymen and janitors. Harry Burks and Charles Chapman helped repair radios. Phil Stanley took over much of the agency's photography assignments. Benjamin W. Case found himself sharpening tools much of the time. He noted, "I filed crosscuts and sharp-ened sickle bars for the mowing machines. Someone loaned me a radio so I could listen to soap operas and news all day. There was only one station available then"—that was CBS affili-ate KGVO.

Case (whose ancestors included farmers, seafarers, bay men, and fishermen) hailed from Shelter Island, located between the north and south forks of Long Island. The island measured "about four miles north to south and seven miles east to west, and the distance around by water is thirty-three miles." From Memorial Day through Labor Day, thousands of New Yorkers thronged to the resort town, while the year-round population numbered about twelve hundred. His father worked as an estate caretaker and boat captain for Artemus Ward. Case recalled, "During the summers most of us started out as caddies at the local golf club and earned maybe $125 for the season. From there, I worked variously for a landscape firm, a truck farmer, helped crew a swordfish boat on weekends, and finally the best paying of all was wait-ing tables at a small night club—no salary, just tips."

Upon graduating from Browne's Business School in New York, Case signed up with the Brooklyn Union Gas Company, progressing from office boy to production statistician. Although Case's ancestors had been Presbyterians, his parents eventually converted to Jehovah's Witness. Although he did not embrace the complete Witness doctrine, "enough of their philosophy rubbed off to convince [my brother and I] that war was wrong and that we could not participate in it. It is my personal feeling that if people followed the teachings of almost any religion, they would come to the same conclusions."

Although a flatlander, Case found the rugged landscape of western Montana refreshing:

> The mountains presented a great contrast—the vastness of it all, white snow-capped mountains never seen before, dry clear atmosphere compared to heat and humidity in New York. . . . The campers even seemed different in their attitude and outlook, perhaps because everyone was here because he wanted to be. . . . Having been doing outside work, I personally felt I was in good shape physically, but after a few hikes, runs around camp, and a session or two on the torture stakes and the obstacle course, all my muscles took notice of the strenuous activity.

Besides sharpening saws, Case helped bring in the hay at Ninemile and chopped firewood. He also volunteered for a plane ride over the Continental Divide to drop cargo at Red Plume Lookout, but the mission turned out to be a disaster. The fiber supply box measured about twenty inches square, was bound with rope, and had a letter taped to the top. Case attached an eight-foot cargo chute to the box. He wrote,

> I kicked it out the door, looked back and couldn't see a thing—no chute. We circled around and saw the look-

out standing with his hands on his hips looking into the canyon which dropped off sharply just north of the tower. Upon arrival at Spotted Bear [the landing strip], we called the lookout to see what had happened, and he said the chute had just streamered, the box hit the top of a snag and disintegrated, falling into the canyon. I asked him if he recovered anything.

"Two lettuce leaves and a piece of the parachute. Tell Shaw to send me up some snoose [chewing tobacco]," and he hung up.

At haying time, many CPSers from rural areas found themselves back on the farm. As fire crews still do at the Ninemile Ranger Station (the only publicly owned ranch in the country), CPSers sweated piling haystacks, pitching the cured hay into a baling machine, and then stacking the bales in the barn. Edwin A. Vail, whose only farming experience had been mowing lawns in Los Angeles County, actually enjoyed haying between fire jumps during the 1944 season. He recalled, "I pitched the hay into the machine that shoved the hay into the baler. Men sitting on each side of the baler tied wires around the bale of hay before it came out to be moved away by other men. Some men, when feeding the hay into the baler, would make a bale a foot too short or too long. That was one reason I was allowed to feed the baler. My hay bales were uniform enough to suit the boss."[2]

The hay, of course, went to feed the horses and mules of the Remount Depot. Some of the men debated "loud and long" whether they did more for the mules than the mules ever did for them, according to Wallace Littel. "Doubts arose occasionally when mules packed them out from some backcountry fire, but during the intervals between fire jumps the labor of haying quickly blotted out such memories and the debate was very one-sided."

While baling hay or on any other job, the men always kept alert for a fire call. One day, Phil Stanley, Ted Lewis, Art Geisler, and Asa Mundell had a surprise as they shocked wheat in the Ninemile fields. Mundell happened to lean on his pitchfork—"just once," he noted—and spotted smoke that he at first thought was coming from the Ninemile barn. However, the fire turned out to be consuming a farmhouse across the road. Mundell recalled,

> When we arrived, a Forest Service person had pulled the hose cart from the barn and we helped him get it over there. But when he turned on the water, the old hose spouted leaks all over. However, with more pressure, a friendly little stream did come to life, and we started dousing the fire. No one had been at home, and so it was just the four of us. The Forest Service man disappeared.
>
> It wasn't necessary for more than two men to hold the hose on the fire, and the fire was so hot that the water made little difference. But Phil and Ted latched onto the hose and kept at it. We could not get into the house to get anything out. But those two kept on hosing it. I don't remember just what Art was doing during this time, but I remember standing astride the top of the roof on the barn calling out any spot fires that appeared in the barn lot, on which they sprayed enough water to put them out.
>
> The family arrived later, shocked to find their house burned to the ground, and the four of us doing them very little good. Eventually we left, and went back to our pitch forks and wheat. It was just one of the variety of fires our camp went on that summer. But it was one we couldn't put out. And like all of our other fires worked on, there were no thanks for our efforts.[3]

Many men had their first and only experience repairing phone lines while waiting for fires. Copper lines strung from poles or trees connected the far-flung lookouts to the dispatchers at the ranger stations. Without these lines of communication that first season, the smoke jumpers would never have known where or when to go to a fire. Many CPSers seemed to have enjoyed the task. At least it got them out into the woods. In addition, the occupation did have its exciting moments, according to Clarence Quay:

> Some of us from Moose Creek were dispatched to maintain about four miles of telephone line up the Freeman Trail. It was a nice day and work was going very well until about the middle of the afternoon. We were getting accustomed to climbing telephone poles and repairing the telephone line.
>
> Ellis Roberts and I walked up to this one pole and since I had on the climbers, I started up the pole. I had not yet reached the top of the pole when I heard a cracking, and felt it also through the pole. Luckily, Ellis held the pole upright until I descended as gingerly as I could to the ground. When Ellis let go of the pole it went crashing down to the ground. Thereafter we did a little more inspecting of poles before climbing them.[4]

Rotted poles were not the only job hazard. The men also experienced some shocking moments. Ralph C. Belzer maintained trails and telephone lines at the Three Forks and Challenge guard stations just south of Glacier National Park. One day the crew hiked a total of twenty-six miles to fulfill its assignment. "The line was Number Nine wire stretched on trees," Belzer recalled. "When you were splicing that wire and were ten or fifteen feet up in a tree with your climbing spurs stuck into a green tree and someone decided to make a call, they would crank that little handle on the old Forest Service phones. Boy, did that ring your bell."

Belzer, a Jehovah's Witness, had been raised on a dryland potato farm about ten miles from Glasgow, Montana. The pay was less than exceptional, according to Belzer, "but we were comfortable, ate good, raised a large garden. Dad butchered beef, hogs, sheep—all of which mother canned. She baked our bread, and mother and dad made pork sausage, liver sausage and hams and bacon, which they smoked in the old smokehouse." When the roads were clear, Belzer rode to school in the back of a truck with a makeshift top over the bed. In snow, they boarded a sledded bus pulled by a team of horses. He wrote, "During summer vacation, four or five of my friends and I would walk or ride our bikes to the Milk River or out to the irrigation ditch west of town to fish or go swimming."

Belzer chose to volunteer for CPS because "a true Christian cannot involve themselves in any world government conflict. The Bible tells us that Christ's heavenly government will soon remove all of this world's governments and replace them with His own government where peace will abide." Belzer's jumping career proved short-lived when he neglected to tuck and roll during a landing. The bad stone bruise on his foot developed into a planter's wart that had to be cut out. "This ended my jumping career," he recalled.

In the summer of 1945, the War Department recruited many CPSers to work on a top-secret operation called "Project Firefly." The previous fall, the Japanese had launched incendiary balloons that ascended to thirty thousand feet to drift across the Pacific Ocean on the jet stream. The balloon's thirty-foot bag was made of lacquered paper and filled with explosive hydrogen. The basket held barometric devices designed to control altitude and to release two small incendiary bombs and one fragmentation bomb. The balloons were to self-destruct after releasing the bombs.

In early November 1944, the Japanese launched ten thousand balloon bombs to celebrate their emperor's birthday. On December 11, two men cutting wood near Kalispell, Montana, found a balloon that had failed to self-destruct. Eventually, officials verified that about three hundred balloons had reached the west coast of North America, from California to Alaska, and some had penetrated as far east as Iowa. Newspapers reported the balloon discovered near Kalispell, but the government, not wanting to let the Japanese know whether their balloon armada had been successful, ordered strict censorship thereafter.

The balloons that were launched during winter started a few small fires, and one balloon bomb killed five children and their mother near Bly, Oregon. Officials began to worry what the balloons might do if they dropped from the sky during a dry summer on tinder-dry forests. The army assigned the 555th Parachute Battalion, an all-black outfit, to help search for the balloons. At Pendleton, Oregon, the infantrymen were trained and equipped to fight fire and to parachute into mountainous terrain. Forest Service instructors Frank Derry and Jack Allen from the Missoula base assisted with the training. Later, about 100 of the paratroopers moved to Chico, California, while about 235 remained at Pendleton. Although a balloon invasion did not materialize, CPSers from Camp 103 drove thousands of miles through the forests with one eye scanning the heavens. One jumper described the task as unrewarding. The 555th was dispatched to help fight some big fires later that summer.

In late summer, Forest Service supervisors often appointed men to harvest seeds of certain tree species. Lee Hebel, along with several others, rode in the back of a stake-bed truck to the Canadian border to find pinecone caches stashed by the squirrels under the banks of dry streambeds. They scooped pinecones into burlap bags and delivered them to the Savenac

Nursery, where the cones were dried and threshed, and the seeds planted in a nursery. Two years later, workers transplanted the seedlings across Region One.

Hebel grew up on a farm near Pennsylvania's Susquehanna River, four miles from the town of Liverpool. "I remember the difficulty the family experienced during the Depression years," he recalled, "simply saving enough money to pay the interest on the farm debt." When Hebel was thirteen, his mother developed breast cancer. "There was just one X-ray machine in Harrisburg, from which mother would return badly burned following treatments." His mother died three years later.

The next year, Hebel began working half time at Weis Pure Food Store in Liverpool for five dollars a week. He later moved to Harrisburg to live with his brother, Donald, and he worked at an uncle's five-and-ten-cent store. He noted, "It is difficult to understand how we could rent a room and eat in restaurants on thirteen dollars weekly pay." Compared to the five dollars a month he later earned as a smoke jumper, Hebel probably considered those times lush living.

During another off-season task at Camp 103, Hebel helped tear down CCC barracks at Camp Rimini, near Helena, Montana, where the army had trained men and dogsled teams for Arctic assignments. The transported barracks were later reconstructed at Hale Air Field in Missoula and became the Region One smoke jumper fire cache and parachute loft after the war.

During the winter, many men remained at Camp Menard rather than transfer to other CPS camps. They scattered across Region One to help out with a variety of understaffed jobs. During the winter of 1944–45, a number of men tended the Ninemile mules that wintered near Perma on the Flathead Indian Reservation, about thirty miles from the Remount Depot. When it snowed heavily, Edwin Vail helped feed hay to the animals. The crew also constructed shelters for the mule foals that would be born in the spring and occasionally roamed the hills burning patches of Russian thistle, a noxious weed. But most of the work entailed "building fences or taking down unwanted fences," according to Vail. He observed, "In the spring of 1945, one fence project was too far away to drive to and from each day. We were put in a cabin near the project. The men worked on the fences while I was chief cook and bottle washer. I cooked on a wood stove which also heated the cabin. It was there I made my first cake to be baked in an oven heated by wood. The cake turned out O.K."

Despite a few gripes, most of the men loved smoke jumping well enough to tolerate practically any job between fires. They looked upon the physically demanding tasks as a continuation of training. Also, no matter what their assignment, the camaraderie—not to mention the beautiful mountains that teemed with wildlife and wildflowers—bolstered their spirits.

"Morale in the smoke jumper unit rises or falls with the barometer and the frequency of lightning storms," observed Wallace Littel. He continued,

> Work between fires, however important or unimportant in itself, becomes merely fill-in, toughening labor between jumps. Thus work which in other CPS camps would be avoided as dull back-breaking routine is accepted here as part of the game. Excellent, in general, relations between Forest Service squad leaders and CPS smoke jumpers help a great deal, as does the variety of work and location, even apart from fire suppression and pre-suppression. There's plenty of spice in life at the smoke jumper's camp.[5]

Constructed in 1939, Camp Menard had followed the standard CCC camp configuration of twenty-three buildings, but in 1943, workers dismantled fourteen buildings and shipped them to Edmonton, Canada, to house workers constructing the Alaska-Canada Highway—leaving eight buildings intact for the CPSers.

Photographs are by Roy Wenger, except as noted.

In 1943, the smoke jumpers trained at the Boy Scouts' Camp Paxson on Seeley Lake. The compound included fifteen small cabins encircling a large lodge and a well-equipped washhouse. "I don't know even if my thoughts of Heaven were any prettier than this" (Warren Shaw).

Ninemile Remount Depot in its early days. (Photograph courtesy of U.S. Forest Service Ninemile Ranger District.)

The training course. "One by one the men run up the first steeply inclined ramp, grip the edge, drop seven feet to the ground and roll, under the watchful eye of the squad leader" (Frank Neufeld).

"Ahead of them hung a rope to climb, from which they stepped to a wooden platform and turned a flip into a rope net" (Frank Neufeld).

The horizontal bars, common at beaches and public parks, were part of the smoke jumpers' obstacle course.

Back bends at the "tank trap."

To practice reaching the ground after being hung up in a tree, the jumpers were hoisted into the air via block and tackle and then used a rope to descend.

Waiting in line to mount the dreaded tower.

The men became so accustomed to jumping after being slapped on the back in training that they would have done so had it been the "devil himself" giving the cue.

CPS smoke jumpers carefully listen to the instructions of Frank Derry, inventor of the Derry-slot parachute.

The Trimotor (foreground) and Travelaire were the workhorses for mountain flying. The slow-flying Trimotor, or Tin Goose, constructed of corrugated aluminum, was perfectly suited for delivering parachutists.

Earl Cooley was the second person ever to parachute to a wildfire—on July 12, 1940. Cooley remained with the Forest Service for many years before retiring. (Photograph circa 2000 by Mark Matthews.)

Waiting for their turn to jump from the plane.

"What can compare to the foot on the step, the rugged mountain below, the wind in your face, the tap on the shoulder, hit the silk. . . . You said it—'Life at its fullest'" (Merlo M. Zimmerman).

David Flaccus, a Pennsylvania Quaker, founded Mountain Press in Missoula after the war. He died in 1994 at age seventy-seven.

Despite the joy that the men found in jumping, they realized that danger lurked with every jump and landing. Many men suffered injuries, mostly to ankles and backs.

Mount Morrell Lookout, northeast of Seeley Lake. This is the original cupola style, which lookouts disliked because they had to climb down stairs to cook and clean house.

On the ground.

Injuries did provide time for introspection.

Jumpers preferred the organized camps on big fires because they provided hot meals, more variety in food, and a chance to wash and rest up.

The CPSers helped bale about six hundred tons of hay in the fields surrounding Ninemile while they waited for the fire season to begin.

CHAPTER NINE

Wild Encounters

On a July day in 1945, Albert Gray, Jr., stood face to face with unbounded fury in the heart of the Rocky Mountains. As a conscientious objector he was used to being harassed, but never with such venom. Born of Methodist parents in Pennsylvania, Gray early on was "taught to avoid violence and encouraged to seek a life of service." His family picture albums never showed any relatives in uniform, nor did his family display medals or guns in their home. "I was active in the Epwouth League of young people of the Methodist Church," he recalled. "At that time, in the 1930s, the great preachers and theologians were pacifists. I read their books and heard them preach . . . war is sin."

In October 1940, Albert and his brother, Paul, registered as conscientious objectors. At first the draft board refused them a 4-E classification because they were "only Methodists" and not "Philadelphia Quakers." But "with support of my father and our pastor, the appeal officer recognized our sincerity and our obstinacy and gave us CO status." Five years later, Gray found himself on a smoke jumper flight from a spike camp at

Cave Junction, Oregon, to a fire in northern California's Klamath National Forest. With no obvious landing spot in the rough terrain, the three-man stick aimed for a clearing about four miles from the smoke. By the time they reached the fire, it had blown up into a conflagration, and the trio radioed for help. The next day, nine American Indian firefighters and forty prisoners of war, arriving on foot, reinforced them. A few days later, after extinguishing the flames, the CPSers hiked out with an American Indian guide.

"There were no trails so the progress was slow," Gray recalled. "The brush was too thick for easy penetration and too high to climb over. The Indian became increasingly agitated. He told us to wait until he found a bear trail which he assumed would be near the ridge. We soon heard his call and joined him. All four of us crawled on hands and knees, each one close behind the other and making good progress."

After a while, Gray suddenly bumped into the rear end of the guide, who had stopped without warning. Gray did not have to see what was blocking their path. He could hear it: "There in the center of the trail was a coiled rattlesnake making angry warning sounds at being disturbed. Fortunately, we had an alert Indian guide, for if I, a city boy, had been in the lead, I'm sure I would have put my hand right on top of that rattler. The snake slowly moved on as if to defy mere humans who had invaded his territory."[1]

Any prolonged Montana experience eventually produces close encounters with animals, whether they be wild or tame. CPSers experienced their share. If a bear did not surprise a man on a wilderness trail, a cow was bound to barge into a streamside camp, even in the mountains. During World War II, packs of wolves still roamed the Canadian border at Glacier National Park, while grizzly bears haunted the backcountry of the Rocky Mountain Front as well as the Mission Mountains on the Flathead Indian Reservation and Yellow-

stone National Park. In the mountains surrounding Ninemile
roamed deer, elk, black bears, coyotes, lynx, and wolverines.
At the more remote smoke jumper bases, even greater and
more diverse populations of animals existed.

Larry Morgan recalled the forests surrounding Cayuse
Landing in the summer of 1944 as being a wildlife wonder-
land. Morgan was raised in the Spokane Valley in Washington, where his father had worked his way through theology
school as a custodian at Spokane University. Although money
was tight, Morgan remembered that "the joy of living was
assured because of the deep undoubting faith of the family
and its committed life within the church." While Morgan was
a junior in high school, his father died of a heart attack, and
the seventeen-year-old got a job earning fifteen cents an hour
to keep food on the table for his mother and sister.

While in CPS, Morgan first became an office clerk for the
Forest Service at Cascade Locks. The first time he applied to
be a smoke jumper, the agency turned him down. He used
the authority of his clerk position to procure his records, and
he discovered that he had been rejected because he was
underweight. The next year he added a few phantom pounds
and was accepted. Like many CPSers, Morgan was enchanted
by his wilderness experience at Cayuse, a small airstrip about
fifty miles northeast of Pierce, Idaho:

> This was a beautiful setting, with Cayuse Creek and
> Kelly Creek running out of the mountains to the south.
> To the east across the creek was a strip of forested areas.
> The higher hills beyond had seen a previous fire and
> was now covered with brush as it waited for the return of
> trees. On top of the ridge above the burn was an aban-
> doned lookout.
>
> Wildlife was abundant in the area. A moose and her
> calf were often seen downstream from camp. We found

it thrilling to see huge bull elk stampede through the trees. A Saturday or Sunday fishing trip up the creek by a couple of ardent fishermen always produced an abundance of large trout to supplement our diet.[2]

Some encounters with animals posed dangerous risks, while others turned into slapstick comedy. While the beauty of animals inspired awe, their unpredictable nature often created a sense of urgency and excitement in the men, causing them to act unpredictably and irrationally themselves. No matter what the circumstances, encounters with animals made for good storytelling at suppertime and at reunions years later.

Even mundane domestic animals inspired their share of tales. The Ninemile mules roamed the pastures around Camp Menard, and cattle grazed on public allotments throughout the forests. After jumper training at Ninemile one summer, Earl Cooley assigned a number of men to the Moose Creek Ranger Station. After several weeks there, Marlyn Shetler, John Shipp, and Emory Garber moved camp to Shearer Airport to clear trails, repair telephone lines, and make hay from the runway pastures. Not long after their arrival, a Hereford bull came around to voice his concerns, according to Shetler:

> He did not like us there. He started bellerin' and pawing the ground. John and I didn't like it and were leery of him. But Emory said, "He was all right. I'm not afraid of him, the old rancher feeds him out of a dish pan."
>
> A couple of weeks went by, then one morning bright and early, there was that old cantankerous bull out by the gate. Finally he got a horn hooked on the middle bar, slid it open, and came in by the cabin.
>
> By this time we were through with breakfast. John

and I were doing the dishes. Emory decided to chase the bull out. He went out and got a shovel and started toward the bull, then decided to put the other two bars down on the gate. John and I were talking, as Emory was going for the gate. John said, "Why don't you tell him to chase him out with his belt. He said he could." So I did.

Emory came back toward the bull pulling his belt out. He stepped in front of the bull, just enough to reach him, and slapped him across the eyes. The bull blinked, shook his head, hit him hard, and threw him fifteen feet. When he landed the bull was there on top of him. I said, "Come on, John, the bull's got him."

He thought I was kidding but followed me out the door. I grabbed the shovel, John grabbed a pulaski. When we got out there the bull was having a ball, he had a whole airport on which to play with Emory.

As soon as we got close, he took off and ran out the gate. We followed and put up the bars. We went back to the cabin and Emory was leaning on the fence. He said, "If you guys hadn't got there when you did, I think I could have got away from him."[3]

Mules and horses often aided the jumpers on fires. After extinguishing a blaze, the men would lug their 110-pound packs through the brush until they reached a trail or road, and then they would stash the gear. A packer would come along later leading a mule or two to carry out the load the rest of the way. On big fires, strings of mules transported extra food and supplies in to the firefighters or brought out the fire camp equipment. The packers rode horses. Sometimes, after an accident, an injured jumper would get to ride out along the trail. Theodore Pfeiffer saw how well trained the horses could be. Pfeiffer had bruised his side and broken an ankle after parachuting onto some rocks. He later observed,

When I woke up, there were two horses and two Forest Service men in the camp. They told us the horses were for Jim and I, and the horses would take us back to camp. They put us on the horses and told us not to touch the reins, the horses knew their way back to camp. One portion of the trip back was along the side of the mountain. I looked to the right and it seemed to go about a mile straight up. When I looked left and down the mountain, this seemed as though it must be five miles straight down. The trail at this time looked about six inches wide and closing. Previously I had been thankful, now I was asking my friend for help.

After this it was an all day ride of not knowing what direction or where we were. One thing that amazed me about this was the horses never stopped either for water or grass. We came to other trails that we crossed. Some came into our trail in a Y. The horses never stopped to ask directions but knew where they were all the time. Just at sunset and ahead of us, was camp. The horses in the mountains must be a special breed and deserve a great deal of respect.[4]

Many men missed their own pet animals at home, whether dog, cat, horse, goat, or cow. One Missoula family who befriended the CPSers thought they could make the men feel more at home at Camp Menard by lending them a dog during the winter. The dog, a Great Dane of massive power and great dignity, was named Chris.

At Christmastime, the men inspected the many small spruce and subalpine fir trees growing on the grounds surrounding the camp before selecting the most perfect specimen to chop down and decorate. They set up the tree in the cookshack near the dining tables. During the long evenings of Christmas week, the men carved, collected, or contrived numerous baubles to add color to the tree. They also strung popcorn on nylon parachute patching thread and draped it around the tree's branches. All the while, Chris the Great Dane lay quietly on the floor, according to Roy Wenger, who recalled,

> We all loved the dog. He was completely domesticated and thoroughly dependent on human direction. To see how all parties would react, we once led him out by the collar to see two deer grazing by our barracks. Chris looked, saw and trembled. The deer, sensing his fear, looked up at him and went back to their grazing.
>
> One evening near Christmas a dozen men lingered at the mess hall tables after dinner. Chris was asleep near the heavily decorated Christmas tree and was making no overt responses to the occasional pats and strokes he received. All was warm, peaceful, and quiet.
>
> No one ever figured out exactly what happened next. Perhaps a mouse ran across his paw or he had a vivid dream or nightmare, but we all saw him stand suddenly on his great long legs, sight an object invisible to us and make a sudden, determined dash into the space between the barracks wall and the Christmas tree.
>
> His paws became entangled in the wires running between the lights and he became frantic, his powerful muscles tensed like a draft horse straining to pull a loaded wagon.
>
> He took off with the whole works, the lights, the tree, the strings of popcorn, and dragged them the length of the barracks, developing in us an entirely new respect for him. We had had no idea that beneath his placid exterior lay strength that, under still incomprehensible provocation, could be mustered for powerful accomplishments.[5]

Although pacifists, most CPSers did not elevate the slaughtering of animals to the same moral level as the killing of humans. Many men had been raised on farms, where chopping the head off a chicken for dinner or slaughtering pigs for sausage was part of the cycle of life. Others were avid hunters who did not hesitate to supplement K rations with some fresh meat, according to Dick Flaharty.

The kid from Chicago made his third and final jump, with Ad Carlson, to a small fire below the lookout tower on Wahoo Peak in the Bitterroots. The smoke chaser assigned to the tower had gone back to high school the week before, Flaharty recalled, "so Ad and I had to take care of this small lightning-set fire just about three hundred yards from the tower. When we radio-phoned in for follow-up orders when we had the fire out, the dispatcher instructed us to remain at the tower and assist the packer in closing the place up for the winter. The packer didn't arrive until the next day so we had some time to kill. As we hiked down to the spring for some fresh water, Ad demonstrated his marksmanship by hitting a fool hen in the head with a rock and we had fresh meat for dinner."

Many hunters in the smoke jumpers' camp marveled over the big-game animals they surprised during their adventures in the woods. Many had seen deer in their travels in the East and Midwest, but majestic elk were often a novelty that evoked awe in such men as William Weber. He wrote, "One of my most memorable fire jumps was a fire in Glacier National Park. We had the fire out within two hours after landing and awoke the next morning to see a beautiful herd of elk in the valley below, not far from our sleeping site."

Charles Schumacher and Lloyd Hulbert got an even closer look at some elk while fighting a two-man fire in the Bitter-roots. With the fire quickly under control, reported Schu-macher (a Mennonite from Bluffton, Ohio), they started mopping up: "We were on our hands and knees to make sure all fire was out so we finished up covered with ashes and soot. At night we slept in the meadow and were scared stiff when a bull elk stood between us and bugled. When you are lying on your back looking up at the beast, they are real big."

Sometimes the CPS greenhorns showed their ignorance of wildlife in naive ways. Dick Flaharty, always the performer and jokester, thought he would try to call in a bull elk one day as he started the long hike out from a fire with a packer. It was the beginning of elk mating season, and the bulls were emitting their eerie flutelike bugle all around. "I started imitating them and before long I was getting answers," Flaharty recalled. "Ad [Carlson] finally stopped dead in his tracks, turned and looked this greenhorn right in the eye and asked, 'Have you ever seen how aggressive a bull elk is in mating season?' I got the message."

Getting stomped or gored by an eight-hundred-pound elk with a six-foot rack full of sharp points was not the only danger in the woods. Sometimes a man could be fatally injured when he was the one to stomp instead of being stomped. Encountering a rattler during the day as Albert Gray did was a hair-raising experience, but stumbling upon one at night was even more terrifying. David Kaufman witnessed firsthand the pandemonium a rattler could provoke during a midnight visit during a fire jump at Meadow Creek in 1945. As the fire burned out of control, the Forest Service called in some of the black paratroopers of the 555th. One night the mixed crews got back to camp at dusk and spread out in their sleeping bags. When one of the firefighters felt something wiggling beneath his bag, he let out a scream and started running, his body still enclosed by the sleeping bag. "I have never seen anybody before, or since, who could run in a sleepingbag, but he went at least fifty yards before he lost it," Kaufman said.[6]

Elk inspired, snakes terrified, but no animal made as great an impression as the bear—perhaps because bears seem nearly human. Skin a bear, cut off its head and hang his carcass and you could swear you were looking at a skinned human. Like most children, many CPSers grew up cuddling stuffed teddy bears. But in the woods, the grizzly bear's behemoth hulk and long claws most likely haunted their dreams.

Just a hint of bear was enough to send some people scurrying for safety, as CPSer Ralph Ziegler testified:

> To tell my bear story I need to draw a map of the camp site [Seeley Lake]. We could not go the most direct way from the bunkhouse to the mess hall because of a fence. One night about twenty fellows were telling bear stories at the bunkhouse. About nine o'clock, we decided to go over to the mess hall for a bedtime snack. We were through the fence and almost to the mess hall when we heard a commotion in the kitchen. We thought a bear was in there and we all ran like mad back to the bunkhouse. One of the Canadian fellows was on crutches because he had broken his ankle in a training jump. He was the first one back to the bunkhouse. I can still see his excited big eyes.
>
> The next morning we found out the cook had made the noise while laying a fire in the cook stove to be ready for the next morning.[7]

Bears could definitely be an annoyance for men camped near high mountain lakes, near rushing streams, or in prime bear habitat where huckleberries grew or where whitebark pine trees produced oil-laden nuts. Many times, smoke jumpers, while intent on battling a fire, forgot that other eyes looked out from the thick forest. That often caused traumatic situations, especially when dinnertime rolled around. On one fire, Dave Flaccus and his mates stashed their sleeping bags and gear away from the fire in thick timber while they dug fire line. Flaccus recalled, "My gear was tucked into a duffel bag, including some fruit, a can of tobacco, a can of juice in the bag. The opening was closed and tied securely. Even with my young fingers, I sometimes had a hard time opening it up. As we approached the camp I saw the tobacco tin glinting in the sun. Nearby lay a crushed and empty juice can and various extra clothes scattered around. Somehow a bear had untied the knot with his hairy claws, reached in the bag, and had a leisurely snack."

The same fate almost visited Merlo Zimmerman's cache of food while he was at a fire camp. Born on a farm near Flanagan, Illinois, Zimmerman spent a happy boyhood in a close-knit community with an uncle, an aunt, and cousins living on the next farm down the road. He wrote, "We were taught the dignity of hard work and were also allowed to enjoy the usual activities of sibling play and rivalry that one would expect to find in a family of four boys." With about twenty-five neighborhood children, he attended a one-room schoolhouse containing five rows of desks and heated by a large coal-burning stove in the corner.

Zimmerman had already reported to a CPS camp in Pennsylvania when the Japanese bombed Pearl Harbor. "I was resting on my bunk," he recalled, "when the radio suddenly blared forth with the news of the attack. I had only served two months of a two year assignment. Quickly the realization sunk in that those two years were now for the duration, which eventually turned out to be four years, one month and twenty-one days." Of those four years, Zimmerman served two summers as a smoke jumper.

Zimmerman's bear encounter occurred when he surprised one stealing a ham that the men had hung in a tree. "I let out a yell and chased that bear until he dropped the ham," he said. "Although it had some big tooth marks in it, it sure tasted good after a day of fire fighting."

Humans love to get close to wild animals. Psychologically, there must be some remnant atavistic brain cells that link us to our wild cousins and make us act stupid around wild animals. CPSer Ivan Moore experienced the excitement of seeing a black bear, but that was not enough to satisfy him. One evening, as he strolled with a friend along a little dirt road past the mess hall at the Haugan Ranger Station, they came to an opening in the woods where two large black bears rooted in the garbage dump. As the two quietly watched, the bears soon lumbered up the side of the hill and disappeared. About a week later, the men returned to the same spot. Moore recalled,

> This time, only the back of a lone bear was visible. Gingerly we approached and circled to leeward. Presently that bear, apparently half-grown, scrambled out of the dump and stared at us. We stood motionless.
>
> Suddenly, like an idiot I whistled, as if calling a dog. The bear, peering through his little pig eyes, came slowly toward us. Closer he came, still closer. The nearer he came the bigger he looked. Then Bill said, "Hey, make a noise opposite from a whistle." I glanced at Bill, and his hair really was standing on end now, but the bear kept coming closer.
>
> In desperation, we jumped up and down shouting and yelling. The bear gave a big woof and took off running up the hill.
>
> I looked around and said to Bill, "What were you going to do with that little piece of rotten wood there in your hand?"
>
> Bill replied: "I was gonna goose you so you'd jump at him and keep him occupied while I ran for help."[8]

No black bear ever charged or physically attacked a CPSer, but in a roundabout way, one bear did cause the most severe injuries sustained by a jumper in 1943. Weir Stone, who had driven his Harley motorcycle to camp, often cruised the mountain roads after dinner. One September evening he invited the camp cook, Glen Corney, for a ride up to the Morrell fire tower. On the way back down to Seeley Lake, the

motorcycle approached the ranger's house where a steep
bank flanked the road. The night before, Roy Wenger had
gone out to chase a bear away from the garbage cans, but the
bear instead had chased Wenger back into the barracks.
Stone turned to ask the cook, "Do you think we will see that
bear that Roy had trouble with last night?" At that moment
the motorcycle was racing about forty-five miles per hour up a
slight hill that made a curve at the top. Just then the bear
appeared on the road. Stone had no time to brake, and the
motorcycle hit the bear dead center. Stone wrote,

> When I came out of my daze and arose, I was sur-
> rounded by Glen, who was dazed, the cycle, and the
> bear. One very unhappy and confused pile. The bear
> was feebly kicking its legs in a death throes, I thought.
> So I stuck my .22 pistol in his ear for the coup de grace.
> That touching of its ear with the pistol woke the bear up
> screaming. It spun around in several short circles and
> then ran up the steep slope. Twice it didn't make it and
> rolled right down on Glen. He didn't mind because he
> had a skull fracture and was out cold.
>
> The third try, the bear made it to the top (about fif-
> teen feet). I stood there panting. I shot at its head and
> then it disappeared over the top.
>
> At the ranger station they heard the cycle coming, then
> the thud, then a scream, then a shot—so they thought
> something had happened and came to investigate.

When the men revived Glen, the injured man said, "Oh,
my God, I hurt all over. What happened?"

"We hit a bear on the cycle," Stone reminded him.

"I've never been on a cycle, let alone hit a bear," Glen
replied.

The next day, Stone returned to the scene and found what

he described as "two narrow strips of blood on the highway about six feet long, from the bear's nose on impact. We hobbled up the bank the next morning, but there was no sign of the bear anywhere."[9]

Fortunately no grizzly bears surprised the CPSers, for that would have been far more dangerous. But many black bears often visited the Ninemile camp and the various outposts. In those days before bear-proof trash containers, rural residents usually discarded their garbage in open pits or gullies. The bears came looking for food, not trouble. They often showed more respect to the CPSers than they received in return. One evening a bear rummaging in a camp garbage pit disturbed Raymond Phibbes and Oliver Petty, who were talking in a nearby cabin. Petty described the scene that followed:

> We went to the back door just in time to see Phil Thomforde poised over the pit with an ax raised in the air. We hollered not to hit the bear, but we were too late. The bear heard us and came up out of the pit. Phil swung the ax with all he had and hit a glancing blow to the side of the bear's head.
>
> The bear walked off about twenty feet and looked back at Phil as if to say, "What the hell are you doing?" Later, the Forest Service packer said he saw a bear with a sore on the side of its head.
>
> Phil was lucky the bear was a pacifist.

CHAPTER TEN

Eyes in the Skies

Billowing dark clouds speared the mountains surrounding the lookout with sharp-toothed brilliant daggers as Bert Olin cringed atop a wooden stool with its leg bottoms capped by glass canisters. Until then, the 1943 fire season had been a dud. A few days earlier, Olin had drawn the short straw among the CPS smoke jumpers stationed at the Big Prairie ranger station in Montana's Bob Marshall Wilderness. He thus earned the dubious prize of living at the "eagle perch" on the mountaintop above, to keep an eye open for smokes. Discontented, Olin feared that he might miss a fire jump.

Tedium soon set in as he constantly scanned the surrounding ridges and valleys through binoculars. After a few days, he could hardly wait until evening, when some of his pals at the ranger station would phone for a chat. Despite Bert's boredom, he was about to experience the most terrifying moment of his life as the huge wet thunderhead blew directly over Tillotson Lookout, pummeling the peak with lightning. The next morning, when the jumpers at Big Prairie could not reach Olin over the telephone, the ranger instructed David Kauffman to take mules, water, and food and a new telephone up to the lookout and check things out. Kauffman, who worked for the Forest Service as a civilian at the time, was the eighth child of a family of fifteen. In two years he would become a CPS smoke jumper himself.

Of his childhood he wrote, "We lived in a very rural area (in northwest Montana) and had plenty of playmates, with so many brothers and sisters to share. As I grew older, of course, there were chores on the agenda, such as weeding the garden, carrying wood for the stove, and learning to milk the cows and care for the livestock. The big deal was learning to drive horses when father thought I was old enough." At sixteen, Kauffman quit school to work in the local sawmill to help support the family. After he contracted tamarack poisoning, he signed on with the Forest Service as a packer. The next year he would petition his draft board for 4-E deferment and request CPS duty.

In 1945, he became a smoke jumper. Kauffman described his CPS experience as "an opportunity to examine my own beliefs and ask myself why I believed as I did." Still later in life he became a doctor.

That summer day in 1943, Kauffman led his mule string up the steep, winding trail to check on Bert Olin. When he came within view of the lookout, he saw Olin sprinting down the trail toward him. Olin's eyes were still wide with excitement and fear, and he could not wait to tell Kauffman of the preceding night. Olin told him,

> I followed directions explicitly. I got on that old big wooden chair on the glass coasters, and I was facing the telephone, and I was getting as far away from anything metal as I could. That lightning struck and all of a sudden one of them hit the lookout. . . . It hit and shook the whole place. And there was a ball of fire that came

out of the telephone and went right to the stove and up the pipe and right out. I couldn't talk for at least ten minutes. I just sat there.

Kauffman noted that Olin "was real happy to see a little company come, and he certainly did not want a second hitch on the lookout."[1]

Although most CPS volunteers did not share Olin's intimate encounter with lightning, many did get an opportunity to live amid the clouds in lookouts. Like smoke jumping, being a lookout provided unique experiences. For many, it also offered some quiet time for reflection and assessment.

During the 1940s, those who manned the lookouts called in most forest fires. Once the agency had designated fire suppression as a top priority, the square wooden structures popped up on many exposed promontories throughout the Rocky Mountains, spaced about ten miles apart. The construction period continued up until the Second World War. Before becoming a smoke jumper, Earl Cooley had helped to raise a number of lookouts and also manned them.

When he first arrived at McCart Lookout, Cooley found nothing more than an alidade board mounted on a high point of the rock, and a tent pitched down the hill. The alidade (a pivoting sighting device) hovered over a map of the area, allowing a lookout to pinpoint the compass bearings of a fire. A lookout familiar with the territory could determine the exact ridge or drainage from which a smoke arose. With sightings from three neighboring lookouts, fire bosses in Missoula could triangulate the location to the nearest foot. Cooley's first assignment at the McCart site was to cut down trees to use as legs for a new tower. He described the process:

I would have to drag the lodgepole timbers almost one-half mile down the ridge. Archie Fulkner, the forest carpenter, had six CCC kids trained to build towers and lookout cabins. They brought up an old bell mare that liked to pull. We trained her by putting a few poles on at a time and having her haul a light load.

We needed at least twenty logs squared to eight-by-eight inches, twenty feet long. Each morning a CCC kid and I would cut the trees, then I would square them with a broadaxe. We'd get them ready to haul down to the lookout, and he would stay at the lookout and watch for fires. When we'd brought all the timbers in, Archie Fulkner came in with his crew and built the tower and installed the precut cabin that had been brought in by packstring.

Cooley's next lookout assignment was Medicine Point, where the ranger instructed him to erect a tower by fall. Cooley faced one major obstacle—the rocky mountaintop was barren of vegetation. The ranger suggested that the crew pull the trees uphill by block and tackle, a hundred feet at a time. With winter closing in, Cooley knew he could not get enough logs up there before the first snow flew. He recalled,

I went around the ridge about one-half mile and found a good supply of lodgepole. They were high on the mountain, churn-butted [wide on the bottom], and required a lot of broadaxe work. Fortunately, we had the mare well trained by then. We could hook on a log and she would head for the lookout, taking her time and resting whenever she felt like it. When she got to the lookout site, the CCC kid would unhook her, turn her around, and send her back. When Archie Fulkner arrived, I helped his crew finish the lookout cabin. We painted the cabin and completed the whole job before we came down in the fall.[2]

Copper telephone lines—sometimes strung from poles, sometimes from trees—connected the lookouts to the local ranger station. The eyes in the skies not only spotted and phoned in smokes, but frequently the men hiked to small lightning strikes to extinguish the incipient fires as they smoldered. Until World War II, only men worked as lookouts. But with the ensuing manpower shortage during the war, the Forest Service trained its first female lookouts, along with many high school students.

The first lookout cabins, built in the late 1920s, were two-story cupola structures, with living quarters below the glassed second story. As lookouts chronically complained about climbing downstairs to cook a meal or grab a drink of water, architects scrapped that style. Only three cupola structures remained intact in Region One in the northern Rockies by the year 2005. By the 1930s, Archie Fulkner and others had begun to construct the classic multiwindowed, square structure with a peaked roof. After the war, when an ever-expanding road system allowed easier transportation of building materials, the agency turned to flat-roofed lookouts set atop concrete bases. Another building boom that occurred during the 1950s saw many cabins sprout atop high metal or wooden towers.

But the postwar construction boom was misleading. With the development of the smoke jumper program, most fire towers had already become obsolete. Smoke jumpers began dousing fires that were once the responsibility of the lookouts. Of even more significance is the expansion of the aerial detection program. Pilots soon surveyed vast tracts of wilderness after bad weather passed through, reporting smokes by radio as they flew over. Sometimes surveillance planes carried smoke jumpers during their runs and dropped them directly onto the fires as the aerial watchers spotted the smoke. Pilots could also buzz drainages hidden from lookouts by ridges or higher peaks.

In June 1945, Region One for the first time experimented with using airplane patrol to replace fire lookouts. The study area covered almost two million acres of roadless area stretching from Flathead Lake east to the plains, north to Glacier

National Park, and south to Seeley Lake. The agency abandoned forty-five lookouts that season but continued manning a dozen strategically located towers in the project dubbed "Continental Unit." During times of high fire danger and following storms, pilots patrolled in Travelaires, carrying two jumpers. A group of a dozen jumpers trained for the mission in Missoula under a recently discharged military officer. CPS smoke jumper Hubert Rohrer enrolled in the program and recalled,

> The training involved a lot of map reading, rotation schedule, location of standbys and other organizational procedures. It was obvious that this was to be a well organized tight ship. The strongest emphasis was given over to teaching us to begin to use twenty-four-hour [military] time, which seemed to be vitally necessary for the success of the project. There were many drills to get us conversant in this all important time language. We were to report to training at O-eight-hundred hours, have lunch break from twelve-hundred hours to thirteen-hundred hours and to return to the house at seventeen-hundred hours. "A.M." and "P.M." were no longer to be part of our thinking.
>
> The fun was that every day at the proper time to leave, Sam Zook would announce loudly and clearly, "Well, it's five o'clock, time for us to go."[3]

Unfortunately for the professional lookouts, the program worked too well. "Soon most national forests had similar projects," Cooley wrote.[4]

Life in a lookout compared favorably to life aboard ship—cramped quarters set in a viewscape with an unending vista. Only this landscape was crammed with mountaintops, ridges, and nearby cliffs instead of waves, whitecaps, and swells. Still, with a little imagination, clouds seemed to float by like great vessels, often scraping their hulls on the mountaintops as if those were reefs. At night, stars and planets appeared to be the streetlights of distant heavenly cities. The full moon shone brightly. Cloudy fronts ebbed and flowed. On summer mornings, fog often filled the valleys and canyons, making them appear to be bodies of water when observed from above. By ten o'clock the air became clear, with not a cloud in the turquoise sky. By midafternoon, though, cumulus clouds popped into existence. Surface heat rising off the mountains sent the clouds billowing higher and higher, expanding into massive battleships with dark gray and black hulls. Oftentimes, lightning streaked from their bellies to the ground and ignited whole trees. Nearby thunderclaps deafened the ear without warning.

The mountaintop offered no sanctuary during a storm. As wind rocked the lookout like a cradle, the thin panes of glass seemed ready to implode. One could only hope that the metal cables wrapped around the structure would hold securely to the rocks below—and that the ground wire would carry off any lightning strikes. The theory that lightning didn't strike the same place twice did not apply to lookouts. Sometimes driving rain splattered the windows. But just as often, there was no rain. That was when lookouts had to be quick on their feet, constantly rotating, trying to pinpoint the location where the umbilical cord of white fire from heaven met the earth.

When there was a strike, a lookout rotated the alidade and took a quick directional reading. When the storm passed, the lookout would check the area for smokes and eventually determine what ridge or drainage had been struck. Sometimes the storms hit at night and lightning exploded the darkness like flashbulbs, causing the dreaming lookout to leap out of bed. If the ribbons of white struck the surrounding ridges, a hit tree often crowned with fire, from a distance looking like the end of a puffed cigar—for a few seconds, a distant red ember would seem to glow, and then it would die out.

Some CPSers took to the storms better than others. After breaking a bone in his foot during a parachute landing, Maynard Shetler was assigned to the Morrell Mountain Lookout. From his perch northeast of Seeley Lake, he looked upon the seemingly endless mountain ridges that stretched across the Bob Marshall Wilderness eighty miles to the Rocky Mountain front. "Life on a lookout during a storm has its moments," he recalled. "You look down on lightning strikes and record them. The phone rings even though disconnected. Every piece of furniture has its own ground wire. A storm is a beautiful sight if you don't think about getting electrocuted yourself."

Few lookouts escape the eye of the storm, but not many get to watch fire explode from their telephones. More often than not, thunderheads peter out near sunset, and the clouds come to rest like fall leaves on a still pond. They often become as colorful, with the great clouds in the west reflecting vermilion, orange, and plum from the afterglow of the sun, while those clouds in the east turn shades of pink and lavender. Viewed from a mountaintop, sunsets and twilight in the north country seem to last half the night.

Lightning did not visit every day. Sometimes it never came, or it might arrive with ample rain to douse the momentary fires. During rainy periods and on lazy summer days, lookouts still had plenty to do. There was always firewood to chop and windows to wash—up to 144 panes in a standard square lookout. Although most supplies arrived by mule, sometimes lookouts had to pack in their own supplies over ten miles of uphill trail. Meals cooked on a woodstove took more time to prepare. Plus, there was another culinary consideration, as Shetler discovered: "Cooking at a high altitude is an art in itself." Shetler swore that he never mastered the art, although he received passing grades from others. "Smoke jumpers

Erling Gamble and Lew Berg brought my mail to me one Sunday (a fourteen mile hike one way)," he wrote. "They ate the pie which I made for them and said it was good, even though it was pitiful in my opinion."

Since water seldom sprang directly from a mountaintop, the lookout had to fetch it by canteen almost every day. Sometimes a lucky lookout found a seep a quarter mile away. Others had to walk farther, up and down steep treacherous goat trails. They usually made water runs in the early morning, when fog still shrouded the valleys and before the sun heated up the hillsides. How much they used depended on how much they enjoyed the hike. CPS smoke jumper Joe Osborn broke an ankle during his initial training at Seeley Lake in 1943 and drew an assignment to Morrell Mountain Lookout. Born in Muncie, Indiana, Osborn was a descendant of many generations of Quakers. With his hurt leg, he did not appreciate fetching water every day. He eventually wrote the following Shakespearean-style ode, "Room without a Bath," about his dilemma:

Oh daintiness, from me forever gone—
But no, 'tis not forever; there within
The bag is water, tempting me to thin
The crust of grime that doth reside upon
This frame of mine. To bathe, or not to bathe?
This question troubleth me. And what about
The dishes soiled, and how can I look out
Through dusty windows, or my whiskers shave?
Perhaps I should no longer wrack my brain
With thoughts about this question. Now I fain
Would go to bed. To sleep, perhaps to dream
Of running water and a shower clean.
To wake and still begrimed arise. To drink,
And once again upon the problem think.
            —JOE OSBORN, Morrell Mountain Lookout, 1943[5]

Shetler, with his broken foot, faced the same two-thousand-foot descent for water on Morrell the following summer. "Needing to make the round trip on a broken foot helped me to conserve water," he confessed.

James Brunk also recalled trips to the spring when he was assigned to assist the regular lookout at Red Plume in 1945. Growing up in a Mennonite family in Harrisonburg, Virginia, Brunk often listened to his mother "read Bible story books to us at first and as we got a little older she read chapters of the Bible to us every night before we went to bed. Major emphases of their training were that we were to love our enemies. One of my early favorite Bible verses was from the Sermon on the Mount: 'Blessed are the peacemakers for they shall be called the children of God.'"

Brunk's boss on the mountaintop was a Canadian veteran, a former Royal Air Force tail gunner. The veteran airman told Brunk that he thought all parachute jumpers were crazed; moreover, he stated that he "would rather go in with a falling airplane than to jump out of it." From the man's looks, Brunk considered that he apparently had followed that course of action during his years in the military: "He had numerous scars, one empty eye socket, and many skin graft patches among his tattoos to prove it." Brunk not only carried water from a spring a half mile down the mountain, but also helped reblaze overgrown trails. When not working, he enjoyed looking at the surrounding mountains, scoping for wildlife through field glasses, and admiring the subalpine wildflowers. He noted, "In the evenings I was reading a book of daily devotional readings, *Abundant Living*, by E. Stanley Jones. Each day I also had my Bible reading program which had been instilled into me by my mother and encouraged by my father."

Like Brunk, Maynard Shetler also found inner peace while stationed on the mountain. He recalled, "After one summer of study on the mountain top—with no books other than the

Bible, and no magazines, I came down anchored in the Word through my study of it. Through this study it became clear to me there was a difference between being a believer, and being a Mennonite or Methodist or a Baptist. Being a member of the church did not necessarily mean you were a believer in Jesus Christ. My study confirmed the biblical basis for being a conscientious objector. War is contrary to everything taught in the New Testament. Nor could I give unconditional allegiance to anyone but God."

Phil Neal possessed the character and personality that thrived in a place of glorious isolation. In fact, he enjoyed sitting atop a mountain more than he did jumping out of airplanes. At that point in his life, Neal seemed to need time to sit in one place to think things over. Born in 1918 (at Newton Square, Pennsylvania), Neal came from a family that did not belong to one of the peace churches. His father worked as a promoter and salesman and led the family on a nomadic life. Neal's one place of "constant return," as he phrased it, was a farm owned by his mother's parents. The transient family life hindered his social adjustment, and Neal became "rather contentious by nature. I became a loner: a group of peers simply meant trouble and harassment—better to go fishing." He also became an independent thinker at an early age. He recalled,

Among my earliest childhood recollections is a feeling of resentment when parents or older relatives would gently say that I was too young to eat this, or do that, or go here or there. To me, it was part of a nefarious plot to subjugate me to magnify the status of elders. I worked on developing logical arguments to expose the sham of such restrictions. I was no mutant: my father scorned established authority if it seemed to contravene his wishes or sentiments and my mother found many things about which to be indignant, though she supported an orderly society.

By 1936, Neal's father had deserted the family. His mother worked through the depression on a Works Progress Administration parent education project. Neal, trying to save some money for college, took a job at a factory on the night shift. At that time, his life began to follow a religious orientation for the first time. Formerly, he had "acquired the bent of avoiding churches"; he soon came to have "increasing contacts" with the Religious Society of Friends. He even began to contemplate enrolling at a Quaker institution—Haverford College. Before beginning school in the fall of 1937, he regularly attended the meetings. He observed, "I respected social gospel, and was confronted with no creed. By the time I entered college I had become a convinced Friend, though admittedly a very incomplete and rough-edged one. My mother also joined, though a different Meeting. Both of us, religious skeptics, were enthusiastic Norman Thomas socialists."

Although he finally found religion, Neal remained spiritually adrift. When confronted with the draft, he eventually based his decision on philosophical rather than religious ideals. He recalled,

I had acquired an anti-military attitude from my mother and the socialists—not to mention the Quakers. In 1940, I equated the military draft with herding—and I wasn't about to be herded. But I reached the rationalization that I could call myself a religious objector (sort of). The local draft board let me by, I think, on my Quaker credentials. Throughout CPS I was uneasy, never feeling absolutely right in my CO stand, though I could not imagine becoming a soldier. A concept of "bad" vs. "worse" began to form in my mind. I felt alienated from society, never admitting to myself that this was destabilizing my life.

At his first CPS camp at Trenton, North Dakota, Neal felt out of place. He still lacked the social skills required for integration into a culture of young strangers thrown together in close quarters. Barracks life slowly eroded what few social tendencies he possessed. He wrote, "Some men, however, adapted constructively. I felt that they had things I didn't have, and feared I never would: loving fiancée or wife; supportive, wider family; solid career on hold. Of course, some men had none of these, yet had good spirits and tranquility. At any rate, I was far from alone in being unhappy for various reasons."

After a brief stint at the camp on what he called the bleak prairie, Neal convinced himself that smoke jumping in the mountains of Montana was for him. He arrived at Camp Menard in June of 1945. But his optimism did not last long. "To be a good jumper one needed inner peace," he noted, "which I did not have. In training, everything went wrong. I encountered one mishap after another—involving equipment, chance injuries, and falls from trees. On my second training jump I bruised a foot in a freak hang up and fall. Rightly judging me accident-prone, Earl Cooley and the trainer squad saw to it that I pulled lookout duty."

The hitch in the tower on Edith Peak, a few miles east of Ninemile, salvaged Neal's summer—and his service record. He took like an eagle to the high lonely and enjoyed watching the chipmunks, birds, deer, elk, and, on one occasion, a cougar that shared the mountain on the long ridge of the Reservation Divide that ran east and west, from Missoula to Superior. He described the experience as "rather calming." In the evenings he chatted with other lookouts over the telephone: "I have good memories of Mrs. McMahon, a sensible and friendly schoolteacher stationed on Cayuse Tower—the one nearest to Ninemile." Yet Neal's bad luck continued to haunt him on the lookout, at least in one humorous event that he recounted. After a storm severed his telephone line, the dispatcher from Ninemile, a man named Smitty, rode up to check things out. Before Smitty followed the line down the mountainside, he instructed Neal to crank the phone at intervals to see if the break was fixed. Neal followed the instructions, and eventually Smitty reconnected the break. But even implicitly following instructions landed Neal in trouble. That evening, Smitty called Neal from headquarters. "Neal, I could shoot you," he sputtered. "Just as I was up to my waist in wet brush trying to pull the busted wire together, you had to crank that phone."

Smitty apparently received quite a jolt. Despite this incident, Neal was given a good rating as a lookout, which partly eased his disappointment over his lost smoke-jumping opportunity.

CHAPTER ELEVEN

Under Fire

On July 29, 1943, when the first fire call finally sounded in the smoke jumpers' office, Earl Cooley called out Phil Stanley's name first—an appropriate gesture, since the Quaker (who would open a photography shop in Missoula after the war) had been the one to propose the idea of training CPSers as smoke jumpers. Joining Stanley on that first jump were Loren Zimmerman and Dave Flaccus. The three tugged on suits that were well padded on the legs, arms, and shoulders and slipped the straps coming from the pant legs over the soles of their boots. Each man checked the large pocket stitched to his lower left leg for his let-down rope and colored streamers. They slipped braces over their ankles and pulled on thin leather gloves. The gloves not only protected their hands during the landing, but the soft leather enabled them to pick out particular load lines for slipping the chutes if needed.

In addition, each man carried a sheathed knife or a switch-blade attached to the top of the reserve chute. "This was the logical result of a concern that a jumper might become hung on the tail of the plane and have to cut himself loose," according to jumper William S. Laughlin. "[Frank] Derry pointed out that he had tried to reach the tail of airplanes but never succeeded, but that the knife was useful for getting out of trees and other purposes."

The men did not clip the chutes onto their jump harnesses—main pack on back, emergency pack on chest—until the plane approached the fire. Then they donned the football helmets with the steel wire mesh masks that protected their faces from being scraped off by branches and stubs. Although Stanley did not record an account of his first fire jump, he probably experienced many of the same things that another CPSer, Frank Neufeld, went through. Neufeld recalled,

> About twenty minutes from the fire, we began putting on our back packs and emergency parachutes. Then we saw the fire on top of a ridge, near a river that looked like a silver ribbon in morning sunlight.
>
> We circled the ridge and picked out grassy clearings, where we were supposed to land. They seemed very small from 2,000 feet up. Our forest squad leader put out two drift chutes to find out which way the wind was blowing. We jumped two at a time, myself first in line.
>
> I fastened my static line and knelt at the open door. The plane made allowances for the wind. The plane motors coughed out, and when the plane pitched into a glide, Carter slapped me on the back.
>
> I did not think. I just jumped. I heard the chute crack viciously over me as it opened. Eureka. I had made it, alone in the sky. I began manipulating my chute and soon spotted the grassy opening and landed safely.
>
> Now, the Ford Trimotor made another pass over us and dropped our fire fighting equipment by parachute. On the next pass it dropped our delicious food—K Rations—and sleeping bags.

> We began to build a fire line around the smoldering
> fire and, by dark, had the fire under control. We ate our
> K Rations and crawled into our sleeping bags. Next day
> we stayed to be sure the fire was contained. The third
> day we hiked out to the nearest road and called head-
> quarters for a ride back to camp.
> I had made my first fire jump. No experience in my
> life has been comparable to this time.

Dave Flaccus briefly reminisced of that first jump that "to suddenly find ourselves drifting down to dense vegetation and
tall trees on a mountain ridge was a great thrill."

Although Stanley, Flaccus, and Zimmerman impressed Forest Service officials with their efforts in putting out their first
fire, their bosses were less impressed by their sartorial splen-
dor. Stanley, with his newly acquired sewing skills learned in
the parachute loft, had patched and darned together a denim
work outfit for himself. He was "pretty proud of the life and
service I had added to the jacket and pants." But the ranger
who picked them up after the fire apparently was a little embarrassed by the state of the smoke jumpers' clothes. "He had the
tact not to mention it to me but apparently [he] was very persuasive with Fire Control at Region I headquarters," Stanley
wrote. "He and my outfit were responsible for getting us a
clothing allowance thereafter."[1]

Earl Cooley gave a more graphic account of the episode.
"While fighting the fire, one man's pants fell apart and his
other clothes were nearly worn out. The ranger at Pierce,
Idaho, bought him a pair of bib overalls. Incidentally, it took
two years to pay for those overalls. The ranger drove the men
back to Missoula by car. He couldn't send them by train with
such clothes." A few days later, Cooley contacted the Washington office. "With almost an act of Congress, provisions were
made to buy logger boots, two pair of pants, three shirts,
socks and gloves for each man."[2]

Over the next few summers, about 250 CPSers got a chance to hit the silk and dig fire line. Most calls were routine, but others, thanks to unforeseen accidents, turned into nightmares. James Brunk looked forward to an enjoyable day of digging fire line as his parachute floated down toward a small fire in the Bitterroot Mountains outside Hamilton, Montana. Seven others waited to follow him out of the plane. Once the line was dug, he could expect a relaxing afternoon of scanning the ashes for tendrils of smoke emanating from remnant embers. By day's end, the crew would take off their gloves and cold trail the fire, feeling with bare hands for hot spots under logs or in deep ash. If they spotted no telltale smokes, they would hike out the following day.

A Mennonite from Edgelawn Crest in Harrisonburg, Virginia, Brunk planned to attend medical school after the war ended. He did not know that he would soon be wishing he already had that degree. After an adjustment to his drift to avoid hitting a tall snag, Brunk tucked and rolled as he hit the ground in the center of the small clearing. He then scrambled to his feet and waved his streamer to the circling airplane to signal the spotter that he was all right. Moments later, two more brilliant white chutes burst open below the Tin Goose. At two thousand feet the chutes seemed to float like thistledown in the air, but as they came closer, they could be seen to fall faster, like wet oak leaves dropping in autumn.

"Watch out," Brunk shouted as one jumper, Archie Keith, swooped in too close over the trees. For a moment Brunk stood terrified as he watched Keith's foot catch the top of an eighty-foot snag. The dead wood snapped off, and the chute folded around Keith, who dropped to the ground like a stone. The upper third of the tree followed him down.

Brunk was not the only one who thought he might have a corpse on his hands. As Keith plummeted toward a pile of brush and rocks below, he also thought that he was a goner, since the splintered treetop seemed to be headed right for him. Upon impact, Keith fractured his right leg near the hip, breaking off a six-inch sliver. His left leg broke near the ankle. But the thick trunk of the tree landed a few feet away with a bone-rattling crash. "I heard the tree hit, I must not be dead," Keith thought.

Brunk quickly wriggled out of his chute harness to attend to Keith, who frantically called out in pain. The other six jumpers had all hung up in trees, but no one was hurt. When they assembled over Keith, they realized that he needed medical attention right away, and they forgot about lining the fire that night. After splinting Keith's leg as best they could, the men cut thin lodgepole pine trees to form twelve-foot shafts, Then they partially rolled their jump jackets around the poles to create a makeshift stretcher. The sun was already setting. One man, the lightest of the team, stayed to monitor the fire as the others prepared for a long night of hiking and hauling: the nearest road waited sixteen miles away.

Carey Evans, Jim Mattocks, Al Thiessen, Johnny Johnson, Brunk, and another man picked up their charge and began the long trek, struggling through head-high brush and a carpet of deadfall that littered the forest floor. Tall snags also often blocked their path. After a short while, they put down their burden, and one of them returned to the fire to retrieve two pulaskis. As the others waited with Keith, Brunk and Thiessen set out ahead, tools in hand, to clear a rough trail. In the dark they made slow progress hacking through the brush. They sweated over and cursed the big logs that blocked their path. Ahead, spooked animals crashed through the brush. Each time they had progressed a hundred yards, they would lay down their tools and walk back to help carry the stretcher forward. Their ordeal was only one example of the danger and hard work that the CPS smoke jumpers could anticipate whenever they dropped to a fire.

During the course of his thirteenth jump, Clarence Dirks of Durham, Kansas, found himself hurtling headfirst toward the earth, his parachute fluttering behind him, half opened. Dirks, whose family immigrated to Idaho after the depression, had worked in the woods as a teenager, felling trees with a two-man crosscut saw, skidding logs with a team of horses, and cross hauling logs onto trucks for the journey to the mill. He then attended Forest Service guard training and was stationed at a remote lookout on Cut-Off Peak in northern Idaho before the war. He recalled, "I would check in every day, and on damp days when the fire danger was low the ranger would let me hike down to the stream toward the end of the day and catch a few trout. Good times." When he received his draft notice, Dirks faced the turmoil that tore apart many CPSers: "Which way to go? Stay with my upbringing as a pacifist, or go along with our government. I decided to go with my family's identity, although I stayed in this mental whirlpool throughout the war."

Stationed first at a CPS camp in Downey, Idaho, Dirks spent a year breaking rock with a sledgehammer. The crushed rock was used to line irrigation ditches. "There was only one good thing about that place," he recalled. "The Mormon girls in the area gave great parties for the CPS men and we all enjoyed that immensely." A year later, Dirks was chosen for the smoke jumper program, thanks in part to his old boss, who had transferred from Idaho to Missoula. But Dirks may have had regrets about volunteering for such a position as he found himself plummeting upside down toward Glacier National Park. "I pulled the rip cord [of the emergency chute] and it fluttered out," he later said. "Normally it would have gone over my head, but I was falling head first and it went over my feet instead. I grabbed the silk and put it over my head, and it opened with the shroud lines wound around my neck. I couldn't look down but when I saw a tree top go by I knew I was ready to land." Needless to say, he survived.

Phil Thomforde, who grew up near Newtown, Pennsylvania, also realized that something had gone wrong during a jump when he found himself floating down on his back with a clear view of a cloudless blue sky. He found it eerily quiet. He later observed, "It didn't take long in this quietness to realize that my chute had not opened automatically, so I quickly reached behind me and ripped the chute cover off. Usually on jumping there would be the jolt as the chute opened up, but this time I really felt it. My glasses might have been lost were it not for the screen on the helmet that covered my face. By this time I hardly had time to pick a landing spot."[3]

Dirks and Thomforde could count themselves among the ranks of the luckiest CPSers. Although no U.S. Forest Service jumper has yet to die because of a malfunction of a round parachute, a couple have been killed after shroud lines wrapped around their necks, and several others have suffered broken bones and injured backs from parachuting.

But surviving the jump was just the beginning. Once on their first fire, the CPSers quickly realized that the fun was over. For many, the experience of digging fire line in stifling heat for up to sixteen hours a day dispersed any illusion that smoke jumping encompassed only the enthralling adrenaline rush that accompanied a leisurely float down from heaven.

After seven training jumps at Ninemile, Ralph Miller thought that "certainly, no work could be this enjoyable." A few fires later, he changed his mind: "The work was hard, the rationale was lacking—several days work on a fire for a thirty minute airplane ride and a two minute parachute jump. I did feel a bit cheated when Merle Hoover and I jumped on one fire, but ended up extinguishing five fires before we left."

CPSer Lee Hebel quickly discovered that exhaustion was one of the most frequently used words in the firefighter lexicon. Those small lightning strikes could flare up and cover so much ground so quickly that a firefighter often felt that ten thousand miles of fire line could not contain it. On one occasion, sixteen additional jumpers joined Hebel on the ground, as there seemed to be fires everywhere. Hebel wrote,

> We started at the stream, on the left flank, building line, throwing dirt—if we could find any among the rocks—on the hot spots. Sawing, chopping, watering down. Mornings were fine, but sweat, work, struggle as we would, when that afternoon hot sun and strong wind went to work, what were young, strong COs to do?
>
> One afternoon as we struggled on a steep area, I believe it was Paul Graber who stated it for all of us. Exhausted, as he crumbled to the ground, he pled, "Dear God, give us strength." He did. When shadows lengthened, after we cleaned up in the stream fed by melting snow, we had a good supper provided by the fire cook, and a sound sleep in those goose downs, until the first rays of dawn.
>
> After a quick breakfast, it was on the line again. And things looked good until the cruel afternoons when the temperature, mountainside, and smoke jumpers would heat up again. Every day that fire grew in spite of all we could do. I don't know how many men were finally fighting the fire.
>
> We were all but exhausted, when on the eighth day we were told to hike out. Smoke chasers came to mop up. Some of these men carried snow in buckets from the northeast side of the border ridge to throw on the Idaho side.[4]

The whole philosophy behind smoke jumping was to hit freshly ignited fires before they had a chance to spread. After most lightning strikes, the negligible flames quickly died down to smolder in the duff. Alan Inglis once jumped a fire that was so small the spotter was "afraid we would not find it once on the ground unless we landed on top of it." The pilot glided in at six hundred feet as Inglis and his partner hit the silk. Inglis noted, "That meant as soon as the chute opened we should be prepared to land, and we did. I landed so close to the fire that I could see the smoke." After shedding their jumping gear, the two dug a fire line around the tree that had been hit. Inglis recalled, "The circle must have been only about as big as a little kid's merry-go-round. Then, what do you do with a smoldering smoke? Well, nature called, so that helped. In fact, it helped so much that we drank all the water we could and peed out the fire."

But once in a while, especially on hot afternoons, the right amount of wind would whip a fire into a force to be reckoned with. As the Ford Trimotor approached the Meadow Creek Fire in the Nez Perce National Forest of northern Idaho, CPSer Roy Piepenburg gauged the scene playing out below:

> I vividly remember the pillars of billowing, gray-black smoke, the occasional leaping orange fingers of flames, and the aroma of acrid, hot gases as we got within jumping range. As we circled the conflagration, we would see through the patches of smoke a silvery thread deep in the valley—Meadow Creek. My heart ached at the sight of towering Douglas firs torching on the steep mountain sides below.

> With near perfect precision, a crew of eight perspiring jumpers lined up in the cabin preparing to depart from the pitching, banking Ford Trimotor. Then, very carefully orchestrated, two jumpers at a time descended, landed and rolled into a welcome green meadow close to the creek.

Some of us commenced digging firelines on the precipitous slopes, while others set up fire camp. The sound of pulaskis slashing through the brush and the occasional pinging, ringing as they tapped hidden rocks, filled the air.

After midday, when hot, turbulent winds raced up the slopes above Meadow Creek, the crews stood with silent resignation—the fire was now fully crowned and out of control. Red hot embers drifted to the opposite side of the scenic canyon and spot fires erupted here and there. The command came out: "It's going to the ridge top. We can't hold it. Drop your tools and packs and run to the valley. There's water down there."

Grimy and hot, we rested, fearful of what the outcome might be.

Bob Searles, who also worked the Meadow Creek Fire, recalled stopping for a rest that was all too short as a tree he leaned against literally exploded into flame. Searles quickly followed the deer, rabbits, and a bear into the nearest creek. With his crewmates, he recalled, "We would duck under the water, and then come up for air, and get soaking wet again. There must have been enough oxygen near the water to give us breathing space. When the crowning was over, we climbed out and went back to work on the fire. We had no relief crew to come in and mop up, so we stayed on the fire until it was out cold, and then hiked out to get a ride to Missoula."

Merlo M. Zimmerman and his three-man crew barely escaped another blowup. They first reached the blaze about eleven in the morning and started digging fire line. Two hours later, the temperature had soared to more than one hundred degrees. Then the wind came up. Zimmerman recalled, "The fire seemed to smolder for a few seconds and then simply exploded, jumping about fifty yards at a time, often uprooting mature trees just by the force of the blast." He continued, "We fled from the fire, buried our parachutes and jumping gear and prepared to submerge in a nearby stream. Fortunately about that time the wind changed and the fire came back down on the ground. We quickly went back to our job."

Less obvious perils were also associated with firefighting. While taking a lunch break during one fire, Alfred Thiessen and his crew witnessed a very common danger as they ate their K rations. They had hunkered down near a cold spring when, according to Thiessen, "suddenly we heard a crashing noise followed by more of the same. In an opening in the brush we saw a large rock two feet or more in diameter come bounding down the hill straight at us. We lost no time in moving over the side to get out of the way. I distinctly remember taking two steps and just then the rock came crashing by us at the exact spot where I had been sitting. Those two steps were necessary; one would not have done it."[5]

Other, more silent killers lurked in the woods. Live trees or dead trees whose roots had been burned out by ground fire could topple unannounced at any moment. Dave Flaccus recalled seeing one of these ghost trees falling toward his crew with only a whisper: "A sighing noise caught our attention and we looked up to see the trunk heading directly at us, and we jumped quickly in opposite directions. The tree crashed exactly between us, splitting the difference."

Then there were times when the only injury that occurred was to a smoke jumper's pride. Poor Calvin Hilty was having a rough enough season in 1945. After two seasons of mostly practice jumps, Hilty was about ready to pack it in. "In fact," he noted, "I had applied for a relief training unit just outside of Washington D.C." Finally, a call came in from the Chelan National Forest in northern Washington for all available jumpers. The men loaded up the carryall and drove to Medford, Oregon, where a U.S. Marines paratroop DC-3 waited at the airstrip. The next morning they awoke at four, arriving at the Wenatchee airport shortly after noon. "The whole town was waiting for us," Hilty observed. "We already felt like heroes." The men devoured a lavish steak dinner with all the trimmings at the best hotel in town. When they returned to the plane, a dozen Forest Service personnel boarded with them to witness the drop. Hilty wrote,

> Well, that was O.K. as we had plenty of room for this historic flight. We circled for half an hour or so to get to 10,000 feet where we were to jump. We were enjoying every minute of it even though the air was rather bumpy. Then I noticed some of the men in green were literally turning a green color to match their suits. They started to scramble for the paper bags and started to heave very seriously.
>
> It was almost humorous until the one I was sitting by missed the bag and a strong whiff of that acrid smell reached me. It made me feel sort of squiggly and I was glad to see the door open and we lined up to jump.
>
> "Oh Lord," I prayed, "I hope I can hold it until I get out of here."
>
> What a relief when I got a breath of fresh air, but with the opening shock of the parachute all of that good dinner started pouring out. I didn't care where I landed. I don't think I even looked down. Apparently I hadn't chewed the steak good enough as the face mask was filling up with that good meal. When I landed in some thorny snow brush I heaved another sigh of relief.
>
> To this day I believe I'm the only smoke jumper that strained a good dinner through his face mask. Maybe I was just too embarrassed to check with any of the rest.[6]

Hilty should have checked. There were others, but their experiences were similar, and one vomit story goes a long way.

A spotter aboard the plane during a fire run tested the nature of the winds by dropping small chutes and gauging how far they blew and how quickly they dropped. If the winds blew too hard, the jumpers would be unable to negotiate their chutes to safe landing areas. During one of his jumps, Laurel R. Sargent found out just how rough riding the winds could be.

Sargent was born in Ness County, Kansas, in a stone house built on the side of a hill "where the wind blew the door open, or shut, depending on its direction." During the depression, he later observed, "the dust blew into six-foot drifts around the stone house, the grass died, the well went dry, and grasshoppers blew in droves." The family survived with "twenty stock cows, four milk cows, four head of work horses, two mules, chickens, turkeys, and no cash flow to worry about since there was no cash."

While in CPS, Sargent first worked at a job building fence line, rain or shine. He learned of the smoke jumper program in 1944.

On this particular fire run, the light Travelaire plowed though rough air for more than an hour to reach the sizable fire in Idaho, where it burned above the steep canyon of the Salmon River. Sargent described the jump:

> We were hanging on to anything available. . . . We made one pass and John yelled, "I'll fly low and drop you on the hillside away from the river." He tossed out a drift chute which promptly disappeared. The pilot managed to bring the Travelaire around and on the second pass I struggled into the door opening, hanging on for dear life, the plane tipped to the right, Johnny pounded me on the back and out I went.
>
> I looked up and saw the tail go overhead, and then collected beautiful strawberry marks on my body when the chute opened. I tried to locate the landing site, but the wind took me up and over the ridge top at forty

miles per hour clearing the snags by at least two hundred feet. About then I noticed the Travelaire had
turned and headed for the safety of the McCall airport
to fly again on a safer day. They didn't even wait around
to see where I landed or if I ever did.

By then I was floating out over the river canyon and
to my dismay, I noticed that instead of getting closer to
the ground, the ground was getting farther away and
the river was getting closer. It occurred to me that the
time had come to try the slipping maneuver that they
had taught us at Ninemile, so I started pulling the lines
down. Either it worked or the wind let up because the
ground started getting closer and when I finally crashed
into the rocky hillside, it felt like a featherbed.

Each jump and each fire became a classroom for the men,
with the subjects often expanding beyond fire and parachuting. The men learned much about their physical and mental
limits as well as the nature of the north woods. "On almost
every fire we had experiences and learned something new,"
observed Dave Flaccus. "How to escape a raging crown fire by
dropping into a small stream bed, hiking endless miles up a
trail from the Salmon River breaks to a landing strip, how a
scorching September day could turn into a freezing snow-
storm overnight."

William S. Laughlin, who was raised in Oregon, found that
ultimate knowledge of smoke jumping lay in the sum of the
details: "The orderly process of packing parachutes, testing
and jumping them, and dropping drift chutes and spotting
the jumpers in the most advantageous place, and then joining them last, became a process in which small variations provided enlargements of details."

The son of a Carnegie librarian, Laughlin had grown potatoes in vacant lots near his home to earn money. He also

picked fruit, worked in a cannery, and pitched hay bales. By the time he volunteered for CPS, he was used to hard work. "My most interesting job," he recalled, "was that of a rock mucker for a cement quarry. It was necessary to lift large stones overhead into a tram car. Drillers and powder monkeys blew off large elements of limestone. Then we broke them into liftable size stones with rock hammers. The more you could lift, the less hammering you needed to do." While working at the quarry, Laughlin formed a lifelong interest in fossils. He frequently discovered shark teeth, crabs, and cephalopods in the rock. Laughlin had earned a masters degree from Haverford College before being drafted. His thesis focused on "the relation between race information and race prejudice." He joined the CPS smoke jumpers in 1943.

On one jump, Laughlin had to improvise a new exit technique while jumping from a plane on which the rear door had not been removed. He wrote, "Each time I opened the door it was blown shut again before I could emerge. Finally, after three or more passes, I found that my back pack was too high for the door so I successfully crawled out. Frank Derry told me afterward that he was about to suggest that I take the parachute off so I could fit through the door."

For some men, the challenges of backwoods life presented even more elementary problems to solve—such as learning how to dissolve the lemonade tablets that came with the K rations. The rations were packed in small waxed boxes measuring about eight inches by four inches by two inches. Each man carried six K rations, or enough for two days. The menu included canned potted meats, cheese, biscuits, and the lemonade tablets. "Except there was no kind of container to mix [the lemonade] in," wrote Alan Inglis. "One of the fellows put the tablet in his aluminum canteen. It dissolved all right, including some of the aluminum. That was a sick CO and we all learned a lesson—don't put an acid in aluminum canteens."

Inglis also thought it would be a good idea to learn how to smoke, reasoning that he would then be able to tolerate more smoke from fires. He made a pipe out of reeds and a hollow twig and borrowed some tobacco. He noted, "I learn slowly, so never mastered smoking of any kind." Inglis did learn how to stay warm on a fire during the night with no sleeping bag. He rolled over a burning log, scraped the hot ashes away, and then lay down on the warm ground. "When we were roused in the morning," he wrote, "I glanced at my socks and there were lots of little burn holes in them and several in the rest of my clothes, but what a wonderful sleep."

For Maynard Shetler, a crucial test of survival involved learning how to boil water without a pot. On a fire near Priest River, Idaho, the men discovered that part of their rations had spoiled, leaving nothing but bouillon to sustain them. However, the bread can in which they usually boiled water had been crushed. Shetler recalled, "I had read somewhere that you can boil water in a paper bag. So we took the paper bag our flashlight batteries were in and filled it half full of water. We cleared a place on the ground in the middle of our campfire and set it down to watch a 'miracle.' The bag burned down to the level of the water. Soon the water boiled. We gave three cheers, dumped in our bouillon and then used our empty cheese cans to dip out our hot drink."[7]

During early August, many CPSers discovered the joy of eating wild foods. While clearing a fire line through the underbrush, John Ainsworth and his crew "went through several patches of huckleberries, at their very best, and a lot of them. So, as we worked along, we could grab handfuls of them to eat. This was my first introduction to them."[8]

Most CPSers became enamored with smoke jumping. They thought it one of the grandest ideas ever formulated, and they wholeheartedly stood behind the system. But there were a few who perceived some flaws in it.

Edwin Vail was among the latter group. Born in Media, Pennsylvania, Vail had grown up in Pasadena, California. His family "always sat down together for breakfast and supper. After supper, dad read the Bible or other spiritual book which we discussed a bit before being allowed to leave the table to play." Vail attended Whittier College after high school, and there he mowed the lawns around the female dorms to pay for his clothes. When he told his draft board that he would apply for conscientious objector status as a Quaker, the head of the board told him "they couldn't guarantee that I could finish college unless I promised to use my chemistry knowledge in a defense plant." Instead of finishing school, Vail volunteered for CPS.

His only gripe about his stay at the camp at Tanbark Flats in California was the "gripers": "If they didn't like CPS, they didn't have to choose class 4-E. There was jail or the armed forces. For me, CPS was fine. It was too bad that a war was the cause of it. Otherwise, I wouldn't have minded ten or more years of the kind of work I did."

Turned down by the Forest Service in 1943, Vail attained a smoke jumper slot the following summer. On August 27, 1945, he was part of a crew dispatched to a fire northwest of Lincoln, Montana. On that trip he became somewhat soured about the whole program and its cost to taxpayers. Vail recalled,

> Three air flights had been made in an effort to find the fire. I was on the fourth flight in the Travelaire when we finally found the fire. Meanwhile the lookout man who had reported the fire had told the Forest Service in Missoula that his wife could run the lookout while he walked over to the small fire and put it out. The office reply was, "No, we will have the smoke jumpers put it out."

After at last finding the fire, we noted that there was a strong wind and if we jumped near the fire, we might land way down in a canyon and then have a long climb to get to the fire. Therefore, our spotter had us jump near the lookout. We then made the same hike to the fire that the lookout man wanted to do in the first place. Arriving at the fire we built it up hot enough, cooked supper on it and put it out easily.

The next day we went back to the lookout where there was a trail, and had an eleven mile hike to the nearest transportation. Forest Service mules had been brought to carry out our chutes and equipment. A Forest Service truck took us to Lincoln where we caught a bus to Helena. There, we caught a train and rode back to Missoula. There was all of that huge expense when one lookout man could have done the same job. We had an enjoyable flight and jump, a trip at the tax-payers' expense. What a waste.[9]

Jumping the fire often proved the simplest part of the process. Returning to the base became more challenging. Usually the men hiked out through wilderness to the nearest trail, but George Anderson received unique instructions on how to get home from one of his assignments. Before Anderson's plane took off, a ranger handed him a bag of nails and told him to build a raft to get back. After extinguishing the fire, he and his crewmates did just that. He wrote,

We loaded our equipment on the raft, which was barely afloat when the three of us got on. I must have been elected captain and was given the pole and told to keep the upstream end of the raft just enough into the current so that it would take us across the river. Everything went fine for a short distance, and then the raft turned end for end, which put me on the downstream end of it. It then proceeded to take us down a set of rapids among huge boulders everywhere. As we were going down the river I would go into the water up to my knees as the front end of the raft took a nose dive. We finally got ashore on the right side of the river about a quarter mile below the Forest Service truck waiting to pick us up.[10]

As they became more experienced, the men gained confidence in their firefighting skills. They located spot fires by sniffing the air; they roamed through vast roadless tracts with only a compass to guide them. But no matter how much time they spent in the backcountry, they could end up looking like fools under certain situations.

So noted Asa Mundell and Al Cramer when they were dispatched on foot to a fire one evening. After parking the pickup truck by the side of the road, they hiked uphill about a mile or so. Al suggested that Asa stay with the packs while Al located and scouted the fire. The lookout had estimated that the smoke was no more than one hundred yards away from the road. A few minutes later Al returned, claiming that he could find no fire but had spotted a smoke up to the north. So the men repacked their gear and headed off on a wild-goose chase, according to Mundell:

> It was getting dark and off we went, trying to keep the smoke in sight of our compass reading, while stumbling down rocky slopes, fording streams, and clawing our way up those steep hills in the dark with our headlights doing little if any good at all.
>
> About one in the morning, we finally reached a flat spot and Al suggested we sleep there and at sunup try to find the fire. I was ready for that, and that little silk and

down sleeping bag was just what I needed. At daybreak
we crawled out. Al indicated he knew now about where
the fire was, and told me to lay out some K rations, and
make some coffee. Al came back in a few minutes, and
said, "We came to the wrong fire, this one is on the
Indian Reservation and we can't work on it. I guess we
have to go back to camp."

So it was off up the hills, climb the cliffs, ford the
streams, and at last find the ridge, and the earlier fire
site. Still no fire. We ran down the hill, got in the pickup
and arrived back at Camp Huson about four-thirty p.m.
Al went in the office and made his report to Earl.

The smoke turned out to have emanated from the top of a
tall snag at the very location first reported. While Cramer and
Mundell humped over hill and dale, a Forest Service
employee had located the smoke, chopped down the tree,
and extinguished the embers. He also told his superiors that
he had found a fresh candy-bar wrapper at the base of the
tree. Mundell suspected Cramer of hoarding. At a reunion in
1989, Earl Cooley reminded Mundell about the incident:
"You guys stood around eating candy bars right under the
tree that was on fire."[11]

On September 10, 1944, the smoke jumpers established
the first full-scale fire camp on the Bell Lake Fire that burned
132 acres, high up on the state divide between Idaho and
Montana. Eight men stationed at Seeley Lake first jumped
the fire. Two days later, thirteen more parachuted in. The Trimotor also dropped a marine pump for use at the lake. Soon
after sunrise on Sunday morning, another squad of eight
men landed with their squad leader, Wag Dodge, who had
been discharged from the army. (In 1949, Dodge would be
one of three survivors of the first tragedy in smoke jumper
history, when a fire killed twelve smoke jumpers and one dis-

trict firefighter at Mann Gulch near the Gates of the Mountains on the Missouri River near Helena, Montana.) The personnel on the fire numbered twenty-nine, a smoke jumper record at that time. Later, a Trimotor dropped boxes of food and equipment. "Because the plane failed to identify the spot by the lake chosen as a fire camp site, the half-dozen planeloads of cargo dropped in the small meadow we had used as a jumping spot, fully a half mile from the camp site," noted Delbert Barley.

Camp cook Dale Yoder, his kitchen helpers—Hubert Rohrer and James Spangler—and two others retrieved the cargo, erected camp, and prepared supper. The jumpers loved the setup. "This, our first relief from dry K rations, tasted delicious," Barley wrote. "Hot meals, more variety in food, a chance to wash and rest up—all these make an organized fire camp vastly preferable to the each-man-for-himself anarchy prevailing before."

On Sunday, nine more men hiked into camp from Darby and Stevensville, to bring the total to forty-one people. As seen through Barley's eyes, camp life was orderly and civilized:

> Approaching the camp along the trail from the fire, the weary firefighter crossed a small creek and immediately stood in the camp clearing. First he deposited his shovel or pulaski in the tool rack by the trail on the right. Fifty feet beyond and to the left he saw the serving table, back of which lay the kitchen with its two stoves and stores of canned goods, oranges, eggs, cookies, and fresh beef—covered by a tent.
>
> Seventy-five yards off the trail to the right were the wash basins at the edge of the lake, with towels hanging on low branches. Close by the trail a pit held a fire at which men could warm and dry themselves. Farther

down the trail the pack mules stood tied to trees, patiently waiting. After a hot supper, tired firefighters rolled out their sleeping bags wherever they could find a level and unoccupied spot.

As happened with many large September fires, snow eventually snuffed out the Bell Lake Fire. The men trudged out with their full fire packs.

No CPS smoke jumper died fighting a fire, although some suffered minor burns. But many barely escaped death and serious injury when landing near the fires. The men had been trained to maneuver their chute so that they could drape the canopy over a treetop in thickly wooded areas. Instructors warned them to avoid hanging the chutes in dead trees, called snags; those rotten, phantom killers could topple or break with the slightest vibration. But even live trees provided their own sources of danger when it came to getting down from them. Jumpers often had to be resourceful to reach ground safely. "I remember one time landing in the top of a snag, next to a green fir," wrote Norman Zook, who grew up on a two-hundred-acre farm at Mio, Michigan. "I thought it would be easy to get to the ground by swinging over to the fir, unstrapping myself from the parachute and climbing down the tree. It was easy going at first, but then I ran out of limbs and the trunk of the tree kept getting bigger and bigger. The bark of the tree was so that I was able to dig in with my fingers and toes until I was close enough to the ground to drop."

Some men found themselves in such dire predicaments after being suspended in trees that they needed help getting down. In one instance, Ralph Spicer found himself hanging upside down with his chute draped below him. His left heel had caught in a notch of a snag about forty-five feet up. His friend, George H. Robinson, found humor in the situation. Years later, Robinson noted, "Always a man who can make the

best of things, Ralph took advantage of this unique posture to
devise several new folk dances of the New-Hungarian school.
Jim Waite finally interrupted this reverie, in a masterful
demonstration of climbers and rope, and lowered Ralph to
the ground."[12]

But Robinson did not escape his own embarrassing
moment, when he was jumping in a high wind and his foot
also got caught in a tree. He recalled,

> This partially deflated my chute, and it blew on past me
> and below, pulling me out of my tree. I then had the
> unique sensation of making a beautiful fifty-foot swan
> dive, falling head first toward rocks and logs. Always the
> perfectionist, I was just extending my arms and arching
> my body to make as little splat as possible when my
> chute snagged on a lower tree, caught me up short and
> ruined my flawless trajectory by swinging me into a tree
> trunk, a few feet off the ground. There are those who
> report that the tree trunk suffered bruises.[13]

CPSer David Flaccus spent his early youth in Europe,
where his father helped assemble an Impressionist art collection (now known as the Barnes Collection, in Philadelphia) for millionaire Albert C. Barnes. David spent his first
grade in a French school but, in his words, "learned
absolutely nothing." Back in the states, Flaccus attended
Quaker schools in Philadelphia, thanks to his mother, whom
he described as "a hater of war and an active worker for
peace in such organizations as the War Resisters League."
During the summers, the Flaccus clan vacationed in upstate
New York and New Hampshire.

After the war, Flaccus learned the printing trade and publishing business. He bought a small press in Portland, Maine,
and moved it to Missoula to begin Mountain Press. The

company became successful with the publication of the popular Roadside Geology and Roadside History series.

On one fire jump out of Missoula, Flaccus had to let himself down from a giant ponderosa pine. "I had landed exactly
on top," he recalled, "had climbed down the branches to the
last limb and found I was still eighty to one hundred feet from
the ground. Nothing to do but use the special rope, drop the
last ten or twelve feet, head for the fire, and worry about the
chute later." When he hit the ground, Flaccus thought that
the worst was over. All he had to do after putting the fire out
was don the climbing spikes to retrieve the chute. But after
studying the tree trunk up to the first branch he was overcome "with mounting concern." With the climbing spikes
strapped to his ankles, he tossed a rope around the tree trunk
and took the ends in both hands. The rope allowed him to
lean back a little from the tree as he climbed to keep the
spikes from slipping out of the bark. At camp he had been
trained to flip the rope up as he climbed, but the technique
would not work on the old-growth pine, for the rope kept
snagging on the large, rough plates of the tree's bark. Eventually, Flaccus gave up on the rope. He noted, "It was a very
scary trip up, hanging on to the bark with my hands, but I did
make it and succeeded in retrieving the chute."

Good luck had followed these men down through the
skies, but others were less fortunate. Alan Inglis and another
CPSer ran into some trouble when they jumped a fire in the
evening, after the wind had supposedly abated. With a loud
thud, Inglis smashed into a tree trunk about three feet in
diameter. He recalled,

> Both feet hit about the same time both hands hit the
> tree. Both legs and arms embraced the tree and my
> whole body hit, including my face mask. I repeat. I was

lucky because my whole body absorbed the shock. My buddy was not so lucky.

He hit a smaller tree with one foot, which broke his ankle. The tree collapsed his chute and dropped him onto a rock, which chipped his hip. I called over to him immediately and he said he was hurt. My let down by rope was at my fastest. He was in pain but not complaining and I immediately signaled the plane with the bright colored steamers that one man was hurt. Then I proceeded to try to keep him comfortable.

I had some strong capsules that the nurse had given me [for a former injury] and I also propped our reserve chutes to cover him and keep him as warm as possible during the night. As it got dark, we could see the glow of the fire we had jumped on. I called and thought I heard someone answer. But we had no more contact. After doing all I could, I went to sleep. I was awakened by rescuers who brought a stretcher. Then we proceeded to carry him out.[14]

Four men carried the stretcher while one person led the way with an axe, trying to determine the best route through the woods. "I don't know which was hardest, carrying or leading," Inglis recalled. "I always carried extra socks which I used this time to tie my hands to the stretcher. It was my hands which gave out first carrying that stretcher." After hours of stumbling through the underbrush in the dark, the rescue team finally discovered a trail, where a horse waited to carry the injured man to a truck. He cried out in pain as the others lifted him into the saddle. But all ended well. Inglis wrote, "Our rescuers pulled out a bottle and told him to drink as much as he could. We had one of the drunkest, happiest, injured Mennonites you ever saw."

During another rescue, Ollie Huset, who had suffered a concussion during a landing, amused some of his rescuers on the way out. "It seems while the stretcher crew was carrying him," wrote Earl Schmidt, "he took pity on them and suggested, 'Why don't one of you get down here and let me help carry this thing a while?' Ad Carlson's reply was, 'Lay down, Ollie, you're rocking the boat.'"

Probably no jumpers suffered more from a backcountry injury or a rescue attempt than did Archie Keith, introduced at the beginning of this chapter, and the men who carried him out sixteen miles in the dead of night on a makeshift stretcher. In the darkness, James Brunk and his fellow CPSers continued to cut through the thick underbrush a hundred yards ahead before returning to advance the stretcher. By morning, twelve hours after they started, the rescuers had progressed only two miles from the fire site. Finally, they gained an area where the brush thinned under a stand of taller trees. An old trail also materialized, but deadfall and logs still blocked the way and slowed their progress. By mid-morning, the rescuers met up with a pair of Forest Service workers who had been sent out to meet them. These men, carrying a crosscut saw, had already cut most of the fallen trees out of the trail from that point on. The going became easier, but Keith still suffered. By noon, about seven miles from the fire site, a crew of eight fresh jumpers landed in a clearing to take up the burden. With them came a basket stretcher and Doctor Amos Little.

Little was one of a dozen military paradoctors who had trained with the smoke jumpers at the end of 1943. When some of the Forest Service trainers had asked Little what procedures they should follow to request his services, he had answered, "Procedure, nothing—call me." Little, a native of Boston, was based in Laramie, Wyoming. Upon arriving at the scene, he administered morphine to the suffering patient. Then the five-foot-tall doctor-soldier took his turn carrying the stretcher, leaving Brunk and his exhausted fellow CPSers to straggle close behind for the remaining nine miles. When the rescue crew came within sight of a cabin located at the end of the road, Little ran ahead to get a cup of coffee. He and his patient still had a long way to go—a seventy-five-mile ride in the back of a pickup truck, much of it along bumpy dirt roads.

Keith spent two and a half months in the hospital wearing casts from waist to right knee and left thigh, a bar across his mid thighs, and a cast on his left lower leg. On November 10, 1945, the Camp 103 newsletter reported, "Archie has been one of the most cheerful patients we have ever seen. . . . He has never complained or become bitter." The Forest Service paid for his care until the camp closed on the first of October. Then Keith was left to his own resources. Such was the life of a CPS smoke jumper under the test of fire.

CHAPTER TWELVE

Home away from Home

In the spring of 1944, Harold Toews applied to become a CPS smoke jumper. He learned of his acceptance while at home on furlough from a camp in Downey, Idaho, and he then took the train to Missoula.

A Forest Service worker welcomed him at the station and put him on the bus to Ninemile. Toews recalled, "He told me and the bus driver I was to get off at the Ninemile marker and Earl Cooley would meet me there. Well, I fell asleep and suddenly the bus stopped and the driver said, Ninemile Corner. I got off, half asleep and looked for my ride, but nobody was there. I looked at the sign and it said Six Mile Corner. I didn't know which way Ninemile Corner was." Whether or not the driver put him out at the wrong stop on purpose, Toews never found out. Meanwhile, his escort, who waited a few miles down the highway, drove back to camp after the bus passed without discharging a passenger. That night, Toews lay down in a ditch beside the road. Even after putting on all the clothes in his suitcase, he shivered through the night while visions of prowling bears and mountain lions chased off sleep. Toews wrote, "I had never been in a forest before. Needless to say, I heard a lot of noises." The next morning a passing road worker pointed the way to Ninemile, and Toews began the six-mile hike in a new pair of cowboy boots. His feet, he later observed, "were full of blisters by the time I got there."

At the juncture of Remount and Sixmile roads stood the white-clapboarded buildings of the famous Ninemile Remount Depot. During the summer of 1929, the Forest Service had found itself shorthanded to deal with a rash of disastrous wildfires—especially for resupplying firefighters in the backcountry. The following winter, Clyde P. Fickles, who requisitioned pack strings for the regional office in Missoula, wondered "why it was not feasible to have somewhere in the region available on short notice a reservoir of trained and equipped packers and pack strings." Regional Forester Major Evan Kelley, a former cavalry officer during World War I, proposed that the agency establish a remount service similar to that of the U.S. Army. Besides being a site from which packers and animals could be quickly dispatched by truck or rail, the depot would also become a training center.

In 1930, the Forest Service secured the lease to the one-square-mile, unoccupied Allen ranch in the Ninemile Valley. A thirty-plus crew of workers mowed two hundred acres of hay, renovated the irrigation system, and built corrals. They also destroyed all the ranch buildings, hauled in a forest lookout as a temporary office, and built other sheds, while in the meantime the crew bivouacked in wall tents. In 1935, the agency bought the ranch outright. Since pastures were limited at Ninemile, workers built corrals and fenced some fields a few miles from the depot, south of the Clark Fork River, between Albert and Tank creeks. By 1944, hundreds of workers from the Civilian Conservation Corps' Camp Ninemile (located three miles north of the site) had helped transform the depot into a Forest Service showcase, under the direct supervision of W. C. "Cap" Evans and the watchful eye of Major Kelley.

Toews limped up to a series of buildings that included several residences, a bunkhouse, a cookhouse, a powder house, and a large barn made with hand-hewn beams. A log fence surrounded the compound. All the clapboarded buildings, as well as the fence, sported a coating of white paint. Green cedar shingles on the roofs gleamed in the spring sunlight. Across from the big barn stood a smaller barn, where the stud horses did their work. Four Cape Cod–style homes with dormers dotted the lawn, a couple of them with covered front porches. Except for the barns, each building harbored polished hardwood floors.

From 1932 to 1936, the Remount Depot served as a breeding ranch. Each stud had a paddock and corral near the stud barn, while the mares foaled in the pastures. The premier stud was Grand Menard, the five-gaited champion of All Western Shows, which the agency bought at auction for twenty-five hundred dollars. When Grand Menard arrived, he greeted a new entourage of forty mares. "He was a big beautiful sorrel," recalled long-time packer Lee Hames, "but did not seem to sire very good colts. Most of his colts seemed to be stubborn, sullen and slow learners. I broke a couple of colts from the horse and was disappointed in them."[1] But most of the breeding operation centered on mules. With breeding stock including one hundred Percheron mares (large draft horses with dark, often dappled coats), the depot raised sixty to seventy foals per year.

After 1936, the depot also served as a firefighting center and a hay ranch. Ten mule strings grazed in individual pastures, with two strings lingering in nearby corrals on standby. When the big brass fire bell clanged, packers herded the mules up one of two loading docks onto the high, staked bed of an R.E.O. Speedwagon—a specially built Kenworth truck with a Greyhound bus chassis. The ten-wheel Speedwagons also featured a cab-over engine, sleeper cab, and dual axles. Average time for departure of the truck from the clanging of the bell was seventeen minutes.

In the fields around Ninemile, workers baled about six hundred tons of hay each summer. Depot farriers shod about twelve hundred head of stock every year. They first wrapped a haltered mule's lead rope around a wooden rack and then tied it off to a metal rack along the wall—a double hitchrack—to enable an easier escape from ornery mules. However, the men working at the depot were said to be just as ornery. "The three meanest people in the world are a Forest Service cook, the packer, and the blacksmith," one assistant forest supervisor observed.[2]

As Toews walked down the dirt driveway, he noted the smart landscaping with flowering bushes—serviceberry, chokecherry, staghorn sumac. Young Douglas fir trees, maples, and cottonwoods had grown tall enough to begin offering some shade. He stopped to peek inside a log-cabin playhouse sitting on the lawn.

Carpenter Charles Engbretson and his fifteen-member CCC crew had built the six-foot by six-foot structure for four-year-old Marilyn Vierhus, daughter of the CCC camp supervisor. For three weeks the men had sneaked out to the woodlot after dinner and on three consecutive Saturdays to finish the surprise gift.

Camp Ninemile was eventually dismantled as carpenters put the finishing touches on the new camp, Menard—which, being only a mile from the depot, was more convenient for interaction between the CCCs and the Forest Service. The playhouse was moved to the depot grounds during the dismantling of Camp Ninemile. When the four-year-old's family left Ninemile, she tacked a "Keep Out" sign to the door of the playhouse, but in later years she was happy that the miniature log cabin had been preserved for other children to enjoy.[3]

Toews admired the small porch of the playhouse and then peeped in one of the three windows. To his surprise, sunlight gleamed off a varnished floor.

A few moments later, in the administration office, Toews explained his predicament to the dispatcher. A driver from the CPS barracks soon picked him up. As Toews rode the mile in the back of the truck, he marveled at the hundreds of mules—most of which would be auctioned off by 1953—that grazed in pastures behind the barn. (Today, many forest administrators who use mule strings for trail building and other backcountry chores still send their animals to winter at the old Ninemile depot.)

The road Toews traveled to the CPS camp paralleled miles of lanes lined with jackleg fences that led through the woods from one pasture to another. In a couple of weeks, Toews would be practicing parachute landings in some of those same pastures. If he had gone in the opposite direction and followed Ninemile Road west, farther into the valley, he would have passed by the airstrip—a simple lane in a meadow where the grass was mown short.

The road heading north from the remount depot gradually climbed through stands of ponderosa pine to the former CCC barracks at Camp Grand Menard, named after the stud horse. The long, single-story CCC barracks, painted red with white trim, stood in the shade of the pines. Constructed in 1939, Camp Menard had followed the standard CCC camp configuration of twenty-three buildings, including a mess hall and three barracks. On July 1, 1942, Congress had abolished the CCC; a year later, workers removed fourteen buildings from Camp Menard and shipped them to Edmonton, Canada, to house workers constructing the Alaska-Canada Highway—leaving eight buildings intact.

The first building Toews approached was the residence of camp supervisor Roy Wenger and his wife, Florence. "It was more space than we needed," Wenger said later.[4] Next was the administration building, housing the offices of the supervisor and treasurer, a library, and a lounge room. Behind that stood the dining hall. Long wooden tables and benches crowded the front half of the dining hall, while the kitchen occupied the rear. Both the mess hall and the library sported hung ceilings made of plywood, rather than open rafters. Outside the buildings, in the oval, stood a red barrel used for burning trash. The men often gathered at this spot for bull sessions before and after meals. In the open woods, a volleyball net stretched between two trees.

The farthest building was the dormitory. Toews walked into an open room lined on both sides with army cots. Clothes hung from hooks and pegs, and footlockers peeked out from under the beds. Along one wall stood a line of small closets, each shared by two men. Photos and pictures adorned the walls—some religious in nature, some of family, with a smattering of pinups, although the camp matron made sure the decorations were not too risqué. Although many CPS men had already bunked in abandoned CCC camps and were familiar with the rustic architecture, the spirit enveloping CPS Camp No. 103 seemed unique. "Here, everything we did was new," recalled Benjamin W. Case. "The campers even seemed different in their attitude and outlook, perhaps because everyone was here because he wanted to be—a volunteer."

Homer Rice knew from the start that he would enjoy smoke jumping, beginning at the moment he walked into the fraternity house in Missoula that the Forest Service rented from Montana State University as a temporary barracks near the town's airfield. Rice noted,

On entering the administrator's office, a man sitting behind a desk was singing a song that went like this: "To hell with Selective Service, to hell with the administration." I was both shocked and giggled at the same time. The camp I had just come from was a Mennonite Camp run by Mennonite personnel, many of whom were active preachers. Life in these camps were well regimented. Every one complied with all the rules and regulations. One even had to go to the "Blue Room" to smoke and anything unseemly had to be secretive. But here the assistant director was verbalizing my very thought. I love this place.

One pleasant change awaited the new recruit. The three peace churches financed all the CPS camps around the country, so administrators cut corners wherever possible. Usually that meant that the menu, uninteresting to begin with, seldom varied, as Roy L. Piepenburg attested: "My work as a survey crew member on the local Missouri River reclamation project appealed to me, since I had always been an outdoor person. I even learned to accept the frequent meals of cabbage and potato soup, since during the Depression that was one of my family's mainstays." The dietary regimen at Camp 103 was vastly different.

Florence Wenger, the camp nutritionist, had been born and raised along with two younger sisters and a younger brother on a two-hundred-acre farm near Fremont, Ohio, that had been in the family since the early 1800s. She recalled "playing in an almost demolished log cabin which had been their first home." The farm lay on a rich Lake Erie floodplain that produced a liberal harvest of good crops year after year. At age five she "would slip a slice of bread, an apple and a cookie into a little gray granite lunch box and run away to school with the older neighbor children." After graduating as valedictorian of her high school class, Florence enrolled at Bowling Green State University, studying to become a home economist. She abandoned those plans when her mother died when the kerosene kitchen stove exploded. Having the responsibility for her three younger siblings, Florence restricted her education to a two-year diploma in early childhood education and landed a job as a first-grade teacher in her hometown school in Elmore:

> At age eighteen, I replaced a thirty-five year veteran teacher in a classroom of thirty-five children. My salary was $810 but was cut to the state minimum, $800, the second year. Soon the combination first and second grade class was eliminated when the teacher married and my class size increased to fifty-four. The bolted-down desks were put on two-by-four skids so rows could be pushed together, leaving almost no room to move about. During the summers I avidly attended Ohio State by borrowing money and working all year to pay it back just in time to borrow again.

After her brothers and sisters had matured, Florence accepted a similar position in the town of Bexley, Ohio, near the state university where Roy Wenger was working on his doctorate in the Bureau of Educational Research. A month after the couple married in July 1943, Roy's draft number came up, and he became the CPS educational director of Camp No. 5 at Colorado Springs. Florence became the dietitian for the camp, which housed about two hundred men. "Here her home economics education served her well," her husband recalled. "She also had an inherent intelligence that had been tested by her experience of managing a farm family of five. She analyzed situations quickly and saw courses of action ahead which did not require ideal facilities but used what was available." During her six months at the Colorado Springs camp, Florence planned the meals, ordered the food, trained the cooks, and fed the men: "all at ninety-three cents a day," said her husband. Some of the food—potatoes, corn, fruit—came directly from Mennonite farms as gifts.[5]

Although there were only sixty men to feed at the smoke jumpers' camp, Florence faced a new challenge. After sharing the first meal in camp with the CPSers, Earl Cooley pulled Roy Wenger aside. As Wenger later recalled, the one-sided conversation went something like this:

> The Forest Service has a long tradition of how to keep men on the job. One important aspect is to feed them unusually well. See to it that they get the finest steaks, the most tasty desserts, and as much as they want to eat. That will keep them going on the fireline and through the deep snow of winter. Florence is doing very well with the money she spends, but we would like a little richer menu. We will bring in a long-time experienced Forest Service cook to work along with your CPS cooks and he will know how to proceed in a traditional way.[6]

The new menu included steaks almost every night, fresh milk, and two desserts. CPSers, resigned to coming last on any priority list, were astonished. David S. Yoder, who later became a cook at Idaho's Moose Creek camp, found it "hard to get adjusted to such good meals." Another CPSer, Chalmer C. Gillin, testified that the conscientious objector smoke jumpers stationed at Cave Junction, Idaho, "ate like kings."

Mealtime at the smoke jumpers' training camp quickly became a major event. Because the men often split up on different projects throughout the day, breakfast and supper provided the best opportunities for the entire community to come together. Each meal generated much excitement and anticipation, not only for the quality of food, but also for the camaraderie. At first, Cooley and other Forest Service personnel tried to institute the gag rule during mealtime, a tradition in logging camps.

If the following description of loggers by Elers Koch, an early forester, is accurate, then Cooley badly misread the character of the CPSers: "A lumberjack is rarely a light-hearted individual, if not morose. One hears little of laughter or jokes in a logging camp. The men eat their enormous meals silently, and sit in the bunkhouses or outside them, tired from the heavy work that necessarily goes with the job of manhandling big logs. It is not that the men are worn out by over-hard work, but heavy manual labor day by day seems to affect a man's nature and take some of the joy out of life."[7]

The garrulous CPSers were a different breed, according to John Scott, a farmboy from Minnesota. When they had a chance to associate with other like-minded fellows, any authority would have found it impossible to stifle their shared interests and goodwill. As for the logger's etiquette, Scott said, "They tried hard to hold to that rule but when you consider they were dealing with a bunch of COs, they gave up and joined in."

Like many men who did not belong to a peace church, Scott had had some trouble convincing his draft board of his sincerity. He recalled that the board members

> were definitely not going to have any COs and that was final, so I jumped back and forth between 1-A and the farming. I kept on appealing and finally in 1943 they said, "You stay home and farm." This tempted me because my dad was seventy-three at the time. But I appealed again. The draft board then sent a federal judge up from the cities. He was a tough looking old boy and I thought, "Here comes Leavenworth." But he

was fair. He said, "I see you've been offered a chance to farm. I think you're sincere." So it was off to CPS. My dad passed away just about a year after I left. He had a heart attack while out feeding livestock at minus twenty degrees Fahrenheit.

Sometimes the men faced a hit-or-miss meal, especially during that first spring training session at Seeley Lake. Camp director Roy Wenger thought that the cook, who prepared three meals a day for seventy men that year, should have at least one day off during the week. Consequently, he assigned two-man teams to relieve the cook once a week. When Norman Kriebel and his partner received the assignment, they found themselves in a predicament. Kriebel confessed to having no cooking experience, and he later noted, "My partner (who shall remain nameless) pleaded equal ignorance. By the appointed day our qualms got the better of us and we tried to get Roy to let us off the hook. Roy gave us a cheerful brush-off and said to get on with it."

About two-thirty in the afternoon, the rookie cooks found the regular cook still hanging around the kitchen on his day off. When they asked him what he was doing, he casually replied that he had "really no place to go." The two novices questioned him about the location of pots and pans and asked if any supplies were off-limits. The cook affirmed that they could use anything, and then he ambled away. After a quick inspection, the two CPSers found that the supply room resembled Mother Hubbard's cupboard with "a two or three pound bone with a few scraps of meat on it, plus a sack of potatoes, some carrots and a few onions . . . about five cans of vegetables, three of them institutional size, an ample supply of bread, and a can of coffee."

When the regular cook reentered the kitchen, Kriebel asked, "How could this have happened? You can't make dinner for seventy people on this."

"It's all we got," the cook muttered, and then he left the building again.

"Cook was an enigma to me; who was he?" Kriebel recalled thinking. "What were his real feelings toward us? Could he be determined to show these religious objectors they couldn't repeat the miracle of the loaves and fishes? Or was he also a victim?" After reviewing the ingredients they had to work with, the two planned to concoct some beef vegetable soup, one of Kriebel's mother's most popular dishes. Kriebel described their venture:

> We found a very large pot, perhaps twenty gallons or more, and put a lot of water in it while revving up the wood fire in the stove to bring it up to a boil. Then dropped in the bone.
>
> It was slow to react, but by four o'clock we were optimistic it would yield a usable beef stock. We added in the cut up potatoes and carrots, plus onions. At five they were still hard and we got worried. Dinner was at five-thirty and early arrivals were already on hand, but the soup was still not edible, and questions and grumblings began to arise. We fended them off with, "It's a surprise."

By six, Kriebel's hungry compatriots appeared ready to mutiny. To avoid being thrown into the soup themselves, the two finally explained what had happened. A half hour later, the men were ready to eat anything as Kriebel dished out the soup, about a quart per person. He recalled, "Surprisingly, they didn't criticize us, and complimented us on the soup."[8]

After meals, many men lounged on the soft carpet of nee-
dles under the stately ponderosa pines, gathering around the
red fire barrel for what they called bull sessions. The talks
often forced individuals to reexamine their beliefs and open
the horizons of their intellects. For William P. Weber, the bull
sessions "were the most interesting and educational part of
the camp life. For it was here that a country boy had the
opportunity to listen and even participate in discussions with
college men and professors on a variety of current subjects.
Through these contacts I realized that there was more to
being opposed to war than the biblical command 'Thou Shalt
Not Kill.' "

The men carried on endless discussions comparing the
appropriateness of serving as a nonmilitary combatant to that
of claiming conscientious objector status. They also argued
over whether the government shafted them by forcing them
to work for practically nothing. "One argument said that we
volunteered to do this so it was right for us to do the work
wholeheartedly without pay," Wenger noted. "The other
extreme argued that we were slaves, forced to work by an all-
powerful government."[9]

Another popular argument centered on the Hutterite
practice of communal property. The men never tired of dis-
cussing this issue with Levi Tschetter, a Hutterite from
Estelline, South Dakota, and a popular figure in camp. The
men also liked to bait Tschetter by asking, "Can only a Hutterite go to Heaven?"

"That question would always generate a couple days worth
of discussion," Wenger said. "Levi would eventually say he
couldn't tell because he wasn't the one to make that decision.
But the next day someone would propose a different angle to
the question and the discussion would start again." Tschetter
was known as Camp 103's favorite Hutterite, according to
Wenger. As a CPSer, Tschetter first worked in soil conserva-

tion at Weeping Water, Nebraska, and later for Glacier National Park. He became a smoke jumper in the summer of 1945 and on one fire suffered burns on his legs when he broke through the earth's crust and fell into hot ashes where a root had burned out.

"Men in CPS looked at their camp experience in various ways," Wenger explained:

> Some emphasized that they were required to do work that was not very important and to do it without pay, but others were determined not to let this irritant cloud their opportunities to do good work in the limited areas open to them. The greatest benefits from this attitude were to the CPSer himself since it spared him from the self-destruction of cynicism and transformed his CPS environment into a school. This was Levi's attitude, and he was one of many who in later years were to say with some feeling, "CPS was my first college."

The men listened respectfully to and learned from each other. If they arrived in camp espousing only the beliefs of their own religion, by the time they left they had often integrated other religious, political, and philosophical points of view into their own belief system. "Several, including myself, worked on bringing those three aspects under one thought system,"[10] Wenger said. In testimony years later, many men, such as Asa Mundell, asserted that the bull sessions affected their spirituality and influenced their outlook on life. Mundell recalled,

> It was a growing period for me, from a strictly pious and holy stance, to a mind-growing experience. It was in CPS that my world view, rationality, and reasoning became a part of my life and my religious faith. It was

through some great discussions with fellow inmates that I got beyond my own naive world of half reason into greater global dimensions. It was like three and a half years of college. . . . Without those years in CPS, I can't imagine what might have happened to me.

Maynard Shetler also experienced spiritual growth at Camp 103, much more than he had at earlier camps. At Ninemile, he learned how to speak up for his own ideals, as well as listen to others. Shetler noted, "The early CPS camps consisted mostly of Mennonites with little conflict on doctrine. The smoke jumpers contained a broad spectrum of beliefs all the way from the radical Pentecostals to modernists. Unity of faith was not one of their strong points. In discussions you either proved your point or you weren't heard."

But the young CPSers did not limit their bull sessions to religion and pacifism. In fact, according to Harry Burks, those subjects ranked second in frequency raised: "Sitting around the stove almost any evening, you can get in a stimulating discussion concerning sweet young things of the opposite sex (fifty percent), religion and pacifism (twenty-five percent), griping (twenty percent), miscellaneous (five per cent.) The one exception to these percentages follows any flurry of fire jumps. Then the topic is one hundred percent jumping and firefighting."[11]

Gather any group of young men together and you'll find a comedian in the crowd. During the 1944 fire season, Dick Flaharty assumed the mantle of jester. Flaharty, a big-city boy from Chicago, had come to camp with a good background in humor.

After his father had abandoned the family, Flaharty and his two brothers moved to Lawrence Hall, a "Home for Good Boys" run by the Humboldt Park Methodist Church in Chicago. His mother took a job close by. By his junior year in high school, Flaharty played drums in a dance band called Courtland Day and His Knights of Rhythm. "We played everything from cheap bistros to the finer hotels and I learned the basics of swing music," Flaharty recalled. After graduating from high school, he began frequenting downtown theaters to listen to the big bands that rolled through town and to study "the techniques of the various drummers." But his greatest skill may have lain in humor. He wrote, "I found myself memorizing the routines of the vaudeville comics who would be sharing the stage with the bands,—and would entertain my friends with repeat performances."

Flaharty caught the acts of such great comedians as Red Skelton, Bob Hope, Milton Berle, and also those who have since been all but forgotten—Ben Blue, Jimmy Savo, Jerry Lester, Billy DeWolf, and Willy Howard. He must have also had some natural talent, because Flaharty was an instant hit with many of the smoke jumpers.

"He had the whole bunch of us in hysterics," wrote George H. Robinson. "First he gave a play in which he took the acting part of every character and he sure was funny. Then he made a speech on why he should be president. I think it was the funniest thing I ever heard and his actions along with his speech just touched it off." For decades, Flaharty continued entertaining the CPSers at reunions held every three years, often also leading them in the singing of hymns and popular folk songs.

Beyond the bull sessions and tomfoolery, the staff organized formal programs to entertain the men, especially during training camp in April and May. These included classes in music, electricity and radio, crafts, and Bible study. Jumper Richard Lehman, a Mennonite from Juniata County in Pennsylvania, learned the art of cushion-top tying in CPS "and continued it after my discharge." He also learned to make hook-latch rugs. During the later camps, the dean of the

School of Forestry at Montana State University visited the camp to teach the principles of silviculture to the men in the evenings.[12] For less formal study, men had access to a number of current best sellers and periodicals in the camp library. During the summer, administrators made sure the magazines and books circulated through the wilderness spike camps as well. "Don't conclude that right after supper all the fellows rush hungrily to the library to pore over a weighty tome on philosophy," wrote Harry Burks. "Actually, the heavier type of literary pursuit is the preoccupation of a distinct minority."[13]

In 1944, under the editorial direction of smoke jumper Gregg Phifer, men at CPS Camp No. 103 published a forty-seven-page, magazine-sized, soft-covered book titled, *Smoke Jumper*. The publication featured many black-and-white photographs of the men training, working, and playing, accompanied by short articles on nearly every aspect of their activities—ranging from why the men chose to go into CPS to setting up a fire camp. Individual volumes sold for seventy-five cents, three copies for two dollars, or "sixty cents in lots of ten or more."

During the winter, those CPSers who remained at Camp 103 published a mimeographed newsletter, first titled "Load Line" and later "Static Line." The half-dozen, double-sided pages featured newsy gossip, round-ups of the fire season, and philosophical musings. Static Line No. 28, released on November 10, 1945, included a Mark Twain–like report on a bridge-building project on the Powell Ranger District, located just over Lolo Pass on the Idaho-Montana border:

Powell Powwow

I thought it would be nice to write you a few lines to let you know that we are still alive, that is some of us are, although I don't think that those three men had any reason for committing suicide. This is a delightful spot only it . . . is rather damp although it seldom rains more than once an hour. . . . We get mail frequently: they tell us it comes in several times a year, unless it gets lost at Powell, or the packers use it to start fires in the mornings, or the mules eat the letters by mistake.

The boss is a fine man and is heartily in favor of reducing the work hours to seventy-two per week since the war is rumored to have ended. Why just today we were permitted to come in an hour early. . . . It ain't every boss who'd let you quit working because it rained six inches in two hours and the motor of the cement mixer was getting wet.

The tents are large and spacious (they were made that way in the Civil War), and there is plenty of room for the ten men assigned to each—if you don't attempt to lie down.

The fishing is swell. . . . There is a small variety of the lesser sperm whale in some of the deeper holes, but the packers object to our using the mules for bait on the end of the six hundred pound cables. . . . Contrary to all reports previously issued from this place there have been no trouble with the native fauna, unless you could count those two men carried off by mountain lions, and I am sure they went along gladly, thankful for the opportunity to give non-violent testimony.

Yes, we like our little home though we don't like the name "Desolation Camp" which has been conferred on it and feel that "Desperation Camp" would be strong enough.

Obediently, your servant,
Bushrod O'Hoolihan

Other frivolous pursuits abounded in camp. The "eight-ball" set gathered around the camp pool and billiard tables, with "an occasional interlude for ping-pong," according to Harry Burks. The volleyball court also attracted many sportsmen. It was the "favorite of all sports," Burks recalled. The men played a no-holds-barred, slam-bang version of the sport. The staff, Forest Service jumpers, squad leaders, and even the nurse joined in. One nurse, Catherine Harder (who eventually married CPS jumper Herb Crocker), probably thought that it was more convenient to be near the scene, since there were frequent injuries to the netters. She wrote, "A fractured nose, broken finger, and more than one gash and black eye are part of the price paid for this fast [volleyball] game."[14]

Catherine Crocker also worried that ticks lurking on the grass and brush around camp might infect the men with Rocky Mountain spotted fever in the spring. She requisitioned some new vaccine to fight the lurking danger and taught a handful of jumpers to administer the shots, having them first practice on oranges and then on her—"to demonstrate my complete confidence in the administration of the vaccine by the deputized jumper." Other jumpers kept a careful record of each injection. Crocker reported no infections or cases of Rocky Mountain spotted fever.[15]

Softball created some interesting situations for the players, especially the layout of the base path between third and home, which was blocked by a tree halfway to home. The forest supervisor had stringently instructed the men not to cut down any trees at Camp Menard, but Earl Cooley thought of a loophole. He instructed the men to dig up the tree by the roots. Cooley recalled,

We had just had the . . . ground repaired a day or so when the ranger came up from the Ninemile station. I had stopped to talk to him about fifty yards from where we had disposed of the tree. He proceeded to tell me that if we just took the tree out, as he pointed to the softball field, and got rid of it no one would ever know the difference.

The jumpers in the back of the pickup started laughing and the ranger didn't know what it was they were laughing about, since we had removed it and he hadn't even noticed that we had taken it out.[16]

On weekends, the men occasionally drove into Missoula for a movie, musical program, lecture, or dates with women they had met. On Sundays, many attended morning church services in town and young people's meeting in the evening. Sunday services at Ninemile were often presided over by a visiting minister from Missoula or one sent out by the Mennonite Central Committee. "The diversity of denominational affiliation sometimes makes our services a real forum on religious philosophy," Burks noted. Some men stationed in Missoula over the winter became more deeply involved in community life. One became an early-morning announcer for the local radio station, another a counselor for a high school group at the Methodist church. Still others volunteered to repaint the community nursery. Missoula also offered a city swimming pool and a roller-skating rink, as well as other places to hang out. Roger's Café was a good place to eat, according to Marshall Jensen.

The spike camps were a different story. There a man had to be more resourceful to amuse himself. During times of high fire danger, the men could not stray far from the telephone. At Moose Creek, Idaho, Sheldon M. Mills liked to throw horseshoes. He noted, "I played one Mennonite jumper dozens of times and was beaten each time except once when I seemed to make all ringers." But the spike camps offered a unique opportunity for many men to learn the fine art of fly-fishing. Just a few yards from the bunkhouses they might cast into blue-ribbon-quality trout streams. Vern Hoffman, stationed at Big Prairie, quickly acquired an expert mentor, fellow CPSer Hubert Blackwell:

> Hubert was a real outdoors type of fellow who grew up in the backwoods of Michigan. He was a real hunter and fisherman and had brought along his equipment. When I saw him flyfishing for those rainbow trout in our mountain stream, I was fascinated and soon became a strong follower of Hubert's expertise. He was happy to loan me his equipment and help me through the early stages of learning the art.
>
> It turned out to be a good place to learn because there was little competition for the abundance of trout in the stream. The rainbows were so abundant that we would tie two flies on our line and most always bring in two trout with one cast. While it was an ideal place for learning fly cast fishing, it turned out to be too ideal, because I have never found a place that good in the fifty years since the summer of 1943.[17]

When David S. Yoder, the cook at Big Prairie, had time off, he likewise headed toward his favorite trout stream: "I had one day a week off, which I often spent away from camp fishing and watching wildlife in the surrounding territory. Where can one feel closer to his Maker than out with nature, in complete solitude?"

Life in the spike camps also led to some problems with personal appearance. By the 1990s, wildland firefighters—both men and women—had become notorious for their often outlandish hairdos. Many men shaved their heads, some shaved portions of their heads, others shaved streaks of hair off their heads. But the tradition of shaved heads stretches as far back as the days of the CPS jumper camp at Cayuse Landing. "Kolmer Spangler, Ray Phibbs, and I were in camp with some others," recalled Harold Toews, "but the three of us were bored out there. So one day we shaved our heads. We thought it was funny until we got a sunburn and our hair came out as bristles. We had real pain and could sleep only if we put our faces on the pillow."

Toews could have hired Larry Morgan to give him a haircut at the Cayuse camp, but the outcome would probably have been the same, according to Morgan:

> As I owned a pair of hand clippers, scissors and a comb, it seemed appropriate to take up barbering at twenty-five cents a head.
>
> My first subject, or victim, was George Iten who had also come to smoke jumpers from Cascade Lock Camp 21. With a towel pinned around his neck to prevent hair from falling into his shirt, I began my work of art. When finished, I felt I had created a masterly job. But after viewing the haircut in a mirror and receiving the comments of his fellow smoke jumpers, George demanded, "Just cut it all off. I'm sure it will look better." I don't remember for sure, but I think I was never paid, and so ended my career as a barber.[18]

There were not many women in camp except for a few cooks at some of the spike camps. At the Ninemile camp, women worked as camp nutritionist, nurse, and matron. The matron made sure the boys did not become too rowdy. She pulled any risqué pinups from the walls and closely monitored the CPSers language and manners. And she allowed no alcohol in camp—not that anyone could afford buying a pail of beer on his five-dollar-a-month salary. But on at least one occasion the young men did get tipsy. None other than their squad boss, Earl Cooley, was to blame. Cooley recalled,

> We were headed back to Ninemile following an all night fire at Welcome Creek in Lolo Forest south of Missoula. . . . Al Cramer, one of the Forest Service jumpers with us in the truck, asked if we could stop in at the Hilander [sic] Brewery and get a case of beer to take back to camp. I went in to get the beer for Al and the manager asked who was in the truck. I told him it was a crew of firefighters returning from fighting a fire down in Lolo. He said for me to have them all come in if they were dry and have some beer.

Cooley, who did not know much about Mennonite history, assumed that the men would be teetotalers. Little did he suspect that many Mennonites, before Prohibition, had been brewmeisters. In Roy Wenger's Ohio community, for example, there had been three breweries run by Mennonites. "The Mennonites were not responsible for the temperance movement," Wenger explained. "Other churches shamed the Mennonites into transferring from making beer to other businesses. But some refused for a time and there became a schism between the 'beer' Amish and the 'nonbeer' Amish." To Cooley's surprise, all but three of the twenty-five-man crew eagerly jumped off the truck and headed into the brewery. He wrote,

> The manager had two gallon cans that he would fill with beer and the jumpers would pass them around.
> When I was picking up Al's case, the manager came into the office with a big smile on his face. I asked how those jumpers were making out with the beer. He

laughed and said, "They are doing O.K." But I decided I had better go in and check on them.

The beer was real refreshing and certainly appreciated, but it was also very effective on empty stomachs and some were beginning to feel some effects of it. I pulled them out of the brewery and we went on back to the camp.

That night about midnight, Florence Wenger came over and knocked on my door and told me I had to get up, that there was some serious trouble in camp. I thought perhaps that someone was sick or had a problem, but then she told me that she had caught one of the jumpers, Phil Stanley to be exact, with a can of beer and wanted me to go over to the dorm and straighten him out.

So to satisfy Florence I went over to the dorm. I turned the lights on, and Loren Zimmerman's feet hit the floor and he asked, "Where's the fire?"

I told him it was over in the superintendent's office and she requested immediate control. After explaining the situation to the crew I went back to bed hoping for a ten a.m. control [the official time limit for extinguishing all fires] the next day.

As word spread about the Forest Service's new method of fighting fires, the media became interested. Paramount Pictures sent a film crew to Ninemile to capture the excitement and danger of a smoke jumper's life. Lowell Sharp and Marlyn Shetler were picked to star in the dousing of a staged fire on the Ninemile grounds. When they arrived at the site that Cooley had picked for the fire, they found everything wet from the rain. They finally got a fire started at the base of a pine tree. Shetler recalled,

The cameraman wanted the fire to go up into the branches of the tree. It wouldn't, so he threw some celluloid film up the tree. The flame at the bottom of the tree caught it and up the fire went. The cameraman waited until the tree was fully involved before he started to film the fire. Lowell and I dug around the fire and put it out. The cameraman was ready to shoot the scene of us leaving the fire with smoke still coming from the fire.

Earl Cooley said, "Oh, no you don't. No pictures of us leaving with smoke still in the fire area." We put the fire completely out, then the cameraman filmed us leaving.

Thus transpired the life of a CPS smoke jumper. They worked hard, played heartily, enjoyed the few creature comforts allowed, and survived the shortcomings of barracks life as best they could. In their personal lives they seemed to thrive and many matured both spiritually and intellectually. As happened with many GIs, the war years became the turning point of their lives, as they quickly matured from boys into men. For many CPSers, their experiences at the smoke jumpers' camp were merely the first footsteps along a path dedicated to social work and personal expansion that would last a lifetime.

CHAPTER THIRTEEN

Lifelong Commitment

On September 2, 1945, the Allies claimed victory over Japan, thus ending World War II. Soon after, enlisted men flocked home, hungry for jobs. At the same time, CPS began to close up shop. The Forest Service decided not to retain any CPS smoke jumpers for the following season, although many supervisors agreed that they would have been a valuable source of experience for training new men. Earl Cooley observed that he probably could have kept fifty of the very best men. He wrote, "Although they had done an admirable job, I decided that they should be released with no exceptions and that we should start anew with returning veterans for the next fire season . . . if these men had been retained, they would have been supervising or instructing returning veterans who would have resented them."[1]

The decision pleased most CPSers, according to Phil Stanley, who occasionally worked for the Forest Service as a photographer after the war: "They all wanted to get home and get on with their lives, just like the returning G.I.s."[2] On January 15, 1946, the last jumper transferred out of CPS Camp No. 103.

Some volunteered for relief deliveries to Europe, tending live-stock on freighters crossing the Atlantic; others finished out the winter at the regular CPS camps. On January 20, 1946, the last of the staff locked up the doors at Camp Menard. "As I remember it," wrote Richard S. Weaver, "[civilian camp direc-tor] Art and Evie Wiebe, another fellow smoke jumper and I loaded up the camp pickup with all the records and remaining CPS office equipment, along with our personal belongings and headed for Missoula and Hale Field."

After being released from CPS later that year, the men returned home to loved ones, uncertain how long society would resent them for remaining true to their convictions. But no matter what the future held, many smoke jumpers considered their CPS experience to be a defining moment of their lives. "CPS definitely had an influence in my life," wrote John Ainsworth. "Four years in the CPS environment with two thirds of it in smoke jumpers was quite a change just as it was for those in the military."

After the war, Ainsworth became an engineer for the Edi-son Company in California for a while before moving back to Montana. He later settled in Yakima, Washington. Since his stint in CPS, Ainsworth has taken "walking tours" with his fam-ily throughout Mexico, Guatemala, Peru, Costa Rica, and Ecuador. As time passed, he became concerned about the treatment of indigenous peoples south of the border. "We regret the actions of the United States Government in Central America the last nine years," he observed in 1990. "We have known some of the Mayans in Guatemala and found them very friendly. They are too gentle to be persecuted as they had been with U.S. military aid. . . . I am sure that I am more aware of world problems, social justice and people's welfare than I would be without the CPS experience." At the Fiftieth Smoke Jumper Association reunion, Ainsworth confided, "I am an engineer. I build things. I don't destroy things."[3]

As they departed Camp Menard and the Ninemile Remount Depot, few men probably realized the extent to which they had helped revolutionize wildland firefighting. The most obvious changes first appeared right at Ninemile. Before the end of the war, in 1945, the Forest Service sold the stallion Grand Menard for $850; three years later, the agency auctioned off the rest of the mares and stallions. "Some of the horses sold fairly well, but some barely brought canner prices," Regional Forester P. D. Hanson recalled.[4] The diminishing reliance on horses and mules marked the beginning of the end of the old way of wildland firefighting. In 1953, the Ninemile Ranger District moved into the structures of the Remount Depot, and the Forest Service auctioned off the last of its stock in 1956.

The agency also abandoned most of the lookout towers. Even before the end of the war, officials began to reevaluate the role of the "eyes in the sky," drastically reducing the numbers of lookout assignments. After a short building boom following the war, many lookouts were blown up or set afire. Others languished into disrepair. Only in the late 1990s did civilian and Forest Service volunteers lobby to restore and save some of the remaining structures, turning them into camping rentals for adventurous souls. Some districts continue to employ lookouts on strategic towers. In fact, Stark Mountain, sitting at the head of the Ninemile Valley, has been manned—or womaned—by the same person for the past thirty years: Virginia Vincent. Vincent was inspired to apply for the job after reading a story about female lookouts in *National Geographic* during World War II.

Not only had the CPS smoke jumpers proved their effectiveness in extinguishing fires, but they had also saved the government money over and above their minuscule paychecks; even if the CPSers had been paid regular wages, their quick control of the fires saved the agency thousands of dollars.

Their first year in action, the smoke jumper squad attacked twice as many fires by parachute as they did on foot, suppressing forty-seven fires, most before they escalated into full-fledged conflagrations. Their efforts saved taxpayers an estimated $75,000, based on comparisons of the cost for a squad of men walking to the fires.[5]

In 1944, officials doubled the smoke jumper force to 120 men, assigning a standby contingent of jumpers to the airfield in Missoula throughout the summer. That same year, the Forest Service deemed the smoke jumpers an official permanent part of its firefighting machine. No longer considered an experiment financed with special funds, the squad received its own budget. As a consequence, many national forests reduced their regular firefighting crews and depended more on smoke jumpers. In 1944, Region Six used a military DC-3 airplane, provided by the U.S. Marine Corps, to drop its jumpers, while the Ford Trimotors and Travelaires remained the workhorses in the other regions.[6]

If anyone still had doubts about the effectiveness of the program, the CPSers clearly proved their worth during the summer of 1945. That year, instructors welcomed about 235 men to the Ninemile training camp, including nearly 100 men who had jumped the previous season. Their ranks also included a few returning war veterans. One of the original Forest Service smoke jumpers, Francis Lufkin, who had jumped in Region Six in 1940, returned to the site of his first jump in Winthrop, Washington, with a crew of 15 CPSers under his leadership. After training that season, other crews dispersed to Missoula; to McCall, Idaho; and to Cave Junction, Oregon.

That year, tinder-dry forests helped spread wildfire throughout many inaccessible areas of Region One. By late September, jumpers barely had time to shower and pack their chutes after returning from one fire call before jumping another. The three regions used smoke jumpers on 296 fires, with a total of 1,236 jumps on twenty-three national forests in Montana, Idaho, Washington, Oregon, and California, plus Yellowstone and Glacier national parks. They also fought fires on Indian reservations, privately owned timberlands, and forests in Canada. A cost analysis covering only three regions indicated a net savings of more than $346,000 for the season. "In many cases, savings on a single fire might have equaled the entire project cost," noted Earl Cooley. "Smoke jumpers were used in large groups to spearhead control on the larger and more threatening fires."[7] By September 1945, Missoula firefighters alone had jumped 181 fires, 26 more than had been jumped from 1940 to 1944.

Hanson, the regional forester, congratulated CPS camp director Arthur J. Wiebe in December 1945. (The Wengers had departed the winter before, after Florence had become pregnant.) There had been twelve hundred forest fires in 1945, he said, but "even so, our total area of burned forest at the close of the season was small. Such an accomplishment was made possible by the splendid action of our air-borne firemen, the smoke jumpers. Many of the fires our jumpers suppressed in the nation's most remote wilderness could have become catastrophic had the jumpers not performed expertly and efficiently. To them goes a large share of the credit of a nationally important job well done."

But the influence of Camp 103 often loomed even larger in the personal lives of the men who made it work. For Luke Birkey of Albany, Oregon, CPS camp was "a time of rethinking a lot of things as we lived so close to each other, with such varied backgrounds. Often the experience was painful, but it was a good time; learning and being stretched." Immediately following his CPS discharge, Luke married Verna Conrad (from his home Mennonite congregation), and the couple moved to Puerto Rico. Verna worked as a nurse while Luke labored as a janitor at a hospital and clinic. He noted, "After three years and four months of CPS I wanted to get on with education and life work. But after more thought, concluded that if the government could take that much of my life without so much as a thank you, it really was not that unreasonable to give an additional eighteen months to the church. We did not regret that decision and volunteered for an additional eighteen months and followed that with another term of three-and-a-half years."

Through the years, Birkey stayed in hospital work, although not in the maintenance department. He eventually became secretary of health and welfare for the Mennonite Board of Missions in Elkhart, Indiana, where he oversaw eight general hospitals, twelve retirement centers or nursing homes, and five child welfare programs. In 1979, the Birkeys moved back to Albany, Oregon, where Luke directed a Mennonite retirement program. When they retired in 1987, the Birkeys moved to Costa Rica for a while to administer a local work-study program for Goshen college students. As far as being a CPS smoke jumper, Birkey wrote,

> I'd do it all again. I was convinced that the Jesus way of non-violence was right. My understanding of this was far too narrow and provincial or incomplete. But CPS became a time of evaluation and maturing as I lived closely with people of conviction but varied backgrounds and perspectives. It was a time to learn, to increase vision of what it meant to be a follower of the Prince of Peace and to be more socially responsible. My fellow CPSers helped enormously in this process and I'm profoundly grateful.

Smoke jumper H. Lee Hebel, following his CPS service, returned to theological school in Gettysburg, Pennsylvania, and eventually became a Lutheran minister. He attested to the importance of CPS by saying, "Throughout Christian ministry I have attempted to relate with Christians of all denominations. I learned that at home, college, and in CPS, and continue to feel that such relationships are extremely important."

For Leland L. Miller, life after smoke jumping led back to the Mennonite community in South Dakota where he and his wife, Mary, farmed for nine years. As farming slowly dragged the couple down financially, Miller took a job with a Caterpillar dealer in Sioux Falls, South Dakota, and the couple "soon were involved in the hard, and sometimes overwhelming, work of starting and building a new church, the Good Shepherd Mennonite Church." In 1966, the Millers moved back to the Northwest, settling in Spokane, Washington, where Leland traveled once again through Idaho and Montana. "I worked for loggers, highway contractors, Snake River Dam contractors, mining contractors, as well as for many small operators doing excavating, yard work, farming, etc. This enabled me to explore this part of the country in much more depth than most natives did. And I loved it in spite of much hard work."

But Miller also found time to volunteer with the local Peace and Justice and Fellowship of Reconciliation chapter. "My interest in political action in the areas of peace and justice has become a high priority," he explained. Miller credited his smoke jumping and other CPS experience with giving him the opportunity for good job experience as well as spiritual guidance:

> I still recall the thrill of seeing mountains, and it began to dawn on many of us that the Midwest was not all there was. I really enjoyed Lapine's [*sic*] wonderful people, interesting work, and beautiful setting. It was there I

learned to fell and trim trees, to climb trees, to run a bulldozer, drive a truck, put out a forest fire, and climb a mountain. But all those things were not as important as learning about human relationships, and best of all, making lifelong friends. In view of all these good things, our loss of freedom didn't seem as crushing to me as it did to many.

Clarence Quay returned to Chester County, Pennsylvania, to his old job at Bethlehem Steel after his discharge from CPS. But he found things had changed. "There was a coolness because I was a conscientious objector," he explained. "After several months I quit and did a number of different things." Quay sold vacuum cleaners, hauled coal from the mines in Frackville, Pennsylvania, operated a bulldozer, drove a dump truck, farmed, and resurfaced roads. After marrying Mary E. Clingaman, Clarence attended the Brethren Bible School in Chicago "to learn more about the Bible." He eventually graduated from McPherson College with a degree in education and psychology. He continued his studies at Bethany Biblical Seminary, earning a master's degree in theology, and spent twenty-four years serving at four different churches. Quay observed,

There have been many experiences that have been a part of my life and I have appreciated nearly all of them. But the total experience of being in CPS, working without pay, being a part of a minority group, learning and sharing together as a group and discovering that, even with different backgrounds and religious beliefs, it is possible (indeed it is an enriching experience) to learn to know one another and share with each other in a sincere and meaningful fellowship. Especially was this true for me with the smoke jumper CPS Camp 103.

After CPS, Kenneth Diller returned to the old Mennonite community near Bluffton, in northwestern Ohio, where he and his brother started up a grain and livestock fattening operation. He married Jeanette Flora, and the couple raised two children on the farm where Diller had been born. He recalled, "Smoke jumping to me had to be the high point in a farmer's life. The nature of the project, with its promise of a mixture of adventure and hard work, seemed to attract some very worthwhile people with whom I'm always able to relate. Although there seems to be no two people who think alike, we found it interesting to consider and respect all points of view."

Dick Flaharty, the camp comedian and jazz drummer, used his musical talents after the war to help support himself and his wife, Betty, while he attended college. "It used to gall Betty, who worked for the Family Service, that I could play my drums one or two evenings a week and earn as much as she would get for a full week of work as a social worker," he noted. The year 1951 proved a busy one for him. He earned a master's degree in social work from Pittsburgh University, witnessed the birth of his first son, and moved his family to Milwaukee, Wisconsin. There he took on his first professional assignment as a group worker and assistant program director at Neighborhood House, a settlement house serving the inner city. Later in life the Flahartys moved to Granada Hills, California, where Dick continued his social work and Betty once again worked for a Family Service agency.

In California, Dick developed a new program, known as the Maud Booth Family Center, for the Volunteers of America–Los Angeles Post. The program provided services ranging from low-cost housing to emotional and vocational counseling for parents and extended child daycare to low-income one-parent families. Dick found his smoke jumper experience invaluable in explaining his philosophies to others who had not learned about the CPS program or who did not understand pacifism.

He observed, "As the years rolled along I found it easier to talk openly about my CO experiences and my pacifist beliefs, in essence making a witness to a philosophy not readily accepted or understood by the majority of our society. Having been a smoke jumper makes it easier to lead into a conversation about CPS contributions to society than talking about surveying watersheds on a soil conservation project."

Roy and Florence Wenger moved back to Ohio after the war. There Roy became the first director of audio-visual education at Kent State University. When he received a Fulbright Lecturer's Grant in 1954, the Wengers, with their three-year-old daughter, Susan, traveled to Japan, where Roy taught at the newly established International Christian University on the outskirts of Tokyo. During the ten-day sea voyage, the Wengers "were tossed about in a typhoon a few days," recalled Florence. In Japan, Florence taught kindergarten at the American School, "which enrolled children of nearly forty nationalities from the foreign community in the Tokyo area." Later, she became director of the elementary division at the school. Roy's one-year sabbatical extended into three years and evolved into a lifelong involvement in international education through study-abroad programs.

Upon returning to Kent State, Roy set up exchange programs for students and professors in a dozen countries around the world, including England, Taiwan, and Tanzania. Florence returned to teaching.

Some summers she would go off and "do my own thing," as she described her travels. One of her African adventures included "traveling by assorted means from Cairo to Cape Horn visiting schools, social agencies, parliaments and mission stations." During that trip, she spent one night sleeping in a cotton storage shed in central Uganda after her car had bogged down in the mud, and another sleepless night in a cottage along the banks of the White Nile as an elephant rubbed its flanks against the bedroom wall.

Another summer, Florence participated in a teacher-education project in Liberia. She recalled, "When, after a long palaver with a village chief, we were able to persuade him to start a school with A.I.D. [Agency for International Development] Assistance and a proviso that twenty percent of the students would be girls, we were thrilled." On a Friends Service Committee project in Powhatan, Virginia, during the 1960s, Florence helped prepare young black children for school integration.

In 1971 Roy helped establish the Center for Peaceful Change, now called the Center for Applied Conflict Management. The program was one of the first in the nation to offer an undergraduate degree in conflict resolution. It stands as a living memorial of the events that occurred on May 4, 1970, when Ohio National Guardsmen killed four people and injured nine others at Kent State during a student protest of the Vietnam War. During that war, Roy often counseled young men about alternative service to the military or imprisonment, but he did not support those who wanted to flee to Canada or Europe, for he believed that objectors had an obligation to serve their country either as a noncombatant or as an example of conscience. However, after the shootings, he questioned whether the government had broken its compact with its citizens.[8]

When Roy retired in 1978 at the age of seventy, he and Florence moved to Missoula, where Susan lived. There he helped establish the Golden College at the University of Montana, an educational program tailored for seniors and retirees. During his retirement, Roy encouraged the CPSers to write about their experiences as smoke jumpers; he later published the memoirs in three volumes to distribute to the families of the men. The Wengers also helped organize reunions for the CPSers every five years.

Before dying in 1989, Florence noted of herself and Roy, "We kept moving and no grass grew under my feet. What part did I enjoy most?—Impossible to answer." Roy died in Missoula on November 30, 2004, at the age of ninety-six.

After the war, most of the CPSers probably figured that they would never again be at odds with their country. Yet less than a decade after being discharged from Civilian Public Service, many men were again called up before draft boards to serve in the Korean War.

Although most of them retained their conscientious objector convictions, a few thought that they had made a mistake the first time by not signing up to fight. For Jonas Hershberger, who had been raised in the Amish faith at Farmerstown, Ohio, the Korean conflict offered him a chance for self-redemption. "The decision to go to the CPS during World War Two was largely due to the teaching of my parents and also because three of my brothers were already serving in the CPS," he wrote. After the war, Hershberger returned to Ohio and tried to live a good Amish life for a while, "but soon I left and bought a car and didn't go to any church. I worked at different jobs for a couple of years, then took a job as a heavy equipment operator. I worked at it for about two years, when I was drafted into the Armed Services in 1950. I took my training in Kentucky and Texas, after which I shipped out to Korea."

However, the majority of the men maintained their conscientious objector convictions during the Korean conflict and long after. CPS smoke jumper Bob Painter, who had become a physician after CPS, found the draft boards less lenient on objectors the second time around. "This time, the draft boards refused to give me a c.o. classification. The next three years, I represented my own case through a series of appeals up to the Presidential appeal. By that time, it was dropped because I was overage. The experience gave me another chance to evaluate and express my own pacifist views, which had become stronger."

Roy Piepenburg also had trouble with the draft during the Korean War. The fact that he had already served twenty months in CPS and received a medical release "seemed irrelevant" to his draft board. Piepenburg's CPS experience served to reinforce his decision to devote his life to pacifism. He recalled,

Regardless of untold difficulties, I realize fully the rare wisdom of my parents' advice to resist war—not only so-called "just wars," but all wars against humanity. After I had learned to live with the ridicule that is so freely dispensed against pacifists, and all constructive non-conformists, an idea caught fire in my mind. I planned to dedicate my life to social reform along avenues that would aid the poor and oppressed in American society. That is how I got involved in Indian education and aboriginal rights. The idea led to my working in numerous Indian communities and boarding schools all the way from the Navaho reservation in Arizona to Yellowknife on the shores of Great Slave Lake in the Northwest Territories of Canada.

As the Vietnam War escalated during the 1960s, so too did the peace movement in the United States. Hundreds of thousands of college students demonstrated against the war, and many youths fled to Canada to avoid the draft. Some spent time in prison as draft evaders, while others lingered in school as long as possible for a college deferment. Others pursued extreme measures to flunk draft physicals, including putting drug user–like needle tracks in their arms and acting in psychotic bizarre manners. Some, like President

George W. Bush, avoided direct combat service by joining the National Guard.

At the time, former CPSers saw their sons facing the same dilemmas that they had experienced. Albert L. Gray, Jr., and his wife, Louise, passed their pacifist convictions on to their three boys, one of whom refused to register for the draft. Roy Piepenburg took no chances. In 1961, when he realized that the United States would become mired militarily in Vietnam, he moved his wife and three young children to Canada. He reflected, "Today I am of the opinion that if we had elected to remain in the United States, both of my sons might have been conscripted and sent to Vietnam." Piepenburg remained in Canada, where he became involved with Project Ploughshares and the Canadian Peace Alliance. He also maintained a continental bond for brotherhood and peace by working with the Mount Diablo Peace Center at Walnut Creek, California.

Like many CPSers, Piepenburg maintained an optimistic view of the world, despite the global turmoil. "What is my vision for the future of humanity?" he wrote in 1993.

> Pacifists, although small in numbers, will link up with staunch environmentalists in a powerful struggle to save our planet. As our survival becomes even more precarious, our intellect, natural resources, and monies will have to be diverted for wholly constructive uses. The military-industrial complex that has held us as hostages for many generations will be rejected universally. Peace will break out, the air, land, and waters will be pure and safe, and happiness will prevail on Earth.

Today, an open field at the Grand Menard picnic grounds, which CPSers referred to as the oval, is the only remainder of the former CCC camp. Returning war veterans continued to train as smoke jumpers at the camp for a few years until the Forest Service built a training facility at Hale Field in Missoula. Shortly after the jumpers abandoned the CCC camp, the government sold the last of the buildings, and the bidders tore them down. A mile south of the picnic area, the handful of green-roofed, white-clapboarded Cape Cod houses, the work barn, the stud barn, the powder house, and the tack shed of the old Remount Depot still gleam in the sunshine. During the winter, mule strings from the various districts throughout Region One graze in the pastures. The dozen mules that comprise the Region One honorary pack team operate out of the station year-round. And every spring, for training jumps, U.S. Forest Service rookie and veteran smoke jumpers board a DC-3 in Missoula to make the short flight above the Clark Fork River west to the Ninemile Valley, where they follow the trajectory of the CPS jumpers who had bailed out over the same hay meadows more than six decades ago.

In a sense, the smoke jumper program proved to be the perfect CPS camp. For the most part, morale remained high and the camaraderie generated what became lifelong friendships. Although a handful of men expressed disappointment with the program and did not return for an encore season, most of the participants felt proud to learn a new skill and excited about experiencing a unique physical feat—floating through the skies—that few civilians ever would. Moreover, the tough physical training and the dangerous work on forest fires assuaged the men's pride. If there ever could be a "moral equivalent of war," then smoke jumping was it. The opportunity offered the CPSer a chance to feel as brave as a soldier, yet he never had to lift a weapon or fire a shot. Plus, he felt he was accomplishing an important mission.

The success of the CPS smoke jumpers also ensured that the nation's forests would be safeguarded during the war years. The importance of the availability of the jumpers increased near the end of summer, when most of the regular fire crews, composed of sixteen- and seventeen-year-olds, returned to school. In the end, the CPSers enabled the Forest Service to continue with its grand experiment of fighting fires by dropping men from the sky. "Undoubtedly we would have had to discontinue the smoke jumper project for the years 1943 to 1945, if we had not had the services of the CPS men," Cooley remarked.[9]

What did the men think about their own experiences? Perhaps the CPSer attitude was best summed up in an unsigned editorial that appeared in the final issue of "Static Line," published on January 26, 1946, after CPS Camp No. 103 was officially closed—with nothing left to do "but some book-keeping":

> If any thing, CPS 103 was a unit of contrasts. Men raced to fires at eighty miles per hour, and walked away at three. Having one of CPS's most stimulating projects, 103 also had some of the dullest. Some men lived in steam-heated homes in Missoula, while others shivered in snow-covered tents. A few men worked at office desks, while the majority, wielding hand tools, sweated or shivered—depending on the season.
>
> Some of the Forest Service personnel were wholehearted, fine-spirited people, a credit to any group, while there were also little bureaucrats. With food the Forest Service was generous to a fault, and petty, even mean, about allowances. Jumping equipment was of the best, while work tools were usually in poor condition.
>
> The contrasts extended to the men themselves. Extremely hard-working and conscientious as a group, yet they were—also as a group—perhaps the most oblivious in CPS to social issues. Smoke jumpers could erect a barracks in record time, then shatter all records for making it messy. The ranges extended from scholars to

lumbermen, from artists to plumbers, from young and impulsive to relatively old and stable.

Yet there was a common thread woven throughout. Each man admitted a flair for the romantic, a taste for thrills. Airmindedness was standard. In general the men liked to do or make things, in preference to philosophizing, or bandying ideologies. Yet there was depth of conviction. Most had a rather highly developed sense of responsibility. Most men combined a desire to do really significant work with a perhaps unexpressed desire to prove to his critics that the CO can have courage. . . . Here was a comradeship, a gathering of men which memory will fondly recall. Here was a big job well done—the protection of the Northwest's forests. Here was a demonstration that pacifists can do as well as preach. Here were a thousand little events, each forever a part of an individual.

Conscription is evil, and conscripted serfdom infinitely more so. Yet, paradoxically, within their framework existed the CPS 103 experience, which will stand out in each man's life.

The thrills, the sweat, the kneeling at the door waiting for the slap, the tension of suiting-up, the exhaustion on the fire lines, volleyball, the horseplay, weekends in Missoula, calihoostics on a May morning, the vertebrae-snapping tower, the congestion in the loft, the sessions in the dorms, the amateur camp programs, the cathedral-like silence of the deep forests: these and many more elements blended to compose 103, the CPS Smoke Jumper Unit.

And so we say goodbye to beautiful 103, camp of enchantment and dreams. And as the dying rays of the sun tint with ethereal scarlet hue the majesty of old Squaw Peak, we hear the throbbing, rhythmic, gentle

(?) chant of the Seepeeyessmen, as they repeat, again and again, "Houi Houahnt Hout!" which when roughly translated [from thick German Mennonite and Brethren accents] signifies: "We want out."[10]

As they fanned out across the country to home and families, the CPS smoke jumpers figured that few men would follow in their footsteps. "Already there is talk that parachuting men to fires will soon be obsolete," mentioned one CPSer.[11] Forest Service visionaries were already dreaming about airplanes that could drop hundreds of gallons of fire retardant at a time, and helicopters that could scoop water out of lakes with big buckets. Eventually, the agency developed that new technology, but the smoke jumper program kept on course at full speed ahead.

Unlike their fathers and grandfathers who fought in World War II, today's smoke jumpers, many of whom lived through the Vietnam era, respect and honor the history of the CPS jumpers. "They were overlooked for too long," said Wayne Williams, a long-time jumper who also served as the information officer at the Smoke Jumper Visitors Center in Missoula at the turn of the Millennium. But it was not long ago that some of the older generation of jumpers and some Forest Service "waffle-bottoms" still held grudges against the conscientious objectors. In July of 1995, about eight hundred members of the National Smoke Jumpers Association gathered in Missoula to renew old friendships, resurrect memories of close calls, and relate countless "war stories." The CPSers decided to simultaneously hold their own reunion under the umbrella of the association.

For the association's first big meeting—held in 1984—they had been overlooked. "It doesn't seem to have been intentional," Williams said. "There wasn't a data base at the time and the invitation list grew by word of mouth."[12]

The climax of the 1995 affair, a Saturday night banquet, featured a lively speech by Secretary of the Interior Bruce Babbitt, followed by a reading of the "definitive" history of smoke jumping. But the document overlooked one important period: it never mentioned the CPSers. "It was deliberate," said Martha Huset, who attended the event with her husband, a former CPS jumper. "From 1942 to 1945 there was a total blank in the history." One daughter of a conscientious objector jumper later cornered the speaker who read the history to ask about the omission. She reported that the excuse was, "We didn't want to bring up anything about cults."[13] Compared to the snubs of the past, Roy Wenger said it was an easy one "to shrug off."[14]

Today, with most outdoor labor having been mechanized, smoke jumping remains one of the few environmentally friendly jobs that still offer excitement and romance for young people. Each spring the Forest Service is overwhelmed with applications for a handful of rookie smoke jumper positions. Why the continuing appeal? Because that style of life couldn't get any better, attested CPS smoke jumper Merlo M. Zimmerman: "Thinking back, what can compare to the foot on the step, the rugged mountain below, the wind in your face, the tap on the shoulder, hit the silk. . . . You said it—'Life at its fullest.'"

Appendix

Letters Home

George H. Robinson documented the gamut of daily events of the smoke jumpers in a remarkable series of letters to his new wife, Betty (née Coppage). A member of a Baptist family from southern New Jersey, Robinson entered CPS duty on December 8, 1942. He first served at the CPS camp at Cooperstown, New York, administered by the American Friends Service Committee. He later transferred to Coleville, California, where these excerpts from his letters begin.[1]

April 10, 1944

I'm all excited today. The American Friends Service Committee just released my name as one of those chosen by the Forest Service for the Smoke Jumpers. It still hasn't been approved by the Selective Service, though. It has taken me a year to get this close. I'm not quite in yet so I shouldn't get so excited. Then there is the possibility I may not qualify after I get up there. It will probably be a month before the transfer comes through.

April 21, 1944

My transfer finally came through. I am supposed to be in Huson, Montana, by May First. I'll have to drop in the office now and see if they will release me. My address will be: Smoke Jumpers, Camp

Huson, Montana. I'll be there for a training period that will cover six weeks and then I will be sent to a spike camp. Huson is about thirty miles northwest of Missoula. Food, housing, bedding and some work clothes are provided by the Forest Service so that completely covers maintenance.

May 1, 1944

It doesn't look as though I am ever going to get away from here. I asked Mr. Haynes if I should leave and he said, "No." I told him I thought they would put me on the ground crew if I didn't get there pretty soon. He said he would send a letter with me. He is also going to ask his father who is in the regional office to put in a good word for me. He wants me to take the big Dodge and trailer on a trip starting Friday. I am to leave for Montana on the night of the tenth.

May 9, 1944—Ninemile, Montana

Well, at last I am here. I took off on my tour of Nevada Saturday morning. Bob Corney was with me. By three o'clock in the afternoon we had covered three hundred miles. We found the D-6 that we had gone after and started for Austin. We unloaded that tractor about ten times before we got it out of the Canyon. Sunday I got the surprise of my life. Here I was three hundred miles from camp and who should I see driving up but Mr. Haynes and John Robbins. Mr. Haynes told me that they wired for me to go right up to Montana. He said he felt responsible for me and didn't want me to end up being a cook for being late so he drove up after me. He drove six hundred miles on his day off just to get me on the earliest train for Montana.

You should have seen the letter he sent with me explaining why he had kept me so long. He even wired Montana and sent a lengthy air-mail–special delivery letter telling them why.

Here I am, the last one to arrive. Training has been under way for two weeks. I hope his letter works.

May 11, 1944

This is a great life. I just barely got in the training course. I had to work like mad to catch up.

Since the dormitories are all full, I have a big tent all to myself. I got a sleepingbag and I guess it will be my bed for at least six weeks.

The country is beautiful and a wonderful camp site. It's different country entirely from Coleville. They have grass and flowers here.

This is about the only camp in which the Forest Service supplies the food. Boy, what food. They tell us it is almost comparable to army food. I honestly don't see how we existed on the food at Coleville. If I don't get fat now, I will miss a good chance. You can have all you can eat. I didn't think food like this existed anymore. We even get dessert twice a day.

I won't get to jump till next week at the earliest. The ones who have been here three weeks jumped today. One fellow broke his leg and about four turned their ankles. I can't wait till I get my 'chute and am up in the plane.

I hope they soon send my trunk. I left Coleville in a bigger hurry than I did Cooperstown, only here I knew I was going, but not when. I packed in the dark and got most of the wrong things.

The Forest Service men out here are young fellows. My foreman is only about twenty-four or twenty-five. He sure is a nice fellow. They know what they are doing out here.

May 15, 1944

Well, I made my first jump this morning and didn't even get a scratch. I don't know how I will do next time. There is nothing to it. You just get in the plane and jump out. I waited a year and about three months for that moment and it was just as I anticipated.

The fellow who jumped ahead of me had quite a time. He was a little nervous and held his hand on the ripcord of his emergency chute. The opening shock of his regular chute caused him to pull the ripcord, then, both chutes opened. They didn't tangle though and he made a good landing.

The fellow right after me was really lucky. He got a shroud line over his chute when it opened, causing him to come down hard. He did a good roll and wasn't hurt a bit.

Another of our squad landed in a tree and another landed in a little creek.

May 16, 1944

We spent most of the day in fire training. Paramount sent a fellow out here for a couple of days. He is going to make a news reel of us.

May 18, 1944

Made my second jump yesterday morning. Since there wasn't a bit of wind, I came down without much of a drift and landed very easily. I am going to try an Eagle chute next time. They steer a lot easier than an Irvin.

We spent all of today on map training and compass work. When a jumper leaves the plane on a fire he is really in the wilderness. Compasses and maps are the only possible means of getting back to civilization.

We have been getting up about 4:30 every morning this week so that we could get our jumping in before the high winds came up. We have made all of our jumps out of a Ford Trimotor so far. About twelve of us go up at one time. There is a single motor plane that holds only about three jumpers.

They drop just about anything to us on a fire. If we signal, they will drop a radio, marine pump, all kinds of fire tools; i.e.: saws, shovels, axes. I'm going to like it a lot.

The more I think of the idea of fighting fire by plane the more practical it seems.

May 21, 1944

It is raining again today. It seems to go from one extreme to another. At Cooperstown it was snow, in Coleville it never rained, and here, rain. I think this must be the rainy season.

My trunk arrived yesterday so I won't have to wash any more clothes.

There goes the dinner bell. You can set your watch at the time the meals are served. Everyone is right on the dot. There is no reason for anyone to work overtime. If you are late, you just miss it entirely.

Everything works the same way. We only work an eight hour day here.

May 22, 1944

Since it snowed almost all day, we had some first aid training. When it cleared off in the afternoon we got out one of the Pacific Marine pumps and were shown how it works.

We usually take a two way radio set down with us. It is only about four-by-four-by-ten inches. It is even smaller and better than the "Walkie-Talkie" of the Army. However, since it is not powerful enough for long distances, they drop us a larger set which can be heard for a distance of up to four thousand miles.

This region is supposed to be the pride of the Forest Service.

Region One is first in just about everything. They have the best
trained rangers, the best maintained roads, the best buildings. This
region originated the fire jumping. I don't think much of the way
they service the trucks, though.

I guess I told you how well the fellows attend the Sunday Services
here. They come out pretty well to the morning devotions, too. I
wish I could learn the names of more of them.

May 24, 1944

It rained all day today and snowed yesterday. Looks as though it
may clear up at last. I'm pretty sure I'm going to be kept here at
Ninemile for the summer.

Oh yes. We get five dollars a month in this camp. That may not
sound like much to you but it sounds good to me. It means that now
I will not only have enough to buy stamps and paper but also have
enough to buy some clothes and still save a little.

May 25, 1944

Made my third jump today. We jumped about fifteen hundred or
two thousand feet so we would have plenty of time to learn how to
handle the chute. The Eagle chute is quicker opening than the Irvin
but it also lets you down faster. We fall about one thousand feet
every minute. We jump three at a time from the Trimotor and one at
a time from the Travelaire.

One of the packers packed one of the chutes inside out today.
There wasn't anything wrong with it except it had to be steered backwards. Some of the chutes are nylon but most of them are silk. All of
the chutes are Army rejects but we fix them over and they are as good
as new. The chutes cost about four hundred dollars a piece. I think
the plane rents for between eighty-five bucks and one hundred bucks
an hour, so you see it costs the Forest Service quite a bit to train us.

May 28, 1944

The living conditions here are pretty swell. Nothing like Cooperstown but a hundred times better than Coleville. I'm living in a tent
but only because it's nicer outside. The barracks are built like the
ones in Coleville, but they are much cleaner. Every two men have a
small closet in which to hang their clothes and it makes the dorms a
lot easier to keep clean.

The mess hall and library have ceilings and are lined with ply-wood. I think this adds a great deal to the meals, too.

May 31, 1944

The Forest Service doesn't fool around with the fellows here because it costs too much to train them. There have been about fifteen disqualified because of their attitude.

The camp is overrun with regular Forest Service foremen but I learned they are just training this year. Next year they will double or triple the squads. They already have a fund of twenty thousand dollars just to build quarters for the jumpers after the war. This is the first year they have done any jumping on a large scale.

It really costs a mint to hire planes. The Forest Service has to guarantee the Johnson Brothers twenty-five thousand dollars a year business. I don't know why they don't buy their own. I guess the reason is that the Johnson Brothers know the mountains by heart. They have been flying ever since planes have been widely used.

June 5, 1944

We have seventy five high school fellows with us for about two weeks. They are here for a course in fire training and lookout work. After they leave, about twenty-five women are coming. They, too, will be trained as lookouts.

We spent most of the day clearing out an irrigation ditch about twenty miles from camp. Most all of the farm land and grazing land in the West is irrigated. The people wouldn't think of planting anything without irrigating because the rainy season is so short and unpredictable.

The work we do in between fires is just fill-in and isn't of much value. However, it is nice heavy work and keeps us in good condition, which is its main purpose.

June 12, 1944

This is going to be a hard letter to write. I asked quite a lot of questions about your coming out here and the answers are very unfavorable. It seems as though the Forest Service is in complete charge here. It is a Forest Service rule in this region that no women folk (even their own wives) are allowed to stay overnight in camp. In this camp they made one exception for the director, but not even the superintendent can have his wife here.

Then for the rest of the fire season we aren't allowed to be more
than five minutes away from camp. It seems as though everything in
the last few days has worked against us but it must be the Lord's will for
the time being. I prayed about it a lot and He must have better plans.

June 15, 1944
   Everything, or about everything, is working in our favor now. I
got the superintendent in a good mood and he said it would be O.K.
for you to come into camp over the weekends. The director has
been on the go for the past couple of days so I haven't had a chance
to talk to him yet.
   There are a couple of people in Missoula including the Congre-
gational minister who come in. Maybe you could come with them. I
will find out tomorrow where you can stay. We won't get to see each
other as much as we would like, but I think things will work out better after you are here.
   I have to go out to a spike camp for about two weeks. You may
arrive before I get back. If I am not back, leave your telephone number and I will call as soon as I get back. We don't know exactly how
long we will be gone. I won't get any mail for that period nor can I
write any letters because I will be about forty-five miles from the
nearest post office and about eleven miles from the nearest house.
   We will be doing some blasting and telephone line repair work. I
was sure lucky to be in camp when you called. That was the first time
in over a year I was on K.P. I was clean-up man in camp.
   They have a small YWCA in Missoula—also the Priess Hotel is a
good place until you can find something better.

[Betty Robinson visited Missoula for a month. It was the first
extended period they had shared since their marriage. Some of the
time, Betty stayed at Ninemile doing volunteer work in the kitchen.]

August 14, 1944
   This has been a hectic day. It rained all day just as it did Sunday. It
doesn't seem like the same place with you gone. It sure was great to
have you here.
   When I left you, I went back to the hotel and slept for awhile.
Then, I borrowed a rain coat and went down to the bus station. I was
just stepping on the bus when I saw Leonard Raney on the street. He
said the camp pick-up was in town so I came back to camp in it.

You should have seen our bed. It had about two washtubs of water inside and a big pool outside. I took it all apart and hung it on the line, but it is still raining so it won't do much good. The tent leaked, too, while we were in town and soaked the pile of work clothes I had on my bed. They absorbed all of the water though and left the bed dry.

August 20, 1944

Colliers magazine sent a couple of reporters out here today to get a story on us for one of the September issues. Vic Carter and Ralph Hand brought them out but didn't mention that we are COs. However, one reporter was not content with the Forest Service view of the unit. She interviewed four or five of the fellows. The Forest Service men almost blew a fuse when one of the fellows said he liked it here because the pay was twice as much as most other camps. When he told her it was sixteen cents a day, it didn't take Vic long to get her away from camp.

They took Johnny Johnson and Jim Jackson out on a fire last week to jump, but Jim Waite was afraid to let them. The wind was really strong and rough. They all got sick. The plane was on its side a good part of the time. It took them forty-five minutes to fly to the fire and fifteen minutes to fly back. When they dropped a test chute, the wind carried it out of sight. They dropped another one after allowing about two miles for wind drift. That, too, went at least two miles beyond the fire.

August 21, 1944

We went back to baling hay again today. The stack we are doing is the one Charlie Rogers got hurt on.

We had to go out on the obstacle course for a while this morning to satisfy a whim of someone in Missoula. I jumped off the tower and my back snapped right into place. It feels perfect now after two weeks of misery.

August 22, 1944

Dale Yoder is chief cook now. Mrs. Peterson went on leave but we doubt if she will come back. When she went she took everything including her cook books. Dale has been doing pretty well and has given us quite a variety but we still get pancakes for breakfast every day. Robutka will be back next week and I guess he will take over then.

We had another accident in the hayfield today but not as serious as Charlie Rogers'. Jim Jackson swung one of those bale hooks at a bale of hay and missed. It caught him under the knee cap. The cut wasn't as bad as the hook going under his knee cap. He'll have a sore leg for awhile.

August 24, 1944

Just about everybody is out on fires up near the Canadian-Washington border. They had a bad storm up there. They have been jumping the fellows right and left. There are about eight of us left here at Ninemile. I am next on the list and expect to get a call either in the next hour or early tomorrow morning.

George Case is cooking now. Dale went out on the fire. Both of them do better than Mrs. Peterson.

August 27, 1944

Some of the fellows from Moose Creek are here at Ninemile for awhile. They just got back from a fire and are waiting for a plane to take them back. The ones are not back from Washington, but we really don't expect them for a week yet. They will probably have to tour the country to get back.

Dave Flaccus and another fellow had to travel fifty miles by boat. They were dropped hundreds of miles from nowhere and really had quite an experience. All of the late fires have been up near Canada. I was next on the list but my turn never came.

August 29, 1944

Wag Dodge just brought most of the Seeley Lake and Big Prairie fellows in to Ninemile. Since most of them haven't jumped, they will be first on the list. We should get some more practice jumps though.

The Seeley Lake fellows came in expecting to jump but Art sent them all up to Helena to tear down those CCC barracks [Camp Rimini] for here and Missoula. The rest of Big Prairie came in tonight. Chuck Chapman came back too, so I guess he will be here for at least a week.

September 1, 1944

We didn't have Bible Class because we didn't have lights. Catherine Harder, the nurse, was supposed to be the leader. Yesterday's storm was pretty bad.

Five of the Big Prairie fellows jumped today so I may get another fire jump yet. You should see the letter the forest supervisor of the Nez Perce National Forest wrote to the regional headquarters in Missoula. He really liked the way we handled the Berg Mountain Fire. He sure did give the smoke jumpers a lot of praise. He knew we were COs, too. (That was the fire on the Salmon River.)

Jim Waite and the fellows in the Missoula office think we should carry out our own equipment which alone weighs ninety-two pounds. When they drop saws and radios, it is well over a hundred pounds. I sure would like to see them lugging all that bulk and weight about forty miles to a road. Last year, Al Cramer had to walk sixty-one miles to get to a trail. About ten miles is the least you can expect. It is tough enough just walking out without packing all that stuff. Art suggested Jim try it out on a twenty mile hike—half of it up hill. He said we are crazy to try to do it. Art said if it wasn't worth a few dollars to send in the mules, he wasn't going to bother carrying it.

September 15, 1944

I have to leave at four a.m. for a fire near Coleville, Washington. It is right along the Canadian border. I probably won't be back for a week, maybe two or three. . . . I just got back from Washington last night at about midnight. We had been working steady with very little sleep for exactly a week. I will start from the beginning and tell you all about it.

I was on KP Thursday a week ago. It was about four p.m. when the fire call came. They wanted eight jumpers for a fire near Moose Creek. All of the side camps that hadn't jumped were at Ninemile so I didn't figure on jumping. Art had me load the truck and round up the men. I did all that and just as they were ready to go, he told me I was to take them in. I had on my slippers so I rushed in and got a pair of shoes and threw them into the truck and took off.

We got into Missoula pretty quick but the eight fellows on standby that were in there had already left. We waited around for about an hour. Then another fire call came in for a fire in the Bitterroots. I rushed them down to the plane and got them off O.K.

When I came back to the loft, Vic Carter said another call had come in from Washington for eight jumpers and that Art wanted me to go on that crew. I wasn't dressed or anything but I wasn't going to miss out because of that. They had previously called Ninemile and had my fire pack and jumping suit on the way. In fact, the fire danger was too great, they had all the jumpers then at Ninemile come into Missoula. There were about forty of them. The truck came in at eleven p.m. I went down to the airport with it and loaded our equipment in the plane. I got to bed about one a.m. and had to get up at four a.m. We ate breakfast and went down to the airport. We took off at five a.m. for Winthrop, Washington. It is about thirty miles from Canada and pretty close to Seattle in the Cascades. Dick Johnson flew us up in the Ford Trimotor. He is really a flier. He has the reputation of being the best mountain pilot in the country and on this trip he really built it up some more. We were flying over Spokane. Most of the fellows were asleep. He said it was about time we woke up, so with that he pushed the stick forward and we went into a power dive for three thousand feet. That woke the fellows up pretty fast.

We followed the Columbia River for quite a ways and flew over Grand Coulee Dam. It sure was pretty, and long to be remembered. Pretty soon we spotted Mount Rainier and Mount Baker and we thought we could see Mount Hood, but weren't certain. We scouted around a little and were over Canada, too. I think.

We landed at Winthrop at eight-thirty a.m. and put on our suits to jump. It was something new for that region and all of the big-wigs of the Forest Service had to go up with us. We had to leave our cargo for a second trip because there were so many of them.

(That reminds me of two of our jumpers and an incident they had. They got a call for two jumpers in Region Six so they flew over there. It was something new for that region, so all of the waffle-bottoms were there. They all got in the plane and Bob Johnson told them it was too much weight to fly. So, they threw out the cargo. About that time two more big shots had arrived to watch the jump. They got in too and Bob said the plane was still too heavy so the big-wigs got their heads together to decide who should not go. They were all about the same grade so the only thing they could decide upon was to let the two jumpers out. Then the plane took off and no one ever did fight the fire and the big-wigs got in a nice plane ride. That actually happened, but I forget who the jumpers were. They were from Cove [sic] Junction, Oregon, though.)

Well, anyway, we took off for a fire that was out of control on Lyall Ridge about twenty miles from Lake Chelan. I have seen rough country, but this was the roughest I have ever seen. It is reputed to be the roughest mountains in the world and is called the Switzerland of America. We skimmed through a canyon with five feet between the wing and a rock cliff. Still another was so narrow that Dick kicked the plane over on its side and flew through that way.

The fire was three hundred acres in size and in virgin timber about six feet through at the base. It was really going to town and was crowning to beat the band. The mountain was about eight thousand feet high. On one side was a rock cliff three thousand feet straight down. The timber side was just about as steep as vegetation would grow on. We baled out on the ridge because that was the only place possible to land. We all headed for trees because if we ever hit the ground, we would roll clear to the bottom. Thiessen really gave us a scare when the wind blew him over the cliff. He guided it back and landed on the edge with his chute hanging over the edge. They went back then to get our cargo.

In the meantime, ten fellows from Cove [sic] Junction came to jump from a navy DC-3 plane. The pilot said he could fly anywhere Johnson could get with the old Ford but when he saw the terrain he changed his mind. A newspaper reporter and a photographer in the plane said beads of sweat stood out on his face when he dropped cargo one thousand feet above the fire. Johnson came in a few minutes later to drop our cargo and hit the treetops with his wheels when he dropped it. Then he dropped four thousand feet into the canyon to drop a fire camp at the base of the fire for eighty walk-in firefighters from the Howe Sound Mining Company. When the captain of the Navy plane saw that, he turned white as a sheet and headed for home. He was supposed to be a crack flier, too.

The eighteen of us jumpers worked for two days and finally got a line around the head and flank of the fire. The next day, the miners got a line across the bottom. We had it almost licked. We really worked and had nothing but K rations to eat.

We got a radio call that we were to pull out and jump on another fire the next morning. We loaded our one hundred and twenty pounds of equipment on our backs and started to stumble down to the lower fire camp over a mile below us. That was really a killer. I was walking down through ashes a foot deep and red hot. My shoes were burning and then I tripped. I fell head first in the hot ashes and would have been there yet if Reimer hadn't helped me up. We all made it down to the bottom O.K.

We ate a hurried meal. Then loaded our chutes and fire packs on a pack string. We walked fifteen miles. Then took a truck to Lake Chelan. The only way out of that country is by boat (they brought the truck up by boat).

We started down the lake which is fifty-four miles long, about a mile wide and one thousand feet deep. We were going to go all the way by boat but since it took so long, we only went forty miles to the nearest road. There, two Forest Service sedans picked us up. A truck took our equipment. They rushed us into Chelan where we ate at about one a.m. We then drove to Winthrop and arrived there at three a.m. Jim Waite was there. He packed our chutes because we were to jump again at five a.m. Two of the fellows tore their chutes so badly that they couldn't pack them and they couldn't jump. I had torn two load lines loose from the canopy of my chute, but I didn't tell Jim because he wouldn't have packed it and then I wouldn't have jumped. I did jump it though and it opened O.K.

Dick had thought he was all through with the plane so he went out on a good drunk. At five a.m. he was so drunk he couldn't stand up. We had to wait for him to sober up. At nine a.m. he was up and stumbling around and after he drank a couple of cups of black coffee, he took off to jump us.

The drinks didn't affect his flying any and he really handled that plane like he always had. We jumped on this fire which was a five acre fire and the ideal for a smoke jumper, at Surprise Lake. The forest supervisor told us to take our time on it and to be sure to take in fishing tackle. We did, too, but never got a chance to use it. The jumping spot was in a little basin covered with grass, at eight thousand feet. The fire was in a rocky section. It couldn't spread very fast. There was a lake one hundred feet from the fire. We had a marine pump and plenty of hose. We thought we would have a swell time there so we worked all that day and half the night on it. We got it under control and were going to just sit back and take it easy for once. Then the walk-in crew came. We thought for sure that we would have a picnic. The plane came in to drop us supplies and we were all set. I had to laugh at one of the fellows who saw us jump. He was watching Dick drop us a fire camp. The chute came off a bag of meat and it fell to earth. When it hit, it just exploded. Even the canned meat could never be found. He said up until then he thought parachuting was O.K. but after he saw that meat hit he would stay on the ground.

It snowed the next day. A radio call came that we were to get back to Winthrop as quickly as possible. We loaded our stuff on three horses and started the thirty mile hike out to Twisp at one p.m. We had only gone a mile when one of the horses fell off the trail and rolled over eight or ten times down the side of a mountain. Somehow he stopped rolling and we rushed down. We held the horse from falling more and cut our equipment loose. The horse then tried to get up again and rolled over again. He managed to get up on his feet again.

All he got was a cut on the leg and some bruises. We loaded him up again and took off in the blizzard. We had to climb two mountains to get out. The snow was really thick. The packer got tired of riding so he asked me to ride awhile. In the next few minutes, I really screwed the works. We came to a creek and the trail divided. The pack horses took the wrong trail so I took off after them to herd them back. I was no sooner out of sight of them when the cinch band that held the saddle on, broke. I couldn't fix it so there I was holding the horse with one hand and the saddle with the other. By this time, the pack horses were a mile away and the snow had covered their tracks. The fellows had gone in some other direction and I was left alone in the middle of nowhere without the faintest idea of which way to go. I finally got the saddle on after a fashion but could not ride in it. I started to lead the horse back and pretty soon I met the packer. He thought something had gone wrong so he came to look for me. He told me how to go. Then he started out to hunt the pack horses. He found them halfway up a rock slide and had a heck of a time getting them back down. I found the fellows, and with a cargo sack we had, we made another cinch. We reached the end of the trail at nine p.m. Dan Deal got off the trail and was lost for about an hour but he finally made it. Then we rode about fifteen miles in an open truck to Twisp where we ate. We pulled into Winthrop about midnight and took a shower and went to bed. I was really dirty and soaked to the skin. I had to wear the wet clothes till I got back here to camp the next night because there was no way to dry them and we were on the go continually. The Ford was all ready for us the next morning to fly us back. Dick stopped at Spokane for gas and disappeared for about four hours. We didn't know where he went or how long he would be gone so we couldn't leave the plane. We finally did get back to camp about midnight though, after fooling around Missoula trying to get a truck to camp.

I forgot to tell you how the fires started. The first one was a lightning strike. The Forest Service had sent in three kids and two drunks to put it out. They did alright but on the way out, they dropped a cigarette in the woods and it really took off then. The other one was man-caused, they think. Two deserters from the army stole a lot of horses and food and headed for the mountains. Fresh tracks were found near the fire. They think they let their campfire get away from them. It is a great life though and I have had four fire jumps now which I think is pretty good.

On the first fire there was a big glacier on the mountain opposite us. We were above snow there, too.

Ed Harkness broke his leg on a fire jump in the Bitterroots. I think it was Leonard Bartel who went over a cliff. His chute caught on the edge of it and he climbed back up it but he sure had a close call. The stories will be thick around here as the fellows come in, but they can't beat our fires. We had three columns and two pictures on the front pages of a Washington paper and for the first time, COs were mentioned with pride. One picture was at least ten-by-ten inches. This jumping is just in my blood now and since I love to fight fires, I am well contented.

September 22, 1944

Well, here I am down in Corvallis, Montana. I will probably be down this way for a couple or three weeks but continue sending my mail to Huson. I left word for them to forward it here.

When we counted the fellows that wanted to use their compensatory time picking apples, we found there were twenty-two of us. The farmers around Corvallis said they could use all of us. We decided we would hire a bus to come down. It cost us a dollar and a half each.

Flaharty was along with us. He kept us in laughter the whole way. We left right after work Thursday and got here about ten o'clock. We sang most of the way. It really was a swell trip. Twelve of us are staying here about two miles from Corvallis at a farmer's by the name of Gander. We averaged about five dollars apiece today, which is pretty poor. We worked from daybreak to sunset, too. Oh well, we have a lot of fun.

Well, I guess I will go to bed now because we are going to get up pretty early. We are sleeping in a little tent in the back yard.

September 26, 1944

I did pretty well yesterday and today; I made about nine dollars and fifty cents, but I have to take one dollar out for meals. This fellow we work for is sure a swell person. He is fair in his dealing and I think he is a Christian, too.

O Boy, did I have some fun today. Mr. Gander had another fellow working for him in the orchard. I happened to get on a tree near him and I wasn't there a minute before he was talking about COs. He said he was a Christian too and gave me all his reasons for mass murder. After I got him to say he believed everything in the Bible, I really went to work with him. He would quote a verse which in itself would support it and then I would quote some following it that would put an entirely different light on the verse. The Lord sure must have been with me because I disproved every argument he set forth. I asked him if he thought Christ would kill and also what he was going to do with all of Christ's direct commands in the New Testament and the Sermon on the Mount. I had a lot of fun and I thought for awhile Mr. Gander was going to tell me to get out because he stopped and listened for about fifteen minutes and then smiled and walked away.

It sure is hard to write because the fellows are all singing and I can't concentrate on what I am writing.

We will finish up with this fellow about tomorrow noon but I don't know where we will go from here. They've got me singing now so I'll have to quit.

October 1, 1944, Sunday Morning—Corvallis, Montana

Well I'm not getting rich very fast here but I am not losing anything so I am still happy. I made about eleven-fifty in the past two days. If we get in a better orchard I should do a lot better. I give them one dollar a day for meals. I brought my sleeping bag with me and sleep in a little tent they put up for us on the lawn. They sure do feed us well here. The people we are picking for are pretty nice people.

Mr. Gander made the remark that we were the leanest bunch of fellows he ever had working for him. He said he has yet to hear one profane word from us. Six of the fellows worked today but the rest of us figured it was Sunday. Frank Neufeld and Oliver Petty went in to Hamilton to church with one of the neighbors but none of the rest of us had clean clothes.

Earl Cooley and the fellows are back from their hunting trip. We heard that they got two elk and four mountain goats. They use high power rifles out here so they don't have to get as close to shoot.

I had to laugh at this farmer. He said that he has had his orchards for about twelve years. In all that time, only two people ever fell from the ladders. The first day all but Loren Zimmerman fell from the top of a fourteen foot ladder. I fell twice and Dick Richfields fell three times.

October 2, 1944

Well, I guess I will stick with the apple picking a few more days. When I told Mr. Erickson that I was going to quit, he almost had a fit. He wanted to know what the trouble was and if the wages weren't right. I told him I figured I'd better quit and find something else to do if I couldn't clear five dollars a day. He said if he didn't get his crop picked in a few days the cold would freeze them—it was nineteen degrees out this morning—and that he didn't care how much he paid as long as he got them picked. When he put it like that what could I do but say I would stay regardless of what he paid me. There are four of us here. He treats us like kings. All of the farmers treat us well.

What I can't understand is that they were all happy when the price of apples went up from a dollar-seventy-five a box to two dollars, and 13 cents a box was top pay for us. Then the price jumped to two-fifty a box and they wanted us to break our necks to pick faster while the price held. Yet, they wouldn't even give us a penny a box raise. I don't get it. One day I will clear ten bucks and the next I will work just as hard and clear two. When the trees are good the apples are easy to pick but when they are bad, so is the picking.

The meals are really good at these farm houses. You should taste the steaks. You can just cut them so easily with a fork. The milk is mostly cream—all for a dollar a day.

October 24, 1944

There is not much doing around here anymore. The whole staff went in to town today. It seems as though there is quite a bit of friction between the Forest Service and the CPS staff. . . .

I don't know what the pow-wow was about today but think it had to do with next year's program.

Some fellows I had forgotten about came back from Soldier Creek. Now we have about twenty fellows in camp. They will be leaving pretty quick though.

Roy said my transfer is causing more trouble than all the rest of them put together but I told him to keep working on it. I've just about decided to hitchhike home. I think I can make it in five days and I think they will grant me that much travel time. I couldn't use it for anything else anyway. I think I will try it. If I see it isn't going to work I can always get a bus or train.

They are talking about closing the Remount next year. I don't think they used the trucks or mules on a fire this year. They have five regular drivers and about a dozen of those big trucks. We must be doing a pretty good job at fire control for them to take a step like that. There is also talk that we are not going to have any lookouts next year. That would save them thousands because there are hundreds of them up here. We will have the whole northwest after us pretty soon if we keep doing them out of their jobs.

There were over twelve hundred jumps made this year counting both practice and fire. Not one fire we got to first caused any serious damage. It was predicted to be the worst fire season in history, too. I'm sort of disappointed that I didn't get more jumps but I guess I turned out to be the luckiest of the bunch.

Catherine says she is going to send me into town this week to have my teeth examined. She is sending everyone in. She is going to Benton, Montana, for the winter but will be back next spring.

December 12, 1944, Seeley Lake, Montana

Didn't make it home.

Well, here I am at Seeley Lake for the winter. I saw the article in *Colliers*. Cochran and Cooley are right in there as true to life as they can be. Did you notice that famous grin of his as he poses for that picture in the mock-up plane. He and Cooley made the perfect foremen. I can hear Earl now as I finish telling him about a fire jump I made: "That was pretty exciting, Robinson, but did I ever tell you about that one I made. . . ." He always had time for the fellows and would rather talk to us than the big shots in the regional office. He went out of his way a hundred times to back us up when some disagreement arose between us and the Forest Service. He has left the unit now to take a job with the timber sales branch of the Forest Ser-

vice. They will look a long while before they find another man half
as good as he is.

I just heard that Bryn Hammerstram [*sic*] got his transfer to
Puerto Rico.

December 22, 1944

We have been married a year and two days and have only had a
few weeks together. Vic promised me a furlough before fire season
starts. I will have to wait until after I put the ice up for the winter and
until he arrives.

The people up here are certainly friendly. I sort of expected
them to avoid me since I am a CO but they have gone out of their
way to do things for me. Three people have invited me to visit with
them. Today when I was down at the post office, three total strangers
invited me out to Christmas dinner. I don't know how many people
have invited me up to the school tonight for the Christmas enter-
tainment. It sure does seem queer. In one section of the country,
everybody just looks daggers at you and in another the people treat
you as a son. I have learned one thing, though. If there is one rabble
rouser in camp, the whole camp gets a bad name.

We have about a foot and a half of snow now. The lake froze before
the snows. I went out today and cleared a path out to deep water. The
ice must be cleared of snow so it can be cut every day. It will keep rising and thus freeze faster and thicker. It was twelve degrees below the
other night and was down to zero tonight by the time I walked the
four miles back from the post office. The eight mile a day walk to and
from the post office is keeping me in good shape.

December 24, 1944

Winter has come to Seeley Lake. It dropped to thirty-five below
zero last night. It doesn't feel as cold as it sounds. I worked outside
with only two sweaters on and didn't even get a bit cold. There is no
wind and the cold does not penetrate unless you stand still.

I got a big package from Nick Helburn the other day. It was filled
with cookies and popcorn. I think he spent the summer up here at
Seeley Lake.

You should see all the applications that came in from Army men
who want a job after the war. I imagine they think all we do is jump on
a fire and then it goes out by itself. If they only knew, the jump only

lasts two minutes at the most. Then comes the period of long hard work that really takes the backbone out of you. The ones that have fought mountain fires before may turn out all right. I'd like to see someone who never has, walking fifty miles out of a fire on which he had to work for about three days without rest, rations and very little water. The young fellows aren't going to like it when they find out they have to spend the summer in a place like Moose Creek or Cayuse Landing. The only way in to those places is by plane. It would be just as bad for a married man, and an older man would not be accepted.

Maynard Shetler was operated on for appendicitis last week. Robutka is going to be operated on for a rupture. One of the fellows in Oregon had an attack of appendicitis, too.

January 13, 1945

You said that some people were wondering if I would stay in smoke jumpers after the war. That question has been settled long ago. The government will not employ anyone who has been in CPS. I really would not want to anyhow. I think it is great work and I really like it, but as soon as I get my release, I am heading for New Jersey. For a year-round place to live, Jersey is hard to beat. New York, California, and Montana are great in the summer, but the winters are not so hot—in more ways than one. When you get away from the towns, there are no churches or anything like that.

January 19, 1945

The supervisor called up and said that when I get the ice ready to cut, he will send the ranger and a crew up to help me. That doesn't sound too good to me because it sounds as though I'm to be up here all alone for the rest of the winter, too. I don't mind being alone, but I don't want to miss out on my furlough. That is all that I've been planning on ever since I have been up here. I told him I thought I could handle it myself. If they send a crew up all the hard work will have been done and I know they won't send anyone else up. They call me the Lone Ranger now.

January 26, 1945

Well, well, well. At last I got some definite news on my furlough. I will be able to take it in March sometime. I called Art Weibe [sic] and told him to sign me up for furlough starting in March and running to the first part of April. Bob Harris who took Earl Cooley's place said training would begin April 15th. I have fifty-four days coming to me but if I can get thirty, I'll be happy.

January 28, 1945
There is a rumor that Johnson is going to give up his flying field. The Forest Service was planning on flying its own planes and hiring their own pilots anyway. This will be after the war. It will be a good chance for someone to get in on the ground floor, though. They will probably hire Slim Phillips and a couple of other pilots of Johnson's that have flown for us. He used to make his pilots fly for three years over the mountains before he would let any of them fly us.

February 8, 1945
Well, we finally started on the ice today. Fickie sent a crew of three men up from the shops in Missoula to help me. We got a lot of it stored today. I think we should be done by Saturday. You should see all the food they brought with them.

February 11, 1945
We have the ice almost harvested. They figured it would take nine men three days. The four of us did it in two and a half.

February 19, 1945
At last. I'm finding out things about my furlough. Everyone is supposed to be working on it. Fickie was transferred to another forest. He will not be here anymore. I should find out soon when I can definitely leave.

I went skiing last night. That is the quickest way I know to get to the hospital. I always wanted to go down a steep hill. First thing off the bat I climbed one and came down—and how I came down. It took me five minutes to unwind my left leg so that it pointed in the same direction as my right. After that, I stayed with the more gentle grades. Since I'm all alone here, I guess I'd better not do too much of it anyhow.

February 24, 1945
Everything is ironed out for my furlough except who is to come up here. I think Mr. Fickie put the deal through for me. Murray

Braden, who is now assistant director, asked Vic for me. Vic said he couldn't send anyone to replace me. I went over his head to the assistant supervisor who said, "Sure." I think I will not even have to pay two-fifty to get to Missoula because the Forest Service is going to send the pickup for me. I wish I could wait until Sunday to leave. If I left at noon Sunday, it would not count as furlough. However, I am not going to take any chances this time. I'm going to get out of here as fast as I can. These Forest Service men change their minds too fast for me.

This will be the last letter. I should be seeing you by Saturday or Sunday. I will probably be leaving Thursday on my furlough.

[George Robinson returned to CPS Camp No. 103 for the 1945 fire season, along with Betty, who roomed in Missoula with another CPS wife, Gerry Braden. Other CPS wives also residing in town that season included Ruth Palmer, Tess Helburn, Betty Case, and Pat Burks. The women often gathered for evening meals, taking turns cooking. When not on fire call, the husbands spent the weekends in town. When Betty Robinson became pregnant, George transferred to Camp Luray, Virginia, on the Skyline Drive in September 1945 so that they would be closer to their families. He worked there until his discharge from CPS duty in April 1946. The Robinsons eventually raised four daughters in southern New Jersey, where George built custom houses and Betty worked as a schoolteacher.]

Notes

INTRODUCTION: CIVILIAN PUBLIC SERVICE

1. Unless otherwise noted, all quotations by the CPS smoke jumpers were extracted from photocopied personal memoirs or letters that were assembled in *CPS Smokejumpers, 1943 to 1946—Life Stories*, vols. 1, 2, and 3, ed. Roy Wenger (Missoula, Mont.: privately printed, 1990–93), pages unnumbered.
2. Mulford and Jacob, *Conscription of Conscience*, 126.
3. Phifer, *Smoke Jumper*, 45.
4. Gingerich, *Service for Peace*, 109.
5. Ibid., 162.
6. Ibid., 213–14.
7. Selective Service System, *Conscientious Objection*, 65.

CHAPTER 1. CONSCIENTIOUS OBJECTION IN AMERICA

1. Bowman, *Brethren and War*, 72.
2. Brock, *Quaker Peace Testimony*, 145.
3. Hartman, *Reminiscences*, 7.
4. Ibid., 8.

5. Ibid.

6. Durnbaugh, *Fruit of the Vine*, 279.

7. Ibid., 276.

8. Brock, *Quaker Peace Testimony*, 170.

9. Cartland, *Southern Heroes*, 254–84.

10. Selective Service System, *Conscientious Objection*, 41.

11. Durnbaugh, *Fruit of the Vine*, 281.

12. Brock, *Quaker Peace Testimony*, 175.

13. Peterson and Fite, *Opponents of War*, 3.

14. Ibid., 13.

15. Durnbaugh, *Fruit of the Vine*, 416.

16. Ibid., 417.

17. Ibid., 422.

18. Peterson and Fite, *Opponents of War*, 136.

19. Bowman, *Brethren and War*, 189.

20. Ibid., 270.

21. Ibid., 280–81.

22. Bush, *Two Kingdoms*, 70.

23. Selective Service System, *Conscientious Objection*, 3–4.

24. Ibid.

25. Anderson, *Peace Was in Their Hearts*, 29.

26. Bowman, *Brethren and War*, 193.

27. Sibley and Jacob, *Conscription of Conscience*, 429.

28. Ibid., 217.

29. Ibid., 429.

30. Bush, *Two Kingdoms*, 75.

31. Ibid., 76.

32. Selective Service System, *Conscientious Objection*, 321.

33. Durnbaugh, *Fruit of the Vine*, 474.

34. Bowman, *Brethren and War*, 311.

35. Selective Service System, *Conscientious Objection*, 321.

36. Ibid., 322.

37. Public Law No. 51, v. 65, Statutes at Large, p. 86 (June 19, 1951).

38. Bush, *Two Kingdoms*, 172.

39. Ibid., 316.

CHAPTER 2. THE HISTORIC PEACE CHURCHES

1. Bush, *Two Kingdoms*, 7.
2. Ibid., 12.
3. Sykes, *The Quakers*, 24.
4. Ibid., 31.
5. Fox, *Journal*, 433.
6. Sykes, *The Quakers*, 137.
7. Brock, *Quaker Peace Testimony*, 88.
8. Clarence Quay, letter to the author, February 12, 1998.
9. Bowman, *Brethren and War*, 93.
10. Ibid., 234.
11. Ibid., 249.
12. Ibid.

CHAPTER 3. YELLOWBELLIES

1. Mundell, *Static Lines and Canopies*, 70–73.
2. Anderson, *Peace Was in Their Hearts*, 10–11.
3. Mundell, *Static Lines and Canopies*, 69–70.
4. Ibid., 70–73.

CHAPTER 4. HARD CHOICES

1. Wilmer Carlsen, interview with the author, 1998.

CHAPTER 5. BIRTH OF SMOKE JUMPING

1. Cooley, *Trimotor and Trail*, 23–24.
2. Ibid., 2.
3. Ibid., 4.
4. Ibid., 6.
5. Pyne, *Fire in America*, chap. 5.
6. U.S. Forest Service, *History of Smoke Jumping*, 1.
7. Cooley, *Trimotor and Trail*, 20.
8. Florek and White, *Tall Timber Pilots*, 127.

9. Cooley, *Trimotor and Trail*, 19–21.
10. Ibid., 21–26.
11. Florek and White, *Tall Timber Pilots*, 44.
12. Cooley, *Trimotor and Trail*, 35.
13. Phil Stanley, interview with the author, 1994.
14. Phifer, *Smoke Jumper*, 30.
15. Sibley and Jacob, *Conscription of Conscience*, 225.
16. Ibid.
17. Ibid., 262.
18. Cooley, *Trimotor and Trail*, 50.

CHAPTER 6. BOOT CAMP

1. Glynn, *Montana's Home Front*, 15–24.
2. Cooley, *Trimotor and Trail*, 51.
3. Ibid.
4. Mundell, *Static Lines and Canopies*, 35.
5. Ibid., 36.
6. Handwritten notes by Roy Wenger, given to author.
7. Ibid.
8. Cooley, *Trimotor and Trail*, 52.
9. Maclean, *Young Men and Fire*, 53.
10. Mundell, *Static Lines and Canopies*, 43.

CHAPTER 7. HIT THE SILK

1. *Time* 89, no. 1 (January 1967), 90.
2. Mundell, *Static Lines and Canopies*, 25.
3. Ibid., 63–64.

CHAPTER 8. THE LONG WAIT

1. Mundell, *Static Lines and Canopies*, 4.
2. Phifer, *Smoke Jumper*, 33.
3. Mundell, *Static Lines and Canopies*, 39.
4. Ibid., 49.
5. Phifer, *Smoke Jumper*, 33.

CHAPTER 9. WILD ENCOUNTERS

1. Mundell, *Static Lines and Canopies*, 19.
2. Ibid., 38.
3. Ibid., 57.
4. Ibid., 46.
5. Ibid., 73.
6. Ibid., 30.
7. Ibid., 75.
8. Ibid., 37.
9. Ibid., 63.

CHAPTER 10. EYES IN THE SKIES

1. Mundell, *Static Lines and Canopies*, 29.
2. Cooley, *Trimotor and Trail*, 15–16.
3. Mundell, *Static Lines and Canopies*, 53.
4. Ibid., 53.
5. Ibid., 44–45.

CHAPTER 11. UNDER FIRE

1. Mundell, *Static Lines and Canopies*, 52.
2. Cooley, *Trimotor and Trail*, 50.
3. Mundell, *Static Lines and Canopies*, 66.
4. Ibid., 21–22.
5. Ibid., 66.
6. Ibid., 23.
7. Ibid., 69.
8. Ibid., 2.
9. Ibid., 68–69.
10. Ibid., 3.
11. Ibid., 39.
12. Ibid., 52.
13. Ibid., 51.
14. Ibid., 54.

CHAPTER 12. HOME AWAY FROM HOME

1. Cohen and Guth, *Pictorial History*, 121–22.
2. Interview with Cap Evans by Greg Munther and Larry Timchak, date unknown. Typescript in files at USFS Ninemile Ranger District.
3. Marilyn Vierhus, interview with the author, July 2005.
4. Roy Wenger, interview with the author, January 19, 1998.
5. Notes written by Roy Wenger, date unknown.
6. Roy Wenger, interview with the author, 1994.
7. Koch, *Forty Years a Forester*, 164.
8. Mundell, *Static Lines and Canopies*, 30–31.
9. Roy Wenger, interview with the author, 1994.
10. Roy Wenger, interview with the author, 1998.
11. Phifer, *Smoke Jumper*, 42.
12. Ibid., 42.
13. Ibid.
14. Ibid., 19.
15. Ibid.
16. Mundell, *Static Lines and Canopies*, 11.
17. Ibid., 26.
18. Ibid., 38.

CHAPTER 13. LIFELONG COMMITMENT

1. Cooley, *Trimotor and Trail*, 65.
2. Phil Stanley, interview with the author, 1995.
3. John Ainsworth, interview with the author, 1995.
4. P. D. Hanson, USFS memo, July 1, 1953.
5. Cooley, *Trimotor and Trail*, 52–53.
6. Ibid., 54.
7. Ibid., 57.
8. Anonymous, "A Service of Celebration for the Life of Roy Wenger."
9. Cooley, *Trimotor and Trail*, 52.
10. "Static Line," no. 30, January 26, 1946 [Huson, Mont.], 1–2.
11. Ibid., 1.
12. Wayne Williams, interview with the author, November 2004.

13. Matthews, "Fighting Fires and Indignities," 11.

14. Roy Wenger, interview with the author, 1995.

APPENDIX: LETTERS HOME

1. Wenger, *CPS Smokejumpers, 1943 to 1946,* vol. 3. Previously published excerpts from Robinson's letters are printed in their entirety in this collection.

Select Bibliography

Anderson, Richard C. *Peace Was in Their Hearts*. Watsonville, Calif.: Correlan Publications, 1990.

Anonymous. *A Service of Celebration for the Life of Roy Wenger*. Missoula, Mont.: privately printed, Dec. 6, 2004.

Bowman, Rufus D. *The Church of the Brethren and War—1708 to 1941*. New York: Garland Publishing, 1971.

Brock, Peter. *The Quaker Peace Testimony—1660 to 1914*. York, U.K.: Sessions Book Trust, 1990.

Bush, Perry. *Two Kingdoms, Two Loyalties: Mennonite Pacifism in Modern America*. Baltimore, Md.: Johns Hopkins University Press, 1998.

Cartland, Fernando G. *Southern Heroes, or the Friends in War Time*. Cambridge, Mass.: Riverside Press, 1895.

Cohen, Stan B., and A. Richard Guth. *Pictorial History of the U.S. Forest Service, 1891–1945: Northern Region*. Missoula, Mont.: Pictorial Histories Publishing, 1991.

Cooley, Earl. *Trimotor and Trail*. Missoula, Mont.: Mountain Press, 1984.

Durnbaugh, Donald R. *Fruit of the Vine: A History of the Brethren, 1708–1995*. Elgin, Ill.: Brethren Press, 1997.

Florek, Larry, and Dale White. *Tall Timber Pilots*. New York: Viking Press, 1953.

Fox, George. *Journal*, vol. 2. New York: Isaac Collins, 1800.

Gingerich, Melvin. *Service for Peace: A History of Mennonite Civilian Public Service.* Akron, Ohio: Mennonite Central Committee, 1949.

Glynn, Gary. *Montana's Home Front during World War II.* Missoula, Mont.: Pictorial Histories Publishing, 1994.

Hartman, Peter S. *Reminiscences of the Civil War.* Ephrata, Penn.: Western Mennonite Publications, 1996.

Koch, Elers. *Forty Years a Forester.* Missoula, Mont.: Mountain Press, 1998.

Matthews, Mark. "Fighting Fires and Indignities." *High Country News* 27, no. 14 (August 7, 1995).

Mundell, Asa, ed. *Static Lines and Canopies—Stories from the Smoke Jumpers of 1943 to 1945.* Beaverton, Ore.: privately printed, 1993.

Peterson, H. C., and Gilbert C. Fite. *Opponents of War, 1917–1918.* Madison: University of Wisconsin Press, 1957.

Phifer, Gregg, ed. *Smoke Jumper.* Missoula, Mont.: Missoulian Publishing, 1944.

Pyne, Steven J. *Fire in America: A Cultural History of Wildland and Rural Fire.* Seattle: University of Washington Press, 1982.

Selective Service System. *Conscientious Objection.* Special Monograph no. 11, vol. 1. Washington, D.C.: Government Printing Office, 1950.

Sibley, Mulford Q., and Philip E. Jacob. *Conscription of Conscience: The American State and the Conscientious Objector, 1940–1947.* Ithaca, N.Y.: Cornell University Press, 1952.

Sykes, John. *The Quakers: A New Look at Their Place in Society.* Philadelphia and New York: J. B. Lippincott, 1959.

U.S. Forest Service. *History of Smoke Jumping.* Seattle, Pacific Northwest National Parks and Forests Association, 1986. Reprint of R1–80-22, originally published by the Northern Region, USDA Forest Service.

Wenger, Roy, ed. *CPS Smokejumpers, 1943 to 1946—Life Stories,* vol. 1. Missoula, Mont.: privately printed, 1990.

Wenger, Roy, ed. *CPS Smokejumpers, 1943 to 1946—Life Stories,* vol. 2. Missoula, Mont.: privately printed, 1992.

Wenger, Roy, ed. *CPS Smokejumpers, 1943 to 1946—Life Stories,* vol. 3. Missoula, Mont.: privately printed, 1993.

Index